CHARLES WESLEY

POET AND THEOLOGIAN

CHARLES WESLEY

POET AND THEOLOGIAN

Edited by

S T Kimbrough, Jr.

KINGSWOOD BOOKS
An Imprint of Abingdon Press
Nashville, Tennessee

CHARLES WESLEY: POET AND THEOLOGIAN
Copyright © 1992 by Abingdon Press

Library of Congress Cataloging-in-Publication Data

Charles Wesley : poet and theologian / edited by S T Kimbrough, Jr.
        p.   cm.
    Includes bibliographical references
    ISBN 0-687-06096-6 (pbk. : alk. paper)
1. Wesley, Charles, 1707–1788—Congresses.   I. Kimbrough, S T, 1936–
BX8495.W4C43   1991   91-30267
287'.092—dc20   CIP

Printed in the United States of America
on recycled, acid-free paper.

Contents*

    * All but three of the chapters in this volume originated as papers presented at the Charles Wesley Publication Colloquium, held at the Center of Theological Inquiry in Princeton, NJ, September 22-24, 1989. Chapter 1 is an English translation of a German article which appeared in the *Theologische Revue* (1988), and chapters 9 and 12 were specially prepared for publication in this volume.

Part III: Charles Wesley and the Church

Foreword*

Very frequently, scholarship in theology is thought to be esoteric or abstract. Properly speaking, it should not be; it should be connected with down-to-earth issues, not only those which arise in universities and churches but much more broadly. Scholarship at the Center of Theological Inquiry has such broad relevance, even if it is pursued here in more concentrated ways. It is intensive because it aims to deal theologically with the fundamental issues of human understanding and life in God's world, what kind of world we live in, how it is best understood and how people are to direct their lives together and individually. There is a fair amount of uncertainty nowadays about how to do these things; and it is this uncertainty which the Center addresses through its work. When I say "deal theologically with the fundamental issues," I mean that we attempt to think these issues through to their foundation in the nature and purposes of God in creation, redemption, and their fulfillment. That may carry the scholars who are members of the Center into the sciences, the social sciences, philosophy, history, culture, language; and it is those areas with which they are occupied as they work as individuals, with each other, and with others with similar concerns elsewhere.

The Center is still relatively young—the building was built only in 1984—and the next years should see it flourish and expand. If it is successful, its work will greatly assist the credibility of theology in the present day, showing the important connection of theology with all areas of human life and understanding. And that will help both the churches and places of learning find the importance of the resources of the religious traditions, particularly the Christian, for life today. I can't think of anything more important to the needs of the world today.

But, you might ask, what does the work of Charles Wesley have to do with such a purpose? In the twenty-nine years I spent in England, many of them teaching in Birmingham, not so very far from the birthplace of Charles Wesley, I learned to understand the special forms which theology takes in England. Theology there does not focus so directly on

---

* When the Charles Wesley Society held its Founding Meeting at the Center of Theological Inquiry, October 10–12, 1990, Daniel W. Hardy, Director of the Center, welcomed the members with the remarks which appear here slightly revised as the Foreword.

matters of belief and doctrine as in some other countries, and there have never been many who concentrated on them. Even if I am one myself, there are few systematic theologians among the English, particularly amongst the Anglicans. They are not so worried about confessions of faith. They are greatly concerned about the presentation of Christian faith, but not usually by confessing the faith or preaching it. Instead, they turn more usually to the presentation of faith in indirect ways. For that reason, they attend to what you might call submerged faith, faith presented in the forms of life itself. Most important are all the basic ways by which life is formed, by nature, personal and social life, and the development of social life in government and politics and law; and the concern of the English is with how God's life (and human responses to it) runs through all these basic ways by which life is formed. Christian faith is, so to speak, submerged in these ways by which life is formed; sound faith is sound life.

Such a way of being concerned about Christian faith is unfamiliar to us who are much more accustomed to faith seen as beliefs, but it is the way most important to the English. One way of submerging Christian faith which I have not mentioned is in language and culture. That is why there is more theology to be found in English literature than in books of theology. Literature is theology for the English; it is the way by which theology comes about, in the formation of literature, the literature by which the self-consciousness of the English is developed in the very process of expressing it. This is theology through the formation of language, and through the formation of language the formation of English consciousness. That, by the way, is why I think Charles Wesley adopts a form of theology which is (at least marginally) more truly English than that of his better-known brother, because the formation of language is itself the way by which he crafts his theology.

Now you may see why I think the study of Charles Wesley is appropriate to the Center of Theological Inquiry, for in studying him you study the formation of Christian faith in the formation of language, and the formation of self-consciousness which goes with it. In a world which is now befuddled by its own language, which—as we might say—resembles "Babel to the nth degree," there are few things more important than finding how Christian faith is realized in the formation of language. Charles Wesley's work is a splendid example of that.

Of course, what is especially fascinating is the texture of the Christian faith which comes to language in his work. That is a much wider subject on which I must not embark right now. But, drawing on my own work on the unity of praise and life, let me say this much. We find in his work a profound appreciation of the inner dynamic of human life with God,

8

one in which God's self-revelation is found in the enlargement of the human spirit. He knew well wherein was God's glory, the glory to which almost all his work is addressed; and he knew better still that the marks of that glory were best found in the growth of the true shape and beauty of human life—God's beauty in the beautification of human life. It is a pity that this is so frequently denigrated as archaic language. In a world like ours, where there is so much falsity and ugliness, such sensitive understanding needs badly to be recovered—God's praise in our re-formation.

It is indeed appropriate that the first Charles Wesley Publication Colloquium, the lectures of which are published in this volume, was held at the Center of Theological Inquiry in September of 1989, and that the Founding Meeting of the Charles Wesley Society convened here in October of 1990. Charles Wesley studies are at the beginning of exciting things. May they and the Society prosper.

Daniel W. Hardy, Director
Center of Theological Inquiry
Princeton, New Jersey

Preface

While Charles Wesley is widely recognized as an author of many significant English language hymns, he is generally not regarded as an astute poet of the seventeenth century. Furthermore, it is common practice to assume the "like mind" of Charles Wesley and his brother John in matters of theology and the church, and Charles has not been viewed as an important theologian and original thinker of the period. Indeed, his brother John has been seen as the theologian and he as the hymn writer.

This volume addresses these views and presents Charles Wesley in a new light: perhaps as not only one of the most prolific English language poets but as one of primary literary significance, albeit mainly in the arena of serious religious poetry. Likewise, the significance of the kind of theological contribution he makes is explored in the context of the broader scope of theology, biblical studies, liturgy, homiletics, and a variety of church traditions: Roman Catholic, Anglican, Methodist, Reformed, and Lutheran.

Misguided views of Charles Wesley and his work are due in part to the inaccessibility of his writing (poetry and prose) to the general public and the church at large. Very little is readily available today. This book provides careful and thorough summaries of his poetical corpus, prose writings, (such as sermons, journal, essays, and letters) and makes available an extensive overview of Wesley's output—its literary, theological, liturgical, and ecumenical significance. In addition, there is an in-depth discussion of the relationship of poetry and hymn writing to theology and biblical interpretation.

The volume breaks new ground, for it reveals much of the uniqueness of Charles Wesley's thought and literature both historically and in relationship to the contemporary church and world. Therefore, it is not surprising that a strong case is made here for the need to publish the complete works of Charles Wesley.

The book fills a major gap in Wesleyan studies and makes significant contributions to English and American church history and hymnody, as well as to the development of theology in England and America as a result of the Wesleyan revival.

The volume consists of three parts:

Part I   — Charles Wesley's Literature
Part II   — Charles Wesley's Theology
Part III — Charles Wesley and the Church

Chapter one is an English translation of the article by Teresa Berger: "Charles Wesley und sein Liedgut: eine Literaturübersicht," *Theologische Revue* 6 (1988), pp. 443–50. She discusses the renaissance of Charles Wesley studies in the last few years and his literature in the light of the primary publications which have addressed it. From the importance of the *1780 Collection* of the Wesleys in *The Works of John Wesley* (vol. 7) series to the contemporary significance of the Wesley Eucharistic hymns and poems in Roman Catholic/Methodist dialogue, she surveys the primary sources and suggests future directions of Charles Wesley studies.

In chapter two Oliver A. Beckerlegge surveys Wesley's poetical corpus and puts to rest the well-meaning but wrong opinion of Charles Wesley's poetry that he wrote almost exclusively hymns. The discussion encompasses the religious and non-religious origins of Wesley's poetry, the wide range of subjects, his relatively unknown satire, and a new look at the question of what constitutes "hymns" and "sacred poems." Beckerlegge covers the primary Wesley publications of hymns and poems, emphasizing Charles's important contributions, and points out the pitfalls of the only existing major collection of Wesley poetry, George Osborn's thirteen-volume work. He treats the development of the Wesley poetry and history of his poems by discussing multiple editions and variant readings, and provides numerous illustrations from Wesley's poetry.

In chapter three Kenneth D. Shields views Wesley within the context of eighteenth-century English poetry and poets. Careful analyses are made of his poetry as one does of any other poet of the period. He makes very clear that a writer of serious religious verse, even hymns, can be a poet of high regard and genius. Shields utilizes Charles Wesley's unpublished poetry as well as his published works. It is the unpublished poetry which includes so many parallels to contemporary poets of Wesley's period. In the arena of literature, as well as in the church, Charles Wesley is to be viewed as an important literary figure. His unpublished poetry shows that he possessed both the ability and capacity to write in the poetical styles popular in the sphere of secular literature.

In chapter four Frank Baker emphasizes the unfortunate dominance of John Wesley's correspondence, while illustrating that Charles's is also of primary importance. Baker once published a volume entitled *Charles Wesley as Revealed in his Letters*,[1] but there has never been a major publication of his letters. A few were published in the *Arminian Magazine* and a few others here and there, but for such a vast number of extant letters (ca. 700) of this important eighteenth-century clergyman and literary figure, it is unfortunate that no edition of the letters has ever appeared.

Baker examines the domestic, courtship, and other family correspondence of Charles Wesley. He points out how the letters introduce largely a new cast of characters and new scenery from without and within the Methodist movement and the Church of England, which is vital to the understanding of eighteenth-century England and the church. The letters also extend the chronological framework of Charles Wesley's life and increase our knowledge of the man and his view of the church and the world.

In chapter five Thomas R. Albin presents an overview of the sermons (one volume of published sermons from the early nineteenth century, the few published during Wesley's lifetime, and the shorthand sermons which Albin recently published with Oliver A. Beckerlegge), essays, and Charles Wesley's *Journal*. The *Journal*, written in a terse and dynamic English style, provides keen insight into the history of the development of Methodism, the Wesley brothers' lifestyle, and English and church society during the period when Charles itinerated, the primary period covered by the *Journal*. Albin shows the importance of the prose writings for understanding Wesley's thought, ethic, ministerial practice, poetry, and life of the Methodist societies in their nascent years.

Part II examines the following aspects of Charles Wesley's theology: theology-as-hymn, theology as informed by the Bible and Wesley's interpretation, theology as liturgy, particularly eucharistic theology. Chapter six provides an exploration of the kind of theologian Thomas A. Langford thinks Charles Wesley is, namely, the creator of a hymn-formed theology. In that light he discusses hymns and theology in general, the theology of Wesley's hymns, and finally Wesley's "theology-as-hymn." Langford characterizes Wesley's theological contribution as follows: Charles Wesley is important "because he creatively provided for the Methodist revival a theological character suited to its self-understanding. He added a distinctive theological dimension to theological expression for the Methodist revival; that is, he kept theology immediately and ineluctibly related to the worship and service of God."[2]

Chapter seven is a discussion of Charles Wesley's relationship to and place in the development of biblical studies in eighteenth-century England. Integral to this discussion are his grasp of biblical languages, his views on biblical literalism and mystical interpretation of scripture. While Wesley profited from many aspects of the development of biblical studies, one of the primary keys to understanding his biblical interpretation lies in the "discovery that the Bible is not only a divine guide for the heart and will, but it is also a thesaurus of immortal poetry and uplifts the imagination."[3]

The author explores how Charles Wesley's hermeneutic of imagination is important for the eighteenth century and the contemporary church: it reinterprets ancient categories, transforms biblical imagery into categories of contemporary experience, and enables personal and social transformation or metamorphosis. The chapter includes many illustrations from Wesley's poetry, a discussion of how his biblical interpretation provides insight into understanding the relationship between the Old and New Testaments, and concludes with a brief look at convergencies and divergencies in Wesley's work with narrative theology.

In chapter eight Laurence Hull Stookey explores the potential contribution of Charles Wesley to liturgical renewal in three areas: ecclesiology, biblical preaching, and Eucharistic theology. Keys to this discussion are Wesley's views of the liturgical assembly, scripture, lectionary, the Eucharist as expressed in his sacred poems and hymns, typology, and eschatology. All of these elements are seen by the author as vital to contemporary liturgical renewal and preaching. Crucial to current ecumenical liturgical renewal and to be learned from Wesley is "his ability to hold in tension things that all too readily are broken apart and scattered if they are deemed theological opposites rather than theological complements."[4]

Part III treats Wesley's relationships to and views of four church traditions to which he responded affirmatively and negatively. His responses are quite varied. Interestingly, his hymns transcend denominational idiosyncracies and have made their way into most significant English language hymnbooks of the last 200 years. The chapters of this part explore Wesley and his work historically, theologically, and in a contemporary context.

Wesley lived and died an Anglican priest. He was devoted to the "old ship," apostolic succession, and a sacramental and evangelical life, faith, and worship. As a poet and writer of hymns, he produced a liturgical literature for which Anglicanism had little or no use, for it was not a hymn singing church. Yet much of his hymnody and religious poetry was directly associated with the *Book of Common Prayer* and Anglican liturgy in general. In chapter nine on Anglicanism Robin A. Leaver maintains that in order to understand Charles Wesley's life, thought, and hymnody one must understand their Anglican roots. He also examines the presence of his hymnody in hymnals of other Anglican evangelicals of the eighteenth century.

Richard P. Heitzenrater scrutinizes erroneous ideas about Charles Wesley and Methodism in chapter ten. He sets Charles here in a new light: that he was not, as often supposed in accordance with his old age recollections, the first Methodist, and was indeed perhaps more Anglican than his brother John. Heitzenrater draws a "new picture" of Charles as a powerful, formative, early force in the Methodist societies but not in "Methodism" as a movement in itself. He radically opposed Methodism as an independent movement. His contribution is, however, much more formative than is often imagined, for the theology of the inner witness of the spirit which permeates his hymns through and through, imbued Methodism from its inception with the liturgical vitality of hymn-theology and sung-theology which engage people where they are.

In chapter eleven Horton Davies highlights the Calvinist-Methodist controversy which resulted in a plethora of anti-Calvinist poems by Charles Wesley. It was in the matter of universal, free grace that Wesley concentrated much of his opposition to Calvin. Interestingly, Wesley is at many points theologically very close to Calvin, and Davies provides a keen analysis of this often neglected area of Wesleyan theology.[5]

In the concluding chapter (twelve) on Roman Catholicism Teresa Berger shows that Wesley in large measure was opposed to it. The conversion of his son Samuel to the Roman Church resulted in a profuse number of poems which provide extensive insight into Wesley's often negative views of Rome. The author, however, casts his importance for the contemporary Roman Church in a very positive light, for his hymns have found their way into Roman Catholic hymnals and his Eucharistic hymns have become the focus of Roman Catholic/Methodist dialogue. They have become a "bridge" to ecumenical and liturgical renewal.

S T Kimbrough, Jr.,
Editor

Acknowledgments

The editor expresses deep gratitude to the authors of this volume and to the following sponsors of the Charles Wesley Publication Colloquium (September 22–24, 1989), at which most of the papers published here were presented:

The Center of Theological Inquiry

The Center of Continuing Education at Princeton Theological Seminary

The Theological School of Drew University, the Ezra Squier Tipple Endowment

The Board of Higher Education and Ministry, The United Methodist Church

The United Methodist Publishing House

First United Methodist Church, Houston, Texas

Mrs. Edward K. Miller

Finally, deep appreciation is due Oliver A. Beckerlegge for assistance in proofreading the text of this volume, the staff of the Center of Theological Inquiry, Patricia Grier and Kate Le Van, for technical and administrative assistance with the Charles Wesley Publication Colloquium and this volume, to the Board of Trustees of the Center of Theological Inquiry and the Center's founder, the late James I. McCord, for vision and assistance in sustaining the Colloquium, and to the current Director of the Center, Daniel W. Hardy, for his continued encouragement and support.

PART I

Charles Wesley's Literature

Chapter 1

CHARLES WESLEY: A LITERARY OVERVIEW[1]

Teresa Berger

Translated by Timothy E. Kimbrough

Even if Charles Wesley can no longer readily be described as the "first Methodist,"[2] he must still continue to be numbered among the founders of the largest church community formed since the Enlightenment. It was Charles Wesley who brought together a group of like-minded individuals at Oxford, thereby forming at least one of the "Methodist cell groups" whose leadership was later assumed by his brother, John. It was also Charles, in 1738, who was the first to experience a personal conversion—three days before John was to have a similar experience. Two key events of the newly emerging Methodist renewal are therefore to be associated with Charles Wesley, even if John is clearly the one to be characterized as "the founder of Methodism."

On the other hand, the hymns of Charles Wesley appear to have had a much greater influence on the sense of community and self-understanding of Methodist churches than, for example, John's sermons or *Explanatory Notes upon the New Testament* which constitute, in part, the "doctrinal standards" of Methodism. Nearly every Methodist is familiar with at least a few of Charles Wesley's hymns, while only a small number would know the writings of John. Still, it cannot be disputed that John provided the actual impetus for the developing movement. His life is to be identified more strongly with the development of Methodism than that of Charles.[3]

Therefore, as one might expect, Charles Wesley was overshadowed by his brother during his life-time and in subsequent historical records and research.[4] I note one recent example. In 1988 the world-wide Methodist Church remembered two important formative events of its early life directly connected with Charles Wesley: (1) the 250th anniversary of the conversion of the Wesley brothers (Charles, May 21, 1738; John, May 24, 1738) and (2) the 200th anniversary of the death of Charles

Wesley (March 29, 1788). Even in this commemorative year, the conversion of John Wesley received more attention than the conversion of Charles and the anniversary of his death.

The literary overview which follows concentrates exclusively on Charles Wesley, particularly his fundamental contribution to developing Methodism: Wesleyan hymnody.

The study of Charles Wesley and Wesleyan hymnody has only recently received an essential tool, namely a critical edition of the most important Methodist hymnbook from the nascent period of the movement: *A Collection of Hymns for the Use of the People Called Methodists*[5] published by John Wesley in 1780. It consisted almost entirely of hymns by Charles Wesley. The first adequate critical edition of this hymnbook appeared in 1983 as a separate volume in a new, critical edition of *The Works of John Wesley*(!).[6] Until recently this was the only Charles Wesley material available in a critical edition. It is high time for the letters, sermons, diary, and a large portion of his poetical works to receive further critical attention and publication.

The new edition of the *1780 Collection* fulfills the demands of critical inquiry quite well. Its introduction outlines the origins and sources of the *1780 Collection*, the theological and literary characteristics of Charles Wesley's hymns, the editorial work of John Wesley, and the reception of Wesleyan hymnody within Methodism. The greatest accomplishment of this edition, however, rests in the publication of the hymnbook itself. For the first time a whole variety of helpful aids are made available with each hymn text: references to the place of first publication, the original length of each text (thereby highlighting the editorial privilege exercised by John Wesley), the variations of earlier editions, and the biblical and literary references upon which Charles Wesley drew. This thorough edition of the *1780 Collection* provides the foundation for any scholarly review of Wesleyan hymnody—even though it includes only about 500 of Charles Wesley's hymns (from a total output of some 9,000 hymns and poems!).

In the meantime another critical edition of Wesleyan poetical work has appeared: *The Unpublished Poetry of Charles Wesley*, edited by S T Kimbrough, Jr. and Oliver A. Beckerlegge.[7] This three-volume work contains well over 1,000 unpublished or partially-unpublished Charles Wesley texts. This work also meets the requirements of a scholarly edition.

A further development has contributed to an essential improvement for the basis of Charles Wesley research. Over roughly the past twenty years, the English-speaking world, in the context of a general renaissance of John Wesley studies, has experienced an increased number of publications which analyze the poetical works of Charles Wesley from a theological perspective. A brief overview of the previous direction of research makes clear that this development of theological inquiry represents progress, when compared with earlier primary emphases on Charles Wesley and his works.

As one might expect, from the beginning the most intensive interest in Methodism was to be found in the English-speaking world. With the expansion of Methodism to North America both England *and* the United States became the locus of interest in Methodism. During the nineteenth century, both countries produced publications on the Methodist movement. These publications, of many varieties, often represented similar directions. For the most part they were historical biographies, frequently belonging to the genre of "devotional literature" written by Methodists for Methodists. An inventory of Methodist literature written between 1733 and 1869 reveals a total of 2,254 titles, 320 of which are biographies.[8] The historical and biographical emphases are especially evident in the works on Charles Wesley.

The biographies which repeatedly described *The Life of the Reverend Charles Wesley, M.A.*[9] offered little variation from one another even in their tables of contents. A detailed description of the family home is followed by references to Charles Wesley's studies at Oxford, with a special emphasis on the emerging development of a strict and systematic "rule of life" with regard to personal piety and good works. The time spent by the two Wesley brothers in the North American colony of Georgia as Anglican clerics and missionaries is often pictured as bleak. Only the encounters with German Pietists seem to shed light on the horizon. Against the bleak background of the American colonial experience, however, the Wesley conversions after their return from Georgia appear in a brighter light. The few days before and after the conversions are frequently described in great detail. Descriptions of the rapid spread of the Methodist renewal movement follow which include the picture of its amazing success, as well as the difficulties it confronted. It is, however, at this point in the history of Methodism that Charles, when compared to John, begins to step into the background. Thus, the biographies, from this point on, concentrate without exception on Charles's remaining contribution within emerging Methodism: his hymnody. All publications value greatly his hymns even though they seldom receive theological analysis. Still, nearly all biographies recognize Charles's hymns as his central and lasting contribution to the Methodist movement.

Many of the biographies, as already mentioned, often have titles which belie the categorization of devotional literature. Charles Wesley is presented as *Poet Preacher,*[10] *Poet of Methodism,*[11] and *Poet of the Evangelical*

23

Revival.[12] Such publications are not restricted to the nineteenth century. One still finds contributions of a similar style in the twentieth century: *Evangelist and Poet*,[13] *Singer of the Evangelical Revival*,[14] (and more specifically!) *Singer of Six Thousand Songs*[15] and *The First Methodist*.[16]

Historical interest in the Wesleys was not, however, exclusively restricted to the devotional literature of the nineteenth century, but also found expression in the first "complete" editions of Wesley's works. Of those editions that dealt with Charles and his poetical work George Osborn's, *The Poetical Works of John and Charles Wesley*,[17] published between 1868 and 1872, is of considerable importance. Even if Osborn's work does not meet today's critical demands, it remains the only place where many Wesley texts are published and accessible. Thomas Jackson's attempt to publish Charles Wesley's *Journal*[18] and complete biography (with considerable autobiographical material),[19] suffered from less than exacting academic standards. Nevertheless, it remains a gold mine of detailed information and autobiographical material for every new biography of Charles Wesley, even though it tends toward hagiography in many places.

Until recently the only published edition of Charles Wesley's sermons was a collection published in 1816 by his wife.[20] For the most part, however, the sermons have proven to be unauthentic. They were indeed preached by Charles but most of them originated from his brother John. A small critical edition of six heretofore unpublished Charles Wesley sermons, however, has now been made available.[21]

There is practically no new satisfactory critical publication of the historical/biographical material available on Charles Wesley, much less a "theological biography" as Martin Schmidt has written on John Wesley. One must continue, for the most part, to rely on the production of popular scholarship.[22] This holds true even for the 1988 Charles Wesley biography by Arnold A. Dallimore,[23] an author from the reformed tradition who is well-known for his biography of George Whitefield. The volume is fairly balanced and his treatment of Wesley is not uncritical. Charles is described as poet, preacher, and proclaimer of the gospel. But even Dallimore includes such generalizations portraying Charles Wesley as "undoubtedly the greatest of all Christian hymn composers"[24] which simply cannot be accepted without question. Furthermore, Dallimore does not really go beyond the information already provided by Jackson 150 years earlier.

Well into the twentieth century, the interest in Charles Wesley, primarily biographical, has shifted to his poetical work from various perspectives.[25] The first group of publications concentrated on the literary characteristics of the texts and the traditions which they assimilated. Henry Bett's *The Hymns of Methodism in their Literary Relations*[26] best represents this method of inquiry. The author respects the poetical works of Charles Wesley as literature, a point of view minimized, to this day, in his opinion. He claims that "the hymns of Methodism constitute the finest body of devotional verse in the English language."[27] Bett's study focuses on the sources and traditions assimilated by the hymns (writings of the Church Fathers, influences of the *Book of Common Prayer*, and other literature). His catalog of criteria for distinguishing between the hymns of John and Charles remains the standard work referred to by all ensuing research attempts.[28]

Though research efforts to resolve the problem of precise authorship in several individual Wesley texts continue, a satisfactory solution has yet to be found. The pioneering work of Bett is, however, not to be diminished thereby. His detailed delineation of the sources was one of the first to analyze and present the various sources upon which Charles Wesley drew for his writing.

The other principal studies of the Wesleyan poetical corpus that fall into this group of publications tend to have a more explicit literary interest. Such volumes include Robert Newton Flew's *The Hymns of Charles Wesley: A Study of Their Structure*,[29] and notably Frank Baker's edition of poetical texts, *Representative Verse of Charles Wesley*,[30] as well as his introduction to this volume which was later published separately and specifically discusses the literary characteristics of Wesley texts. This introduction appeared in an expanded edition for the 1988 anniversary celebration.[31] Seen strictly from the point of view of literary criticism very little attention has been devoted to the work of Charles Wesley. Donald Davie's chapter on "The Classicism of Charles Wesley" in his book *Purity of Diction in English Verse* is a notable exception.[32]

One of the questions raised by Davie's chapter, however, is subject to continuing debate among those devoted to Wesley studies. What is Charles Wesley's relationship to Romanticism? Does he serve as a forerunner of Romanticism or are his ties to the Classicism of "The Augustan Age" too strong to shake?[33] Whatever the outcome, the debate seems to me to be of little value. After all, the placement of the Wesleyan poetical corpus is not really in question here. Rather, the debate should focus on the placement of an entire group of poets from the period of late Classicism who began to include elements of Romanticism. Charles Wesley is but one of these poets and certainly not the best example to be used in the resolution of this question as to their status between Classicism and Romanticism.

Theological interest in the poetical texts of Charles Wesley began to surface almost simultaneously with publications concerned with a more

25

literary focus. This interest in theology leads us to the second group of twentieth-century publications on Wesley's work. The 1940s produced two works by J. Ernest Rattenbury often cited for prompting a number of subsequent theological inquiries. The attempt at theological analysis in Rattenbury's *Evangelical Doctrines of Charles Wesley's Hymns*[34] and *The Eucharistic Hymns of John and Charles Wesley*[35] remain standard reference works consistently acknowledged in more recent studies along similar themes. *The Hymns of Wesley and Watts*,[36] the collection of lectures by the Congregationalist Bernard L. Manning, and the short book of George H. Findlay, *Christ's Standard Bearer*,[37] are to be noted at this point even though they straddle the fence separating literary inquiry from the theological. Findlay, in particular, after a few introductory notes on literary characteristics (he devotes an entire chapter to the use of the exclamation point in the hymns!) explores questions of content and themes suggested by key words within the hymns. Neither book takes as its subject the whole Wesleyan poetical corpus but rather looks specifically at the *1780 Collection*.

Detailed theological analysis of Wesley's poetical work has surfaced during the last twenty years taking the form of dissertations from England and, in particular, the USA. It could almost be referred to as a Charles Wesley renaissance which appears to be focusing on his theological legacy rather than renewed interest in his biography.

The dissertations which examine the theological perspective of the Wesleyan works are almost always organized by theme. The dissertations of James Dale, *The Theological and Literary Qualities of the Poetry of Charles Wesley in Relation to the Standards of his Age*,[38] and Gilbert L. Morris, *Imagery in the Hymns of Charles Wesley*,[39] combine literary and theological inquiry. Dale's thesis attempts to establish Charles Wesley as a classicist of the "Augustan Age" as opposed to a poet with early-Romanticist expression. This work, however, also provides important insight into the relationship between poetical form and religious witness in the Wesleyan writings. Morris's scholarly dissertation explores, in detail, the colorful language of 300 representative Charles Wesley hymns.

In contrast to the above, the dissertations of Barbara Ann Welch, *Charles Wesley and the Celebrations of Evangelical Experience*,[40] James C. Ekrut, *Universal Redemption, Assurance of Salvation, and Christian Perfection in the Hymns of Charles Wesley, With Poetic Analyses and Tune Examples*,[41] James A. Townsend, *Feelings Related to Assurance in Charles Wesley's Hymns*,[42] and John R. Tyson, *Charles Wesley's Theology of the Cross: An Examination of the Theology and Method of Charles Wesley as Seen in His Doctrine of the Atonement*,[43] provide primarily theological insight. With nearly 1,000 pages, Tyson's dissertation is the most exhaustive theological examination of Charles Wesley's hymns to date. The author uses detailed word and motif studies in examining the soteriological center of Wesley's legacy. His study has led him to believe that Charles Wesley is an important theologian, often underrated. Presumably, this conclusion led him to continue his work on Charles Wesley beyond his dissertation. In 1986, his book describing Wesley's teaching on sanctification was published and characterized as a "biographical and theological inquiry."[44] Three years later, Tyson published a collection of selected Charles Wesley texts as an introduction to his life and work.[45]

I have completed (1989) an inquiry into the theological interpretation of the *1780 Collection*.[46] This study allowed the theological themes and their interpretation to be suggested by the *1780 Collection* itself, rather than by approaching Wesleyan hymnody with presumptions about suitable themes to explore, looking to have them confirmed. Craig Gallaway, in his 1988 dissertation, focused on an understanding of the presence of Christ in the hymns of the *1780 Collection*.[47] Wilma Jean Quantrille dealt with the doctrine of the Holy Trinity in her 1989 dissertation.[48]

So much for the review of the development of Charles Wesley research. A brief look at the works about Charles Wesley produced in German establishes that principal contributions to Wesley research have come primarily from English-speaking countries. Interest in Methodism in German-speaking countries has never been great for a variety of reasons. True, some[49] have been able to highlight specific aspects of John Wesley's life and theology as well as that of developing Methodist communities, but outside Methodist circles little interest in Charles Wesley has been generated. Even among German-speaking Methodists interest in Charles Wesley and his hymns has been quite limited.[50] This neglect is, in large measure, attributable to the influence of nineteenth-century North American revival hymns on the hymnody of German-speaking Methodism, which served to obscure the importance of original Wesleyan hymnody on the movement.[51]

The Methodist bishop John L. Nuelsen's *John Wesley und das deutsche Kirchenlied*,[52] and Erika Mayer's dissertation, *Charles Wesleys Hymnen. Eine Untersuchung und literarische Würdigung*,[53] must be cited as exceptions to the general lack of interest in Wesley studies among German-speaking peoples. Nuelsen's study is the first to examine thoroughly the hymns of German Pietism which John Wesley encountered and translated while in North America. His examination of this subject remains a standard reference work. One might also note the contributions of Franz Hildebrandt[54] (a Lutheran who emigrated to England and became a Methodist) and the work of Martin Schmidt.[55] They, at least, suggest a certain interest in Methodism outside Methodist circles.

In 1988, the 250th anniversary of the conversion of the Wesley brothers, as well as the 200th anniversary of Charles Wesley's death, an abundance of literature appeared (at least in the English-speaking world). By definition, a significant portion of this literature was "devotional" in nature. After all, a faith community was celebrating the seminal experiences of its founders, without which it would not have been born. To a certain extent serious scholarly projects cannot be planned according to anniversary celebrations. As a result, new scholarly revelations were not necessarily to be expected.

In light of the foregoing history of Wesleyan research, it should come as no surprise that even in the year in which Charles Wesley's conversion and death were commemorated, interest in Charles Wesley[56] took second place to interest in his brother, John. Signs, however, were emerging indicating an increased interest in Wesleyan hymnody.[57]

This review of Wesleyan studies makes clear that further research into the theological interpretation of the Wesleyan works is warranted. It is apparent that until now the soteriological emphases of the Wesleyan works have received the most attention, and rightly so. But a new and thorough study of the eucharistic hymns might prove to be as rewarding as an analysis of the poetical texts of Wesley associated with the church year.[58] Above all, an important area for future Charles Wesley research will include work on critical editions of primary literature as well as exhaustive historical/biographical studies.[59] Further research concerns might also include an examination of the traditions assimilated by Charles Wesley in his poetical works from the Holy Scriptures[60] to *Paradise Lost*.[61]

Finally, one might also hope that in the wake of the ecumenical overtures churches are making toward one another the research concerns of other traditions might well become the concerns of one's own. *A Rapture of Praise*, by H. A. Hodges and A. M. Allchin,[62] is a fine example of ecumenical research on the Wesleys. It provides a collection of Wesleyan poetical texts chosen by both authors along with their commentary from an Anglican perspective. The Roman Catholic priest Francis Frost's "Biblical Imagery and Religious Experience in the Hymns of the Wesleys"[63] is also worthy of note.

Charles Wesley's works—his sermons, diaries, letters, and poetical texts—deserve the attention of scholars from many Christian communities. In order to give researchers access to this Wesleyan work, a critical edition of the complete works of Charles Wesley is sorely needed. It is astounding, considering the above review, how much research has been produced without such a resource. An edition of Wesley's "complete works" published today would stand on ground considerably more solid than in years past. Thus, this literary overview concludes by emphasizing the fundamental importance of a complete and critical edition of Charles Wesley's works for the sake of future research.

Chapter 2

CHARLES WESLEY'S POETICAL CORPUS

Oliver A. Beckerlegge

In his book *John Wesley as Editor and Author,* Walter Herbert writes:

> He believed with that much maligned critic John Dennis that if poetry is
> the language of the emotions, and if the sublimity of poetry is dependent
> upon the sublimity of its subject, then, since the religious emotion is the
> most powerful and universal of all, the sublimest poetry will be that which
> treats religious topics. Furthermore (they believed) since Christianity is the
> sublimest possible conception of religion, Christian poetry ought to be the
> sublimest possible poetry.[1]

That is a judgment that until recently has been very rarely admitted.
Though, as Frank Baker pointed out,[2] Charles Wesley wrote some 9,000
poems, totalling some 180,000 lines, three times the output of Words-
worth and exceeding even that of Browning, and though 96% of that
output was in lyric verse, Wesley has rarely been recognized by antholo-
gists of English poetry. He does not figure, for instance, in Palgrave's
Golden Treasury, even though it is a "treasury" of songs and lyrics; there
are none in the two volumes of *One Hundred Best Poems* (1903–04); none
in a very large anthology, *A Casquet of Gems* (1900) though that work
contains four poems by Isaac Watts, and very many by James Thomson
and Samuel Rogers; none in *Children of the Poets* (1888); none in *The Poet's
Life of Christ* (1922). The series of Aldine Poets, running to some three
score volumes, does not admit him, though the well-nigh forgotten
Robert Beattie and Charles Churchill have three volumes between them.
Last but not least, the *Oxford Book of English Verse,* edited by Quiller
Couch (1900), the *New Oxford Book of English Verse* (1922), the recent
Oxford Library of English Poetry (1986) all include one poem only, in each
case "Wrestling Jacob," and the *New Oxford Book of Eighteenth Century
Verse* (edited by Lonsdale, 1954) has but four. Charles Wesley has fared
very little better in distinctively Christian anthologies. *Lyra Christiana*
(1888) has two poems by Wesley but ten by the forgotten Lord Kinloch;

but the number of those is in truth remarkably small. But at other times
he can, and does not infrequently, pull out all the stops, as organists say.
Think of the closing verses of the hymn, "Father of Everlasting Grace":

> So shall we pray and never cease,
> So shall we thankfully confess,
>   Thy wisdom, truth, and power, and love;
> With joy unspeakable adore,
> And bless and praise Thee evermore,
>   And serve Thee as thy hosts above;
>
> Till, added to that heavenly choir,
> We raise our songs of triumph higher,
>   And praise Thee in a bolder strain,
> Out-soar the first-born seraph's flight,
> And sing, with all our friends in light,
>   Thy everlasting love to man.

Consider three verses from "Come On, My Partners in Distress":

> Beyond the bounds of time and space,
> Look forward to that heavenly place,
>   The saints' secure abode:
> On faith's strong eagle-pinions rise,
> And force your passage to the skies,
>   And scale the mount of God.
>
> That great mysterious Deity
> We soon with open face shall see;
>   The beatific sight
> Shall fill heaven's sounding courts with praise,
> And wide diffuse the golden blaze
>   Of everlasting light.
>
> The Father shining on His throne,
> The glorious co-eternal Son,
>   The Spirit, one and seven
> Conspire our rapture to complete;
> And lo! we fall before his feet,
>   And silence heightens heaven.

Look at the following verse:

> Thou, Jesu, Thou my breast inspire,
> And touch my lips with hallowed fire,
>   And loose a stammering infant's tongue;
> Prepare the vessel of thy grace,
> Adorn me with the robes of praise,
>   And mercy shall be all my song:
> Mercy for all who know not God,
> Mercy for all in Jesu's blood,
>   Mercy that earth and heaven transcends;
> Love, that o'rewhelms the saints in light,
> The length, and breadth, and depth, and height
>   Of love divine which never ends.

One thinks also of that glorious hymn in which Christ's "proffered benefits," the "plenitude of gospel grace," are rehearsed and offered for adoration, culminating in:

> The guiltless shame, the sweet distress,
> The unutterable tenderness,
> The genuine, meek humility,
> The wonder—Why such love to me?
>
> The o'rewhelming power of saving grace,
> The sight that veils the seraph's face,
> The speechless awe that dares not move,
> And all the silent heaven of love.

This reminds us of the amazing series of paradoxes and antitheses in "Thou Hidden Source of Calm Repose." These, and many, many more hymns, can surely lay claim to satisfying Keats's dictum that "poetry should please by fine excess." And it will have been noted that I have not quoted "Wrestling Jacob," or that packed verse in "And Can It Be." If this be so, if Wesley's hymns do indeed rise to the heights I have claimed for them, then they abundantly deserve to be placed within reach of all who delight in fine English, as well as of those who, like us, find them a rich aid in our devotion and our faith.

Wesley's Sacred and Secular Verse

I have referred so far to what we normally call "hymns." In point of fact, though by far the major proportion of his verse took the form of hymns, he wrote verse on almost every imaginable kind of subject, and it is worth remembering always that he used the word "hymn" to cover much religious verse that one would never think of singing. In *Hymns on*

God's Everlasting Love (1741), Hymn XVIII, entitled "The Horrible Decree," contains the verse:

> The righteous God consign'd
> Them over to their doom,
> And sent the Saviour of mankind
> To damn them from the womb;
> To damn for falling short
> Of what they could not do,
> For not believing the report
> Of that which was not true.

Not even in the boisterous days of eighteenth-century Calvinist controversy would one sing that verse in worship!

Frank Baker's *Representative Verse of Charles Wesley* is precisely what its title claims to be: representative verse, giving examples of the various sorts of poetry which Charles wrote. In the selection, the editor divides the first two sections into "Hymns" and "Sacred Poems"; it will be recalled immediately that "Hymns and Sacred Poems" was a favorite title of the Wesleys; and the difficulty in distinguishing between the two types of verse is illustrated by the fact that Dr. Baker includes seven so-called "hymns" in the section of "sacred poems." And yet, to complicate the issue further, John Wesley included some of those "sacred poems" in his *1780 Collection*—which goes to prove, perhaps, that Methodist hymnbooks have always been "intended for use in private devotion as well as in public worship."[5] This is especially true of the *Short Hymns on Select Passages of the Holy Scriptures* of 1762 and the many other such never published in Charles Wesley's lifetime. Other "hymns" were written for use in restricted circles. One thinks of his *Hymns for the Use of Families* (1767), covering every aspect of family life: for a woman near the time of her travail, on the death of a child, on sending a child to boarding school, on moving into a new house; one need not go on. Such were no doubt intended to be read, perhaps even on occasion to be sung, in the family circle only, as others, such as those "for malefactors," would be read in the condemned cell—in Death Row.

But a noticeable number of Charles Wesley's verses have far other than "religious" origin. It seems likely, for instance, that in his school and university days he translated passages form the Latin classics into English—a few fragments still remain—and that this led him to composition in the same contemporary medium of heroic couplets. In this verse form he wrote a number of poetical "epistles," one to his brother, another to George Whitefield, another to Zinzendorf, and so on. These have a "religious" aspect of course, as they were addressed to fellow preachers of the gospel. But other long poems in continuous rather than stanza form have no such background. His "American War," written in Hudibrastics, is a bitter satire on the conduct of the War of Independence by the British commander, Sir William Howe; how far his strictures were justified is perhaps a matter of some dispute. Allied to his effusion is a considerable corpus of hymns and verses on patriotism, the "hymns" mainly being sacred poems sympathizing with the plight of those loyalists who as a result of the war had fled to their native land and, like so many refugees, had not met with the warmest of welcomes. He voices their complaints:

> From dire rebellion's rage we fled
> (Proscrib'd and singled out to bleed)
>   And left our all behind,
> Wanderers and Emigrants once more
> On Britain's hospitable shore
>   A sanctuary to find.
>
> But who with open arms receives
> The poor, the loyal Fugitives,
>   Or generous Pity shows? . . .

His political Toryism cannot abide such men as Charles James Fox and his like, the radicals of their day, and other short poems show Charles Wesley's keen interest in the political scene. He sees such men as being the contemporary parallels to his *bête noire*, Oliver Cromwell, and other sacred poems are consequently prayers for the King. Some of these poems, arising out of the events of the time, such as the Fortyfive, the Seven Year's War, an earthquake, the Gordon Riots, etc., were indeed hymns, issued in pamphlet form, to be used at the services which were held—what we called in the early 1940s "national days of prayer." Other events which captured momentarily the nation's attention also called forth short poems, entirely secular in theme.

On the other hand, his love poems to his beloved Sally are far from secular. They are verse-prayers that his hopes of marriage may not be in vain, or they are prayers for his wife—so much so that some have, with very little alteration, been turned into hymns for public worship. Not unnaturally, Charles Wesley being who he was, his concerns for his family expressed themselves in similar verses, whether it be when one of his infant children was ill or died, or when later he was heartbroken at the (temporary) apostasy of his son Samuel to Rome; all these occasions summoned forth verse-prayers. But the *pater familias* not only prayed for his children, he played with them; so we find a cluster of light-hearted jingles to amuse them:

> There are, by fond Mamma supplied,
> Six reasons against Sammi's Ride:
> Because a different turn he takes,
> Because his back, or finger aches;
> Because 'tis wet, because 'tis dry;
> Because it may be by and by,
> Or any other reason why.

Lastly, the death of friends called for epitaphs, and these again sometimes took the form of continuous lines, and sometimes the form of what he would call hymns. Altogether there was hardly an aspect of life, personal, ecclesiastical, or national, that he did not handle, and hardly a poetical form (saving only blank verse) which he did not use.

If therefore, we are to judge Wesley as a poet, we must look at all his verse; we must be able to compare him as a satirist with his contemporaries; and his epigram on Charles James Fox bears comparison with any of his day:

> Clodius, inspir'd with fierce inveterate hate,
> With furious faction shook his Roman state;
> His country to destroy was the design
> Of daring, dark, atrocious Catiline;
> But both assassins meet in Fox alone
> And perfect wickedness is all his own.[6]

And if scholars are to make these comparisons, the material must be made available; not only his hymns, but his "sacred poems," his poetical epistles, his love poems, his verse (often, though by no means always, with a religious background) on contemporary events and family affairs, even the jingles he composed to amuse his children, everything, in fact, must appear in a definitive edition. The vast majority has admittedly been already published, but it is very difficult to find; Osborn's thirteen volumes of 1868–72 are all but unobtainable, and they are in any case not a critical edition. But if we can produce such, then perhaps it will be possible to judge him as a poet, doing our best to ignore the spiritual content of his verse, if that indeed be possible or even desirable; we may then perhaps be able to solve the age-old question: can a hymn be great poetry? Furthermore, if we can have before us all his hymns, the church will be able to judge afresh his place in hymnody. J. Ernest Rattenbury considered "It would be possible today to publish hundreds of his forgotten hymns which, if their authorship were unrecognized, would be hailed as exceptionally fine, and if wedded to melodious tunes would certainly become popular."[7] That judgment admittedly speaks of "hymns"—but at the same time speaks of them as being "exceedingly fine."

A Complete Edition of Charles Wesley's Works

If we then agree that a complete edition of Charles Wesley's poetry is a consummation devoutly to be wished, what are the issues at stake, the problems that have to be solved? In the first place, we can divide his poetical works into three groups: (a) those published in the many books and hymn pamphlets in his lifetime; (b) the thirteen volumes of Osborn, which contain the first group together with much else; and (c) those that have never been published until the appearance of the three volumes of *The Unpublished Poetry of Charles Wesley* (1988-1992). Each group, particularly the first two, presents its own problems. In all, some one hundred publications in Charles Wesley's lifetime contain work by him. But we cannot set about publishing all these in a simple straightforward way, seriatim.

In the first place, some of them contain work other than by Charles. The earliest volumes were, according to the title pages, "published by John Wesley, M.A." or "published by John Wesley, M.A. . . . and Charles Wesley, M.A.," a phrase, which on reflection, is ambiguous. "Published" does not necessarily mean "composed"! Leaving out the *Charlestown Collection* (1737) which has nothing by Charles, the first four or five collections contain poems of varied origin; these are the 1738 *Collection of Psalms and Hymns*, the *Hymns and Sacred Poems* of 1739 and 1740, the *Collection of Psalms and Hymns* of 1741, and the *Hymns and Sacred Poems* of 1742. In the 1738 volume there are only two that *may* be by Charles Wesley; in 1739 there is very little of his verse in Part I and a minority of material in Part II, though those poems include the conversion hymn and the great hymns for Christmas and Easter. In the 1740 *Hymns and Sacred Poems* almost all is by Charles, but the 1741 *Collection*, "published by John Wesley," which has the same title as the 1738 volume, served the same purpose, and possibly was intended to replace it, has some fifteen hymns only which may be of Charles's authorship. The 1742 *Hymns and Sacred Poems* which bears both names on the title page, is almost entirely Charles Wesley, and the others are not by Watts, or Herbert, and so on, but by John. But the question as to the criteria by which we judge which of the "uncertain" hymns are by Charles Wesley, and not their unidentified authors, or his brother, is a matter which will have to be examined later.

In the second place, some hymns and poems appear in more than one of these volumes; we shall clearly have to collate these, as we shall have to collate the texts of the various editions—the 1739 *Hymns and Sacred Poems* went through five English editions, and the 1741 *Collection of Psalms and Hymns* had fourteen editions in Wesley's lifetime (we must ignore those issued after his death, and those published in America, with which he had clearly nothing to do.) The 1742 *Collection of Hymns*, by John and Charles Wesley, is taken entirely from the 1739 *Hymns and Sacred Poems;* the *Hymns and Sacred Poems* of 1747 is compiled from hymns from the same 1739 volume, together with hymns from *Hymns on God's Everlasting Love* (1741) and the 1742 *Hymns and Sacred Poems*. In all, twenty-five publications are taken entirely from other volumes. Then again, many of John Wesley's works, particularly short pamphlets, include hymns at the close, sometimes in the first edition onwards, sometimes in later editions only (depending, possibly, sometimes on whether the printer had a page or so to spare); there are at least fifteen of these. Other hymns, presumably hymns that early became popular, were reprinted individually, and sometimes no doubt pirated, though it must be said that some of these instances we know only through entries in Strahan's ledgers, no copy presumably having survived. On the other hand, at least three hymns were published on their own in advance, as it seems, of their appearance in collections: such are "The Life of Faith" and "The Means of Grace," both of which later appeared in *Hymns and Sacred Poems* of 1740, and, supremely, "The Whole Armour of God" which, appearing first in an undated broadsheet of 1742, later is found in the *Hymns and Sacred Poems* of 1749. In such cases, which of the two, separate or collected, do we regard as definitive? Yet other hymns and poems appeared simply as individual publications: such are the "Epistle to George Whitefield," the "Elegy on George Whitefield," the "Epistle to John Wesley," the "Elegy on Robert Jones," and so on; there are at least eight of these. I imagine we take it for granted that the texts of hymns reprinted at the end of other publications are not authoritative; but they cannot be completely ignored.

Summing up, one volume (the *Charlestown Collection*) has no hymns of Charles Wesley; eight volumes contain his works together with that of others; thirty-four were publications of his own work, varying from eight-page pamphlets to works in two volumes; eighteen were hymns or poems published separately, of which eight appeared nowhere else; at least fifteen publications contained one or more hymns as a sort of appendix to a prose work, and twenty-five were collections, large or small, extracted from earlier works. One should add that in some cases an entry might as easily, and with justification, be differently classified.

The second main group consists of the poems contained in Osborn's thirteen volumes, leaving out all those poems already covered by group (a), and of course those that are indisputably the work of John. Among these are the various translations from the German, etc., and those hymns and psalms that are adaptations from other poets. While I personally am not convinced that all translations are *ipso facto* by John (Frank Baker has shown,[8] and I agree, that two hymns in particular appearing in the *Moral and Sacred Poems* are translations and are almost certainly by Charles), I think we must ascribe all such to John in the absence of very strong evidence to the contrary, and therefore exclude them from our Charles Wesley corpus. But, as far as I know, there is no certain case of Charles Wesley adapting or improving the work of other poets other than that of his brothers John and Samuel, whereas John had almost a passion for making use of, and adapting, other people's work, whether it be verse or prose; so that we exclude from our consideration all the hymns that are adaptations of Herbert, Norris, Prior, and others; in the earlier publications of 1738, 1739, 1740, and 1741 the many psalm versions, whether it be the New Version, or Watts, show minor variations, and these must all be ascribed to John, and therefore excluded.

The church, and scholarship in general, has reason to be grateful to Osborn for his work, for it made the contents of rare volumes available; and some early editions are *very* rare; there are, for instance, only two extant copies each of the *Charlestown* and 1738 *Collection* first editions. Now, after well over a century, Osborn himself is very difficult to find. But what is more important, perhaps, is that the thirteen volumes have serious drawbacks: in the first place, the spelling and general styling is modernized without any indication in the Introduction or elsewhere as to the principles governing such modernization; there are no indications as to how or when the texts varied from edition to edition; and far too often, in those cases where Osborn has added hitherto unpublished material, he selects verses from a poem, again without indication of when or why.

This brings us to our third group, the three volumes of *The Unpublished Poetry of Charles Wesley* (1988-1991). These include, in addition to the new material, those poems in their entirety of which Osborn published only part; but, because of the exigencies of costs, these three volumes contain only a minimum of variant readings, and those only in exceptional cases.

I am taking it for granted that we must, without question, think in terms of an edition with the full critical apparatus of the Bicentennial

Edition of John Wesley's *Works*, that is to say, with fitting introductory chapters, variant readings, (especially comparing the published version with the manuscripts where possible), the history of the various editions of each original volume, with stemma, and so on, or odious comparisons will be made! This will involve collation of the various editions of Charles Wesley's lifetime—and of the Nativity Hymns there were some twenty-six editions. As we have seen, this problem is further complicated by the fact that some of the hymns were in volumes, or appeared at the end of volumes as an appendix, which John Wesley no doubt supervised as they went through successive editions. Clearly Charles Wesley had, as has been hinted, no supervision of volumes reprinted in America; how far can we say the same for those reprinted in Ireland? Now Charles Wesley was in Ireland from September 1747 to March 1748, a period of six months, and during that time no less than nine collections of hymns were printed in Dublin by the printer Powell, with whom Charles Wesley dined and spent other time. Is it unreasonable to suggest that Charles placed orders while he was there, and supervised the printing? In the autumn of 1748 he was back in Ireland and there met the printer Harrison in Cork. Again, two items were printed by Harrison about that date as well as five of his brother's shorter publications; is it not likely that Charles again was in charge? All his productions otherwise seem (for many bear no indication of either place or printer) to have been printed in either London or Bristol, apart from one printed in Newcastle in 1751, and Charles was there in August of that year. So it would not be safe to assume he did not read the proofs of all those British editions.

We have referred to the fact that Osborn "modernized" the styling of the poems, as regards punctuation, capitalization, spelling, and general appearance. What are we to do? Charles Wesley's own style developed in the course of nearly half a century. We can see this in two ways: first, by comparing early and late printings of the same work, and, second, by comparing the first edition of an early work with the first edition of a late work. A comparison of the first edition of the *Whitsuntide Hymns* (1746) with an unnumbered edition of forty years later (1786) shows the earlier edition to be heavily capitalized, in accordance with Charles's practice and the custom of the day. This shows itself not only in that every noun, and other significant words, begin with a capital in 1746, whereas 1786 follows modern usage much more closely; but important words appear printed entirely in capitals: THE PROPHECY, PROMISE, GIFT, THE GRACE, GOD, and so on; all these disappear in 1786. In 1746 unpronounced *e*'s and *i*'s are not printed: Orig'nal, Spir't, join'd, purchas'd, and others too numerous to list; all these are restored in 1786, very often with the apostrophe placed above the *e* in the case of

41

past participles; words are italicized in 1746 for the sake of emphasis, while in 1786 italics are reserved for proper names (as also in 1746). Spellings are modernized: chear, chace, Paradice, woud'st, compleat, Seraphick in 1746 give way to their modern form forty years later; though shew, burthen, and rent (as a verb) are still retained. A similar difference is found if we compare, say, the *Hymns and Sacred Poems* of 1742 with *The Protestant Association* of 1781, though the later publication still frequently printed nouns with an initial capital. We have, of course, to bear in mind that we may well have to do with a particular printer's conventions as much as with Charles Wesley's changing style; it depends on how far the one imposed his preference on the other, and how far Charles Wesley insisted, or not, on his own preferences. And that we may never know. Summing up, perhaps we ought to say that the style in this edition should be that of the printing, spelling, etc. of the 1780s in which Charles Wesley acquiesced. This would then be faithful to Wesley and at the same time be sufficiently in tune with modern styling as not to make reading difficult.

Two other questions arise. If we, as we should, show all the variant readings, i.e. demonstrate the history of a poem, including its occasional erratic variants, do we also take into account the original manuscript reading if the manuscript still exists? I suppose we must, for thereby we are able both to assess the meaning of a poem and the way in which the poet worked; our understanding of both poet and poem is enhanced. As I have already said, one always takes it for granted that anything published after Charles Wesley's death, anything for which he was not responsible, is excluded from consideration. This is certainly, in my judgment, the correct procedure in the majority of cases; but should we not take cognizance of the way in which well-known, favorite hymns have been treated? To take the most obvious example, the hymn "Glory to God and Praise, and Love" is far better known by the first line of its seventh verse, "O for a thousand tongues to sing," and we cannot ignore that!

We still have to face the question of the authorship of many volumes. Of all the collections, from the three volumes of the *Moral and Sacred Poems* to the twelve-page hymn pamphlets to the single hymns at the end of tracts, very few, comparatively, bear Charles Wesley's name; indeed, a high proportion bear no name at all; others bear John Wesley's name only as publisher; others bear both names. It is natural to assume that John saw through the press those publications bearing his name, even though work by Charles may have been included, whether they be hymnbooks containing work by both brothers—and by others—or, for example, *A Word to a Protestant* which, in some editions, contains three hymns by Charles. I suspect we can assume the same in the cases of publications bearing the name of both brothers; John as the senior, the organizer, the businessman, would naturally take responsibility, as he would in the cases of those anonymous collections containing hymns of mixed authorship. Charles clearly was responsible for his own publications; indeed, in one or two cases John found grounds to criticize some hymns which he had not seen before their appearance in print; such were the two volumes of the *Short Hymns on Select Passages of the Holy Scriptures* of 1762. We are left with the considerable number of anonymous works, many of them slight in bulk.

Wesley scholars are aware of the tradition, originally publicized by Samuel Bradburn, that the brothers agreed not to distinguish their hymns, which information Bradburn claimed to have received from John Wesley himself. And while many nineteenth-century hymnbooks were content to print simply "Wesley" as the author, with a note "not certain whether John or Charles," most scholars have found the problem too intriguing to ignore. Osborn said that "his own inquiries have led him to think it likely that Mr. John Wesley contributed more largely to these joint publications than is commonly supposed; and that the habit of attributing almost everything found in them to his brother, is scarcely consistent with a due regard to accuracy."[9] But he adduced no evidence whatever in support of his claim. Henry Bett[10] and Frank Baker,[11] chiefly, have attempted to draw up criteria whereby it was hoped to identify the work of the brothers, with some degree of likelihood if not certainty. Baker's criteria are not identical with Bett's; and others, notably J. E. Rattenbury and Newton Flew, together with the editors of Volume 7 of the Oxford/Bicentennial Edition of John Wesley's *Works*, have also varied in their judgment. All of which, of course, suggests how uncertain are any conclusions and ascriptions. That does not mean that the chances of a hymn or poem having been composed by John or Charles are equal. We have sufficient verse in Charles's hand, or published by him, or ascribed to him by his brother, for us to be sure that the vast majority are of Charles's authorship. Apart from the consideration of criteria, did John's fantastic work schedule allow him time for composition? If he had spent time in versifying, would not his journal or his diary, every minute accounted for, have betrayed the fact? The authors already cited suggest the particular hymns that either are known to be, or may well be, John's; but the question may rather be: Are there perhaps hymns that have been hitherto ascribed to John which in fact were written by Charles? Two translations from the German, for instance, (and we have traditionally assumed that all such were John's) may well be by Charles because of their meter and phraseology, both of which are unlike John's known preferences. We cannot spend time now examining this question in detail; the places where the study can be made have already been indicated. Herbert sums up the situation when he says, "Unless some as yet undiscovered evidence is brought to light, we must refrain from attribution to John Wesley any of the poetry except pieces such as those we have been reviewing, which can be definitely proved to have been his."[12] He amplifies this in a note: "A letter from the Rev. John Telford written some months before his lamented death assured me that he believed, as I do, that the only entirely original poem definitely attributable to John Wesley is that on Grace Murray."[13] So I suggest that in any definitive edition of Charles Wesley we must include all that is not indisputably John's work, with perhaps an indication of those few poems which may conceivably be his brother's.

In any edition of Charles Wesley's complete works, the poetry, I suspect, will be the largest individual section, perhaps even greater in sheer bulk than all the rest of his writings put together. The great majority is largely unknown; the two or three hundred hymns in contemporary hymnbooks comprise the poetry on which his popular reputation rests—and that is a smaller body of sacred poetry than was familiar a couple of generations ago. The British 1876 Wesleyan Hymnbook contained 706 hymns of Charles Wesley's (certain or probable) to 320 by all other writers; and those 320 included the work of John and the two Samuel Wesleys, father and son. And if all those 706 hymns were not all equally known, at any rate they were all in the book used by perhaps a couple of million Methodists every Sunday, and cannot fail to have been known in some degree, especially as the hymnbook was used in class meetings and in private devotion as well as in chapel on Sunday. But nowadays others are beginning to discover and appreciate Charles Wesley; the work of Bett and, I suspect, Bernard Manning (precisely because he was not a Methodist) are beginning to bear fruit. In the last very few years there have been a number of selections of Charles Wesley's poetry published, each with a critical and appreciative introduction; one thinks of the work of Allchin & Hodge, and in 1988, Timothy Dudley-Smith—all three Anglicans—in addition to the study-anthologies of John Lawson, H. G. Tunnicliffe, Gordon Wakefield, Alan Kay, and of course S T Kimbrough, Jr. To publish in a full-scale edition all the poetry of Charles Wesley can only lead to even wider knowledge and appreciation. English scholarship and Christian piety demand it of us. Let us not fail future generations.

Chapter 3

CHARLES WESLEY AS POET

Kenneth D. Shields

One cannot read any scholar on the hymns and poetry of Charles Wesley without hearing the same question raised again and again: Why do so few, especially in the literary and academic worlds, value his hymns as poetry? In the splendid 1983 edition of the *1780 Collection*, Oliver Beckerlegge states:

> During recent years attention has been drawn to the high literary quality of much of Charles Wesley's verse. Although too many scholars remain who assume that a hymnwriter may not also possess poetical gifts of a high order, the dark ages of fifty years ago, when hymns were automatically excluded from any consideration of English poetry, are happily past.[1]

S T Kimbrough, Jr., in his Foreword to *The Unpublished Poetry of Charles Wesley* (1988) asserts: "Charles Wesley is indubitably one of the important literary figures of the eighteenth century and one of the most outstanding Christian poets in English history."[2] Yet Peter Levi, Professor of Poetry at Oxford University, in his recently published *Penguin Book of English Christian Verse* (1984) includes only "Wrestling Jacob" in his selection. Collections of eighteenth-century poetry for academic use either have nothing of Wesley's or only "Wrestling Jacob" and an occasional hymn, usually "Hark! The Herald Angels Sing."

Underlying the question are a variety of complex further questions which lie at the heart of both the practice of Wesley and the nature of poetry in his century as well as modern criteria used by critics to evaluate his work. I shall try to identify the questions I find most useful for an understanding of Charles Wesley's hymns and poems, and as one whose job is to teach the poetry of the eighteenth century, I will ask you to examine with me several texts more carefully and compare them with another poet's work. Literary criticism has sometimes been described as placing one text beside another, and I shall ask you to do that with me. But first some background.

45

Both John and Charles Wesley were at Oxford during the period when the poetry of Alexander Pope became the standard against which all other poetry was measured, and the poetry Pope aspired to was not that of his contemporaries but those classical masters, Virgil and Horace. Both John and Charles greatly admired Pope's poetry and the standards he established. Pope died in 1744 when Charles Wesley was thirty seven. Given the religious interest and commitment of the Wesleys, we might have expected John Milton and George Herbert to have figured more largely as an influence than in fact they did. Milton, however, was also an influence by indirection through other eighteenth-century poets who wrote what may be called the "biblical sublime," poets such as James Thomson (*The Seasons*) and the evangelical poets, Edward Young (*Night Thoughts*) and James Hervey (*Meditations Among the Tombs*). We know more about what John Wesley's taste in poetry was than we do of Charles's because his letters are available in accessible form. Hopefully with further publication of Charles Wesley's letters we can speak more definitively on what he read. From what we do know, John's reading was much wider, and he was more aware of his world than was Charles.

What was their literary world like? Poetry in that century was supported and sustained by patrons, men and women of social standing and wealth. Although a very few, Alexander Pope and Samuel Johnson being notable exceptions, were able to support themselves through their writing, most poetry of the time was written by men and women either in academic posts (Thomas Gray, for example) or priests in the Church of England like Charles Churchill who neglected his parish and lived in London to be near the center of the literary world. To be a poet in the eighteenth century was to write for a comparatively small group of worldly people, largely of the upper class, who represented for Methodists generally and Charles in particular many of the things against which he preached.

That Charles Wesley understood the ambiguities of that audience and the dangers it represented is clear at least in relation to music. Blessed with an extraordinarily precocious musician son, and his namesake, he recognized the need to get for him the training and instruction in music which his talents demanded. At the same time, that meant at least marginally to become involved in a world that Charles shrank from out of fear for his son's immortal soul. That fear became indeed real for him when his other son Samuel, only slightly less gifted than his brother, became involved with a musical circle centered in the Portuguese Roman Catholic chapel and embraced the Roman Catholic faith.

It is my belief that Charles Wesley could have become a significant poet as defined by the literary world of his time, but it is my contention that he chose not to pursue his talents in that direction. William Cowper, in contrast, wrote both hymns for the parish services at Olney and poems in the fashionable literary genres for a London audience. The poetry and music patronized by the court and the social circles and discussed in the literary coffee houses and periodicals of the time was rejected by Wesley. This can be seen both in what he did not do and what he did. Nonetheless his hymns and poems could only have been written in the eighteenth century and reflect the literary taste for clarity, simplicity, and purity of diction which Charles clearly expresses and John states as the standards which governed his selection and editing of Charles's hymns for the great *Collection of Hymns for the People Called Methodists*. In his Preface to that collection, he states:

> May I be permitted to add a few words with regard to the poetry? Then I will speak to those who are judges thereof, with all freedom and unreserve. To these I may say, without offence: (1). In these hymns there is no doggerel, no botches, nothing put in to patch up the rhyme, no feeble expletives. (2). Here is nothing turgid or bombast[ic] on the one hand, nor low and creeping on the other. (3). Here are no *cant* expressions, no words without meaning. Those who impute this to us know not what they say. We talk common sense (whether they understand it or not) both in verse and prose, and use no word but in a fixed and determinate sense. (4). Here are (allow me to say) both the purity, the strength, and the elegance of the English language—and at the same time the utmost simplicity and plain-ness, suited to every capacity. Lastly, I desire men of taste to judge—these are the only competent judges—whether there is not in some of the following verses that true spirit of poetry, such as cannot be acquired by art and labour, but must be the gift of nature. By labour a man may become a tolerable imitator of Spenser, Shakespeare, or Milton, and may heap together pretty compound epithets, as 'pale-eyed,' 'meek-eyed,' and the like. But unless he is born a poet he will never attain the genuine *spirit of poetry*.[3]

Few of the over 4,600 hymns and poems published in his lifetime conform to the major kinds of poetry practiced by Pope and his contemporaries. Only occasionally does he use the decasyllabic or heroic couplet; when he does so, it is for satirical purposes, such as in his "Epistle to Whitefield" (1771). He did not write moral essays or epistles, the usual forms to satirize the ills of the day or to chastise publicly gross sinners against God or the social standards. In his unpublished poems he did attempt these "secular" forms more frequently, but many of these have only now appeared in print, and some appear to have been left unfinished and unrevised.

What he chose to write are hymns and poems which cannot be properly called lyrics as the lyric was understood by his contemporaries.

The lyric was understood as a genre suitable for private occasions, thoughts, and feelings such as pass between a lover and his lass. Eighteenth-century poetry was overwhelmingly concerned with public poetry written for public occasions. As a result, the lyric was little valued. It also carried a slightly negative association, since it was used in the late seventeenth and early eighteenth century for erotic poetry. Isaac Watts called his sacred poems "lyrics," by which he meant to stress their simplicity in form and diction.

The form Wesley's writing took was influenced less by its serious content than by the audience for which he wrote and the occasions on which his hymns were to be sung. The verse form familiar to the generally uneducated and illiterate (which meant at the time not just the inability to read and write but to be ignorant of the classics) was the ballad, the poetry of the people; but the ballad was also attracting the interest of poets since collectors were beginning their work of preservation of that ancient body of poetry, and imitations of varying kinds of ballads were becoming fashionable. Gray's "Elegy: Written in a country Church Yard" is the best known example of a highly sophisticated adaptation of the ballad stanza for an urban, educated, academic reader. Professor Frank Baker has distinguished nearly one hundred stanza forms, or what in hymnody are called meters, in Charles Wesley's hymns. Most of these may be fairly described as variations on the common ballad measures rather than lyrics.

Practically speaking, the verse forms Wesley used had to conform to the metrical demands of the limited musical settings available to him and his audience. Because of his musical knowledge, however, his stanzas are more varied and sophisticated than those written earlier in the century. (The relationship between hymn text and musical setting needs much more attention. The studies done by the late Erik Routley give us a place to start, especially his *The Musical Wesleys* (1968) and his books and articles dealing more generally with hymnody. But much more remains to be done.) The stanzas Wesley uses are not usual in poetry, then or now, and strike the ear most oddly when separated from their musical setting. He seems to have composed with the tunes running in his head, the music determining his meters and placement of accent or stress. From my reading of his poetry, I believe Wesley wrote primarily not to be read but to be sung. There are many references in John Wesley's letters to the singing of Charles's texts, but few references to the reading of his hymns.

The appropriate diction for poetry was continually debated during the whole century and Wesley reflects the taste for the Senecan style, a chastened, less metaphorical diction. Wesley's diction is notable for its use of biblical language. One of the most frequently quoted comments on Charles Wesley's use of scriptural language is that by Rattenbury: "A skilful man, if the Bible were lost, might extract much of it from Wesley's hymns."[4] The full annotation of some of the hymns in the *1780 Collection* in the Bicentennial Edition of John Wesley's *Works* demonstrates how almost every line, every phrase, can be identified with a specific reference to Scripture. This thoroughly biblical language is seen by most as one of the splendid qualities of his hymns and poems. To understand Wesley's use of scriptural language it may be helpful to place such usage within poetic practices of the eighteenth century.

It appears probable that most school boys in England were taught the rudiments of versification by asking them to do metrical paraphrases of the Psalms. Found among the juvenile writings of almost all the poets of the time are such metrical exercises. Further, at the heart of instruction both in school and university was the translation of classical texts, especially the Latin Augustan poets, Horace, Virgil, Ovid, and the late Augustan Juvenal. These poets, with Homer, were seen as the foundation of the learning of an educated man. They carried enormous authority and were reverenced as "the Ancients." A reader who knows his Homer, Virgil, and Horace will find their writings as sub-text to almost all that was written by Milton, Dryden, Pope, and the other major writers of the century. For those not literate in the classical languages, there were numerous translations by major writers, including Dryden's *Aeneid* and Pope's *Iliad* and *Odyssey*, all translated into heroic couplets, the line of poetry felt to be proper for heroic poems. Access to a knowledge of the Ancients distinguished a man of letters from the middle class whose education was functional and concerned with the practical needs of the counting house and the language of commercial contracts. But shared by both the merchants from the city—usually from a Puritan background and now making up the primary support for the Evangelical Revival within the Church of England—and the upper class public school and university educated men of letters was a knowledge of the English Bible and the Book of Common Prayer, both of which carried an authority almost equal to that of Homer, Virgil, and Horace. The language of the Book of Common Prayer, as well as of the litanies and collects, was thoroughly biblical. Nonconformity also limited the language used in chapel services to the words of the Bible. For both church and chapel, the Psalms, the hymnbook of Jesus, became their hymnbook as well, especially in the metrical versions of Sternhold and Hopkins and in the eighteenth-century version by Tate (the poet laureate) and Brady.

The eighteenth-century hymn as Wesley knew it sprang both from this use of biblical language in worship and from current practices in secular poetry, especially that known as "imitation." In the practice of the time, distinctions were clearly drawn between (1) the *authoritative text*, whether Virgil or the Bible, (2) a *translation* of that text into English (which if it was to be valued must be exact and as faithful as possible), (3) a *metrical paraphrase* of that text which permitted some freedom necessary to turn it into verse but not a substantive divergence, and (4) finally, what was called "an *imitation*." In an "imitation" the classical text remains as a distinguishable sub-text, sometimes actually printed at the bottom of the page to encourage comparison with the original for those whose memories might not be exact. But ordinarily the reader is paid the compliment of the poet's assuming he will know the text well enough to follow without such help. (There is, of course, a kind of snobbery going on with such poetry.) In an "imitation," the English text loosely follows the general organization and arrangement of the classical text but substitutes English places, figures, flowers and imagery. Rome becomes London, Augustus becomes George the III, and in the case of biblical imitations, the Hebrew Psalms are turned into distinctive Christian poems as in many of Charles Wesley's Psalms.

To understand and appreciate such poetry requires a level of classical education that effectively excludes all but an extremely few modern readers. Even in the eighteenth century, it excluded all but those who had the leisure, the wealth, and the university education that distinguished a class within the upper class. When the young Sam Johnson wished to leave Lichfield for the literary circles of London, he sent ahead of his arrival as a kind of poetic introduction, his poem "London," an imitation of the third satire of Juvenal. The major poem of his career was "The Vanity of Human Wishes," an imitation of the tenth satire of Juvenal. "Imitation" was a kind of poem which carried status among the most sophisticated and learned. It is hard to think of it as a form that could flourish outside the academic quadrangles of Oxford and Cambridge. Isaac Watts, however, included imitations in his collection of sacred poems, *Horae Lyricae* (1727).

What such practice did for Charles Wesley was not only to allow but to encourage a freedom in the use of biblical narrative and language. For example, although Isaac Watts "Christianized" the Psalms for use in Nonconformist chapel worship, he was never as free as Wesley in his "imitations" of the Psalms. Look, for example, at Wesley's "imitation" of the twenty-third Psalm:

50

Jesus the good Shepherd is;
   Jesus died the sheep to save;
He is mine, and I am His;
   All I want in Him I have—
Life, and health, and rest, and food,
All the plentitude of God.

Jesus loves and guards His own;
   Me in verdant pastures feeds;
Makes me quietly lie down,
   By the streams of comfort leads:
Following Him where'er He goes,
Silent joy my heart o'erflows.

He in sickness makes me whole,
   Guides into the paths of peace;
He revives my fainting soul,
   'Stablishes in righteousness;
Who for me vouchsafed to die,
Loves me still—I know not why!

Unappalled by guilty fear,
   Through the mortal vail I go;
My eternal Life is near;
   Thee my Life in death I know;
Bless Thy chastening, cheering rod,
Die into the arms of God!

Till that welcome hour I see,
   Thou before my foes dost feed;
Bidd'st me sit and feast with Thee,
   Pour'st Thy oil upon my head,
Giv'st me all I ask, and more,
Makes my cup of joy run o'er.

Love divine shall still embrace,
   Love shall keep me to the end;
Surely all my happy days
   I shall in Thy temple spend,
Till I to Thy house remove,
Thy eternal house above![5]

This is not Charles Wesley at his best. Other Psalm imitations are more successful, usually when he is less bound to the biblical text. The familiar, "O for a heart to praise my God," for example, is an imitation of part of Psalm 51, but perhaps because that Psalm is less familiar and less lodged in the mind, the imitation stands somewhat freer from its sub-text.

In his psalm imitations, we see Wesley following an accepted poetic practice of the time in substituting Christian theology for Jewish. Also supporting his practice is the Christian, especially evangelical, attitude that the Hebrew Scriptures are the "*Old* Testament," to be valued largely for its messianic prophecies and to be interpreted through Christian eyes to free the gospel of Christ latent in it. Such a cavalier attitude toward the Bible Jesus knew as Scripture, may offend both Christian and Jew today, but it was uncritically accepted by Wesley.

It is only a short step from imitation to the free use of biblical language which characterizes the diction of Wesley's hymns and poems. Commonly the phrases and imagery are drawn not from a single passage but from all over the Bible. Although Wesley gains authority, perhaps, by his use of biblical language, it is at times a source of poetic weakness. In such instances the language and imagery drawn from Scripture has lost the metaphorical power it had in its biblical context. Wesley seems drawn too often to the sweeping and grand abstractions such as "God our righteousness," and when he does use a concrete detail—such as "worm"—to describe sinful humankind, or his use of blood imagery, there is no indication that he *sees* what he says. We can see this by comparing Richard Crashaw's "They have left thee naked Lord," with Charles Wesley's "With glorious clouds encompassed round."

Crashaw wrote a century before Wesley and before the Royal Society encouraged the less metaphoric style we call modern English.

> Th' have left thee naked Lord, O that they had!
> This Garment too I would they had deny'd.
> Thee with thy selfe they have too richly clad,
> Opening the purple wardrobe in thy side.
> O never could there bee Garments too good
> For thee to weare, But these of thine owne blood.[6]

The imagery is extraordinarily vivid and compellingly personal. The scene upon which the poet meditates is objectively and starkly presented. Though the picture created is that of the central event in Christian faith, the diction is not scriptural. At its heart lies a rational, intellectual awareness inseparable from the feelings evoked. The mind is required as much as the feelings. The first line is an objective, descriptive statement. "The Lord," with all that title implies, has been left exposed, humiliated, vulnerable, naked. But then the paradox that drives the poem is introduced, contradicting the statement. The second part of the line concludes with a cry of anguish from the heart: "O that they had!" for He is not left naked after all. The imagery of garments follows with logical rigor. The "I" of the speaker is used only once in the poem, and his response to what he sees before him focuses not on himself and his feelings but on what has been done to his Lord. The ironies continue to unfold. Robed with himself is rich robing indeed. He is his own wardrobe and is clothed with himself. But is there any other garment, no matter how kingly, rich enough, good enough, for him to wear but his own blood?

This poem of metaphysical wit displays that inseparable union of thought and feeling, subject and object, that characterized the School of Donne and the practice of George Herbert, the Wesleys' favorite poet from the seventeenth century. It is a poem that requires no musical setting since it carries its own music with it. Additional sounds might violate it, and certainly the kind of settings available at the time would have trivialized its impact. (It has been set to music recently by Daniel Pinkham as an anthem for Lent.) This is not a poem written for "public use." It is a meditative poem primarily to be read in private devotion in which the poem aids the reader in what was known as "composition of place," a process of making vividly present a central event crucial to Christian faith.

Crashaw's use of language is precise and concrete. His use of blood imagery is precise and powerful. It is real blood, not a theological abstraction. For him words create pictures. Charles Wesley, following evangelical practice, is more concerned with the effect of words rather than their power to create or recreate a scene.

By the eighteenth century such metaphysical poetry was no longer in fashion. We know from John Wesley's own "editing" of George Herbert's poetry for the *1780 Collection* that he at least did not know quite how to respond to such intense writing. Wesley's "With glorious clouds encompassed round"[7] uses some of the same imagery, but it is a hymn text rather than a poem.

> With glorious clouds encompassed round,
>   Whom angels dimly see,
> Will the Unsearchable be found,
>   Or God appear to me?
>
> Will he forsake his throne above,
>   Himself to worms impart?
> Answer, thou Man of grief and love,
>   And speak it to my heart!

In manifested love explain
　Thy wonderful design:
What meant the suffering son of man,
　The streaming blood divine?

Didst thou not in our flesh appear,
　And live and die below
That I may now perceive thee near,
　And my Redeemer know?

Come then, and to my soul reveal
　The heights and depths of grace,
The wounds which all my sorrows heal,
　That dear disfigured face.

Before my eyes of faith confessed
　Stand forth a slaughtered Lamb,
And wrap me in thy crimson vest,
　And tell me all thy name.

Jehovah in thy person show,
　Jehovah crucified
And then the pard'ning God I know,
　And feel the blood applied.

I view the Lamb in his own light
　Whom angels dimly see,
And gaze, transported at the sight,
　To all eternity.

The first stanza begins well. The controlling image is that of "seeing" God. He is "encompassed," i.e., circled, by "glorious clouds," clouds which are made full of glory by the source of light who is God himself. But even the angels can only "dimly see" what is beyond seeing or finding, who cannot be seen by attempting to do so and so is "the Unsearchable." The fourth line makes God the subject of revelation not its object. If God is to be seen by angels or by "me," it will be at *God's* choosing, *God's* self-revelation.

The second stanza is framed as a wondering rhetorical question. Will God forsake a "throne above" to "impart Himself" to "worms"? The question answers itself. But the choice of "worms" as an image of sinful humankind, if it creates any picture at all, is a false one. God after all became incarnate in the *flesh* to redeem *humankind*; he was not incarnate in a worm. Milton has Satan "imbrute" himself in a worm, a snake, in order to seduce Eve, but Christ became a second Adam. The question is posed to the Man defined by "grief" and "love." His answer must be addressed not to the mind or reason but to the *heart* of the questioner. Only through grief and love can the "wonderful design" be shown forth.

Wesley next focuses on images drawn from the crucifixion where love and grief or suffering are joined into a concrete answer to the question which now becomes more specific: "What meant the suffering Son of man, / The streaming blood divine?"

Stanza four is an insensitive intrusion. All four lines shift from the vividness of the streaming blood, now emblematic in the poem for grief and love, to abstractions. Wesley seems not to trust the power of imagery to communicate his message. The evangelical takes over and insists on focusing on the question of assurance, *his* assurance, the subjective response, rather than the objective character of God's mighty acts in Jesus Christ. It is as if the gospel can have no real meaning or reality unless there is a subjective response.

The fifth stanza continues this concentration on "my soul" as the point of revelation and slips further into clichéd abstraction—"The heights and depths of grace." But the last two lines once again come to the rescue with "Those wounds" and "that dear disfigured face." At this point there is an effective imaging forth of the gospel with metaphoric strength, and the simple alliteration of "dear disfigured" gives focus and emphasis.

Stanza six stresses seeing with "eyes of faith" and slips into symbols created by theological abstraction.

> Before my eyes of faith confessed
> Stand forth a slaughtered Lamb,
> And wrap me in thy crimson vest,
> And tell me all thy name.

Unfortunately the "slaughtered Lamb" and "crimson vest" of the "blood applied" dominate the concluding stanzas. The eyes of faith appear to look too much inwardly to search for evidences of righteousness rather than outwardly to that suffering love which reveals the heart of God.

The concluding stanza returns to the first, repeating line two, and the poet now views the Lamb "in His own light"—that is, not obscured by clouds no matter how glorious—and transported gazes at the sight eternally.

When Wesley is at his best, he is concrete and specific and his private struggles for assurance fall away as he envisions the objective nature of grace. Perhaps the best hymn to illustrate this is "O for a thousand tongues."[8]

Glory to God, and praise, and love
   Be ever, ever given,
By saints below, and saints above,
   The church in earth and heaven.

On this glad day the glorious Sun
   Of Righteousness arose;
On my benighted soul He shone,
   And filled it with repose.

Sudden expired the legal strife;
   'Twas then I ceased to grieve;
My second, real, living life
   I then began to live.

Then with my *heart* I first believed,
   Believed with faith divine;
Power with the Holy Ghost received
   To call the Saviour *mine*.

I felt my Lord's atoning blood
   Close to *my* soul applied;
Me, me he loved—the Son of God
   For *me*, for *me* He died!

I found, and owned his promise true,
   Ascertained of *my* part;
My pardon passed in heaven I *knew*,
   When written on my heart.

O for a thousand tongues to sing
   My dear Redeemer's praise!
The glories of my God and King,
   The triumphs of His grace.

My gracious Master, and my God,
   Assist me to proclaim,
To spread through all the earth abroad
   The honors of Thy name.

Jesus, the name that charms our fears,
   That bids our sorrows cease;
'Tis music in the sinner's ears,
   'Tis life, and health, and peace!

He breaks the power of cancelled sin,
   He sets the prisoner free;
His blood can make the foulest clean,
   His blood availed for me.

He speaks; and listening to His voice,
   New life the dead receive,
The mournful, broken hearts rejoice,
   The humble poor *believe*.

Hear Him, ye deaf; His praise, ye dumb,
   Your loosened tongues employ;
Ye blind, behold your Saviour come;
   And leap, ye lame, for joy.

Look unto Him, ye nations; own
   Your God, ye fallen race!
Look, and be saved through faith alone;
   Be justified by grace!

See all your sins on Jesus laid;
   The Lamb of God was slain,
His soul was once an offering made
   For *every soul* of man.

Harlots, and publicans, and thieves
   In holy triumph join;
Saved is the sinner that believes
   From crimes as great as mine.

Murderers, and all ye hellish crew,
   Ye sons of lust and pride,
Believe the Saviour died for you;
   For me the Saviour died.

Awake from guilty nature's sleep,
   And Christ shall give you light,
Cast all your sins into the deep,
   And wash the Ethiop white.

With me, your chief, you then shall *know*,
   Shall feel your sins forgiven;
Anticipate your heaven below,
   And own that love is heaven.

The hymn as he wrote it runs to eighteen verses; the hymn as usually reprinted now includes only six verses. *The United Methodist Hymnal* (1989) adds the concluding verse of the original for a total of seven in the musical version, but prints all but verse seventeen of the original on a facing page.

The hymn opens rather too bouncingly:

> Glory to God, and praise and love
> Be ever, ever given,
> By saints below, and saints above,
> The church in earth and heaven.

The stanza chosen is the old ballad or common measure 8.6.8.6, a notation that describes syllable count rather than patterns of stress. It is the same stanza used for "With glorious clouds encompassed round."

The content of the lines is hardly objectionable to any Christian, but it is expressed in language so frequently used that it becomes clichéd. Language from the liturgy when used in poetry has the disadvantage sometimes of being too familiar, but that familiarity can be pleasing in its own way. Here the patterning of stress renders it less effective. The second stanza uses the biblical title "Sun of Righteousness," as the controlling image, a sun, with a pun on Son of God, rising and shining on his benighted soul. It is a metaphor used frequently by Wesley in other hymns and by many of his contemporary hymn writers such as William Cowper. In stanza five, he applies the atoning blood to his own case:

> I felt my Lord's atoning blood
> Close to *my* soul applied;
> *Me, me* He loved—the Son of God
> For *me*, for *me* He died!

This too is characteristic of Wesley's practice. Instead of showing us by images which draw the reader in to share the experience, he tells us, with emphasis added, of his experience rather than pointing outward to what God has done for all and in which all can share. He does generalize from his own experience by arguing that what God has done for him, God can do for others, but the focus tends to fall regularly on the exemplary nature of his own experience. With stanza seven, the hymn as we know it begins.

> O for a thousand tongues to sing
> My dear Redeemer's praise!
> The glories of my God and King,
> The triumphs of His grace.

The "thousand tongues" turns outward, suggesting the sharing with others and "The triumphs of His grace," though abstract, yet points to the objective mighty acts of God that are the basis for his joy.

That concreteness and objectivity continue through the succeeding stanzas.

> He speaks; and listening to His voice,
>   New life the dead receive,
> The mournful, broken hearts rejoice,
>   The humble poor believe.
>
> Hear Him, ye deaf; His praise, ye dumb,
>   Your loosened tongues employ;
> Ye blind, behold your Saviour come;
>   And leap, ye lame, for joy.

Here his lines come alive as poetry. He plays with paradoxes that become oxymorons. Broken hearts rejoice, the deaf hear, the blind see, the lame leap for joy. The patterns of stress follow the argument and with a pleasing irregularity avoid the pounding felt in the first stanza.

Unfortunately the remaining six stanzas do not sustain the same quality. John Wesley must be thanked for his good taste and judicious editing of this text for the *1780 Collection*.

To what extent did Charles Wesley participate in the selection of verses used? Can we judge from this text that Charles was uncritical of his own writing? He seems not to know when to cut and discard, and he seems insensitive to serious lapses in taste which sometimes occur.

His method of composition seems to have been to write rather spontaneously without much revision. He has good closure usually, but at other times the hymns are simply too long. When a hymn extends beyond six stanzas, the writer must expect singers to pick and choose what they will sing. Formal considerations of the piece are weakened along with the progression of logic or development of key images from verse to verse. As we know from the Wesley letters, however, such carving up of hymns was commonplace among Methodists. This is not to say that some longer poems and hymns are not successful when read.

Wesley wrote clusters of hymns on the same or similar themes, frequently using the same language and imagery. It is as if, rather than re-writing, he simply makes another try, keeping the first rather than discarding it, and this leads to much repetitiveness. Even in his shorter collections, such as his Eucharistic hymns, which I greatly admire, the reader's attention is dulled by the repetition. His apparent method of writing may also help explain the huge number of hymns and poems he wrote. Quite simply, from the point of view of his literary reputation, he needed to write less and revise more. No one, no matter how skilled a poet he may be, can write the thousands of hymns he did without producing chaff. The single thing which would do more for the literary reputation of Charles Wesley than any other would be the publication of a single volume of his poetry selected with care and taste.

Poetry of quality impresses the reader with its *economy* of language (what John Wesley meant by the term "strength," defined by Johnson in his *Dictionary* as "much meaning in few words"), its shapeliness of form, its intellectual vigor, and the sensuous qualities that bring the reader into the experience of the poem. The thought should be passionate and the passion disciplined by reason. The versification should not be extrinsic; the rhythm, the rhymes, the use of pauses, the patterns of imagery should make for a whole. Charles Wesley is frequently a good poet in his hymns. But he is at his best when his lines are sung to the right musical settings. Less frequently can he be read with admiration by an informed, experienced reader of poetry who does not share his theological outlook.

With the exception of Wesley's imitation of Psalm 23, the hymns and poems we have examined thus far were published in the *1780 Collection*. Slightly more than half of his poems and hymns were published during his lifetime. As we saw with "O for a thousand tongues," the published texts, usually edited by John Wesley, leave unanswered the question of the final intention of Charles Wesley the poet. The problems of establishing a text for unpublished material are also complex. Are unpublished hymns ones rejected by John Wesley? Were they never intended for publication? Are the manuscripts to be considered as we consider writers' journals, as the place where seeds sprout or fail to, as the case may be, the more promising transplanted, watered and nurtured into flowers, shrubs, bushes, and trees? Are they more properly to be seen as works in progress? Or, are they, as in some cases they appear to be, finished or nearly so, but private, never intended for any eyes but his own, and concerned with family matters improper for circulation outside the family?

Charles Wesley is so identified with the Wesleyan Revival and its hymns and as the younger brother of John Wesley that we hardly know the private man. Yet in many ways it is this poet whom I find most interesting, both for what his until now unpublished poetry reveals about him as a man, and as a poet writing more within the literary conventions of the eighteenth century. The Wesleys were public men. Charles wrote his hymns for public use in meetings for preaching and for use in class meetings and for devotional, private reading. Even the more devotional poems were "public poems" designed to explore matters common to

Christians seeking a disciplined life of obedience to God's will. Those published hymns which tradition associates with private occasions in the life of Charles Wesley—such as those written on the anniversaries of his "conversion"—are not private and do not depend on readers knowing anything about the life of Wesley for their effectiveness. So it was with some eagerness I turned to those poems Charles wrote for few if any eyes but his own.

The hymns have been helpfully commented on by many others. What is now finally possible, since the publication in 1988 of the first volume of *The Unpublished Poetry of Charles Wesley* edited by S T Kimbrough, Jr. and Oliver A. Beckerlegge, is an evaluation of Charles Wesley as a poet based on a broader scope of poetry. We are all deeply indebted to them for making available this body of Wesley's poetry. With the completion of their work, we will for the first time have in print all of Charles Wesley's hymns and poems. If only Osborn, the nineteenth-century editor of his work, had been as careful.

Let me describe the volume in general terms before turning to a closer evaluation of a few of the poems. The poems drawn from various manuscripts are arranged into five sections: The American War and other Poems on Patriotism, Epistles, Courtship and Marriage, Family Hymns and Poems, and finally a small group of eight written on John Wesley's marriage.

It has long been known that both John and Charles Wesley strongly opposed the rebellion of the American colonists against the Lord's anointed. In these poems on the American War and Patriotism, we see Charles, not as a genteel, thoughtful Tory, but as an angry and uncritical supporter of the crown. George III is presented as almost saintly, and those who question or oppose his policies, whether John Wilkes at home or the American colonists abroad, are presented as demonic and witting pawns of Satan. His language is intemperate and abusive.

His most common form to express his anger is the octosyllabic couplet, a form made popular for rough and ready satire by Samuel Butler's *Hudibras* (the first part of which appeared in 1663) directed against the Puritans and in support of Charles II. The tone, style, and language of Wesley's poems are at times Hudibrastic. Otherwise the tone is uniformly one of moral outrage. Wesley is never uncertain about God's will in this conflict, and anyone who differs from his views is treated as a traitor to king and country and as a defier of God. He impugns their motives, loyalty, and character. Howe, the general of His Majesty's forces, becomes the primary object of his attacks. The Loyalists who were forced to flee to Canada or to England are seen as martyrs, and he campaigns for reparations for them.

Political propaganda rarely makes for significant poetry, and Charles Wesley seems unaware of the complexity of the questions he addresses. In these poems Wesley is the evangelist of his king and is not concerned with finishing and polishing his lines. It should be noted, however, that it is conventional in such poetry to cultivate a certain roughness. Those who came through the debates and scurrilous exchanges between parties during the Civil War of the previous century had mastered a language of abuse that was only slightly more refined in the hands of Wesley's contemporaries. Expressing his anger, even fury, is enough for Wesley.

Since Charles (or perhaps John) Wesley chose not to publish these pieces, one must ask if they were written with publication in mind? Were they circulated in manuscript, a common practice at the time? Were they viewed as possibly dangerous and better given a limited circulation ? By whom were they read? At the time of composition, Wesley was in his late sixties, a public figure well known to many through his hymns and his preaching. Did he feel it improper to enter into public debate in this form?

The second section, titled "Epistles," is one of the more interesting and valuable from the point of view of literary questions. All six are written in heroic couplets, which the epistle form requires. The epistle was a popular form among the leading poets of the century. The form itself comes from the practice of Horace, and Alexander Pope's effective use of it was greatly admired. It was Pope whose usage also made the term "epistle" synonymous with "moral essay." It is a form which comes to Wesley, then, with the double authority of Horace and Pope and its use by them as a vehicle for the public discussion of current issues. Both Horace and Pope's epistles were satirical in style, and Pope's finest writing was in this form.

Wesley's epistles reflect the conflicts generated early in the Methodist Revival between the Evangelical Movement proper, which was Calvinistic and predestinarian, and the Wesleyans, who were Arminian and universalist. The epistles as a group are addressed to "To Moravians, Predestinarians, and Methodists. By a Clergyman of the Church of England." The Moravians, of course, had not many years earlier been important to the shaping of some early Methodist practices, including the singing of hymns. But their tendency to "Quietism" and, one must add, their not conforming to the Established Church, make them the object of Wesley's attack.

But the note which is struck early and repeatedly throughout all six is that of personal betrayal by friends. The first epistle, and the finest in terms of poetry, is "An Epistle to a Friend. Written in the year 1743." This poem is found in two manuscripts, one in shorthand, the other with gaps that suggest it was never finished. This epistle mourns the disaffection and falling away of some who were in the original group of Oxford Methodists, including Ingham, Gambold, Delamotte, and Whitefield. Wesley reminds the Friend to whom the epistle is addressed of the great love to God and to each other that had characterized these young men as they set out on their journey of faith. The quietism of the Moravians and the predestination of the Calvinists, he suggests, have seduced some from their pressing on to Christian perfection.

> They heard, they listen'd to the soothing Tale,
> They let the Foe with flesh and blood prevail,
> No more continued in the written Word,
> But vilely cast away both Shield and Sword,
> Gave up the Cause of Christ to Satan's Hands,
> Rejected GOD'S, and bow'd to Man's Commands.
> No longer now their watch the Watchmen keep,
> But love to slumber, and lie down in sleep,
> Their eye-lids in *Poor Sinnership* they close,
> Or, rock'd in Calvin's Arms, supinely doze.[9]

The final couplet is worthy of Pope himself.

Ingham not only left his "Mother Church and native land," he compounded his apostasy by disowning

> . . . the truth his pen did once maintain
> And Ingham now brings up the ghostly train;
> Abandoned to his headstrong carnal will,
> A monstrous compound of elect and still,
> Poor [   ] Ingham quits the glorious strife
> And sells his God and churches for a wife.[10]

This view of marriage as in some way a betrayal of the group is one we will see again in his courtship poems.

Some of the best lines in this epistle are those on Whitefield.

> Meek, patient, humble, wise above his years,
> Unbrib'd by Pleasures, and unmov'd by Fears,
> From Strength to Strength the young apostle goes,
> Pours like a Torrent, and the Land o'reflows:
> To distant Climes his healing doctrine brings,
> And joins the Morning's with the Eagle's Wings,
> Resistless wins his way with rapid Zeal,
> Turns the World upside down, and shakes the Gates of
>   Hell.[11]

But this "Poor piteous youth, while innocent of thought / His feeble mind the dear infection caught"—that is Predestination—"Drank the venomous tongue," and came to stand "In Calvin's cause Against his Brethren," and "warns with moving sobs and flowing eyes / Against those Wesleys, Papists in disguise."[12] In 1755 Charles wrote another Epistle to Whitefield celebrating their reunion which was not published until after Whitefield's death.

Wesley's knowledge and reading of Dryden and Pope are clearly indicated in these lines, some of which echo Pope's *Dunciad*, Book II. His use of triplets and the parenthesis to loosen the bounds of the couplet to permit a freer flow from couplet to couplet reflects the practice of Dryden; Wesley's use of the alexandrine is his own. Pope in his "Essay on Criticism" warns against its abuse by lesser writers when he describes the twelve syllable line "That Like a wounded snake, drags its slow length along." Unfortunately Wesley did not heed the warning and ends too many of his verse paragraphs with one.

The diction is vigorous and strong. The satire is often pointed and sharp. On the whole, these epistles have many good lines. After the death of Pope in 1744, there was increasing concern with the morality of verse satire. This may be the reason these were not published.

The poems on his courtship of Sarah Gwynne and those on his son Samuel are among the most troubling in the volume. The first six poems on his courtship show Wesley wrestling with the question of knowing the divine will in his courtship. He asks for a sign, some unmistakable leading to what God wills. But there is also a deeply troubling note. Can he love Sarah without loving God less? Will loving a creature lessen his love and zeal for God? And will doing so lead to the loss of his immortal soul? If so, it might be better to embrace death and go to God whose love must be all consuming. The phrase, "Horror of offending Thee," occurs twice in two different poems. Typical of this group, and among the more curious is "Jesus, hear, my God, my All." The first and last two verses illustrate the tone.

> Jesus, hear, my God, my All,
> An helpless Sinner's Cry
> Sore perplex'd to Thee I call,
> To thee for Succour fly:
>
>
> O resolve the Painful Doubt,
> And lead me by a Way unknown,
> Cut the Knot of Life, and cut
> Ten thousand Knots in one.[13]

Wesley suggests this hymn poem be sung "to the tune of 'Jesus, let thy pitying eye,'" which requires the two line refrain be sung twice with each stanza.

> Yet for Mercy sake restore
> The Comfort of thy Grace,
> Saviour, let me die, once more
> To see thy smiling Face,
> Purge away my Sinful Blot,
> And then take home thy Banish'd One,
> Cut the Knot of Life, and cut
> Ten thousand Knots in One.
>
> Horror of Offending Thee
> Extorts the sad Request,
> End the Fearful Misery,
> And take me into Rest,
> Now bind up whom Thou hast smote,
> Revive and raise me to thy Throne,
> Cut the Knot of Life, and cut
> Ten thousand Knots in One.[14]

This note of desiring death continues even in those poems apparently written after he and Sarah marry. It is deeply troubling to see this forty-year old man with a young wife so torn between her and God. And why the suggestion of a tune to sing it by? It may have been the tune in his head that he used for his meter. There is something grotesque about it all. But the real key to this is the seriousness with which both Wesleys took Luke 14:25–33 and other calls to perfection.

These courtship poems and those he wrote concerned with his anxious concern over his son Samuel's conversion to the Roman Catholic Church are the most painful and private. Why he wrote them and with whom he shared them is not clear. Some appear in more than one manuscript and with some variation in diction or form. His poems on Samuel are so full of both pain and anger, one wonders again if they were intended for his eyes only.

I think it is clear that Charles used verse as a way of disciplining his thoughts and feelings. He uses the act of ordering words into lines of verse not so much to create poems as to externalize his pain and anger, to examine it, and gain some control. In "Farewell, my All of Earthly Hope," verses four and five are scored out, but restored by his daughter Sally Wesley:

Keep (for I nothing else desire)
The bush unburnt amidst the fire,
   And freely I resign
My child for a few moments lent
(My Child no longer!) I consent
   To see his face no more.

Receive me! and accept my pain!
Nor let him view my parting scene
   Or catch my parting breath!
Nor let the hast'ner of my end,
Th'unconscious Parricide, attend
   To trouble me in death![15]

This is the anger of a father whose will has been thwarted by a beloved son. Here we see Wesley driven to curse his son and to disown him. In the verse that follows, he prays that God may find some way to redeem Samuel, but Wesley does not propose a reconciliation with his son this side of the grave. God, hopefully, will find a way to restore Samuel, but Charles remains unforgiving and angry. One gets a glimpse in such a poem of the Charles who could furiously attack his brother John when Charles felt he knew God's will with absolute clarity and was certain John was obstinately refusing to see things his way. Late in his life, Charles and his son were reconciled, and it is worth remembering he had scored out these lines.

I began with the question of why the hymns and poems of Charles Wesley are not given more recognition by the literary establishment. By now it should be clear that the answer to that question is by no means simple, but some answers may be suggested. (1) Few of Wesley's poems and hymns, taken as wholes, taken at full length rather than the shortened, edited versions we are more familiar with, have the focused shapeliness that poetry at its best requires. This is not to say that individual stanzas and some pieces are not good. I have included "Wrestling Jacob" for your close reading because I share the general recognition of its achievement. (2) Wesley's chief weaknesses lie in his metrics and his diction. His metrics are determined by the musical settings which do not allow for the flexibility and variety in patterns of stress which poetry requires. The music forces him into anapestic and trochaic meters which clash jarringly with his serious matter when read rather than sung. At other times he uses anapestic meter properly, from an eighteenth-century point of view, for comic or satiric ends.

His biblical diction, which gives strength to his hymns for use in worship, sometimes loses its metaphoric and allusive power when lifted from specific scriptural contexts. He draws too much from the more abstract language of the New Testament and not enough from the narratives and rich sensuous language of the Hebrew scriptures. (Watts's "Christ Hath a Garden Walled Around," provides an example of how powerfully such language can be when adapted for Christian purposes.) I suspect Charles may have been uncomfortable—John certainly was— with the language of the Song of Songs. Wesley has great strengths also, and he is at his best in narrative poems, such as "Wrestling Jacob" and the Good Samaritan poems on the parable in Luke now available in Volume II of *The Unpublished Poetry of Charles Wesley*.

But the question as posed is fundamentally flawed. We see from his unpublished verse that he could write poetry in the genres that literary people of his time respected. But Charles Wesley did not choose to write for that audience. He chose instead to employ his considerable talents to serve his Lord as a priest and evangel of His Word. In his pursuit of Christian Perfection, he rejected the world of literature and the pursuit of a literary reputation. He wrote for the humble people who joined him on a journey of faith. If the learned and sophisticated wished to come along, and some certainly did, they must come as sinners saved by grace. Why do we ask that he be measured by standards of success that he himself rejected? Why do we wish for him a literary reputation he did not seek? Charles Wesley made his choice, and I for one, believe he made the right one.

APPENDIX

I. *Wrestling Jacob*[16]

1. Come, O Thou Traveller unknown,
    Whom still I hold, but cannot see,
  My company before is gone,
    And I am left alone with Thee;
  With Thee all night I mean to stay,
  And wrestle till the break of day.

2. I need not tell Thee who I am,
    My misery or sin declare,
  Thyself hast called me by my name,
    Look on Thy hands, and read it there;
  But who, I ask Thee, who art Thou?
  Tell me Thy name, and tell me now.

3. In vain Thou strugglest to get free,
    I never will unloose my hold;
  Art thou the Man that died for me?
    The secret of Thy love unfold;
  Wrestling I will not let Thee go
  Till I Thy name, Thy nature know.

4. Wilt Thou not yet to me reveal
    Thy new, unutterable name?
  Tell me, I still beseech Thee, tell;
    To know it now resolved I am;
  Wrestling I will not let Thee go
  Till I Thy name, Thy nature know.

5. 'Tis all in vain to hold Thy tongue,
    Or touch the hollow of my thigh;
  Though every sinew be unstrung,
    Out of my arms Thou shalt not fly;
  Wrestling I will not let Thee go
  Till I Thy name, Thy nature know.

6. What tho' my shrinking flesh complain,
    And murmur to contend so long,
  I rise superior to my pain,
    When I am weak then I am strong;
  And when my all of strength shall fail,
  I shall with the God-man prevail.

7. My strength is gone, my nature dies,
    I sink beneath Thy weighty hand,
Faint to revive, and fall to rise;
    I fall, and yet by faith I stand,
I stand, and will not let Thee go,
Till I Thy name, Thy nature know.

8. Yield to me now; for I am weak,
    But confident in self-despair:
Speak to my heart, in blessings speak,
    Be conquered by my instant prayer;
Speak, or Thou never hence shalt move,
And tell me if Thy name is LOVE.

9. 'Tis Love! 'Tis Love! Thou diedst for me;
    I hear Thy whisper in my heart:
The morning breaks, the shadows flee:
    Pure UNIVERSAL LOVE Thou art;
To me, to all Thy bowels move;
Thy nature, and Thy name is LOVE.

10. My prayer hath power with God; the grace
    Unspeakable I now receive,
Through faith I see Thee face to face;
    I see Thee face to face, and live:
In vain I have not wept and strove;
Thy nature, and Thy name is LOVE.

11. I know Thee, Saviour, who Thou art,
    Jesus, the feeble sinner's Friend;
Nor wilt Thou with the night depart,
    But stay, and love me to the end;
Thy mercies never shall remove;
Thy nature, and Thy name is LOVE.

12. The Sun of Righteousness on me
    Hath rose with healing in His wings;
Withered my nature's strength, from Thee
    My soul its life and succour brings;
My help is all laid up above;
Thy nature, and Thy name is LOVE.

13. Contented now upon my thigh
 I halt, till life's short journey end;
All helplessness, all weakness, I
 On Thee alone for strength depend,
Nor have I power from Thee to move
Thy nature, and Thy name is LOVE.

14. Lame as I am, I take the prey,
 Hell, earth, and sin with ease o'recome;
I leap for joy, pursue my way,
 And as a bounding hart fly home,
Thro' all eternity to prove,
Thy nature, and Thy name is LOVE.

II. *The Church the Garden of Christ;*[17] Sol. Song 4:12, 14, 15, and 5:1

1. We are a Garden wall'd around,
Chosen and made peculiar Ground;
A little spot inclos'd by Grace
Out of the World's wide Wilderness.

2. Like trees of Myrrh and Spice we stand
Planted by God the Father's Hand;
And all his Springs in *Sion* flow,
To make the young Plantation grow.

3. Awake, O heavenly Wind, and come,
Blow on this Garden of Perfume;
Spirit Divine, descend and breathe
A gracious Gale on Plants beneath.

4. Make our best Spices flow abroad
To entertain our Saviour-God:
And Faith, and Love, and Joy appear,
And every Grace be active here.

5. Let my Beloved come, and taste
His pleasant Fruits at his own Feast.
I *come, my Spouse,* I come, he crys,
With Love and Pleasure in his Eyes.

6. Our Lord into his Garden comes,
Well pleas'd to smell our poor Perfume,
And calls us to a Feast divine,
Sweeter than Honey, Milk, or Wine.

7. *Eat of the Tree of Life, my Friends,*
   The Blessings that my Father sends;
   Your Taste shall all my Dainties prove,
   And drink abundance of my Love.

8. *Jesus,* we will frequent thy Board,
   And sing the Bounties of our Lord:
   But the rich Food on which we live
   Demands more Praise than Tongue can give.

(Isaac Watts)

Chapter 4

CHARLES WESLEY'S LETTERS

Frank Baker

The letters of John Wesley have remained treasured personal relics and prized historical documents for two centuries. As precious symbols of the founder of Methodism they have been eagerly sought throughout the world, and cherished for their literary content as well as their increasing commercial value: their direct simplicity, their forthright challenge, their homely wit, their concern for human sin and sorrow. No such fame has come to the letters of Charles Wesley. Just as the hymns of brother Charles undoubtedly overshadowed those of John, so the journals and letters of John overshadowed those of Charles. Yet if we are to understand John Wesley fully, let alone understand early Methodism, we must not neglect the prose writings of Charles. True, for over a hundred and forty years the bulk of Charles's journals have been known—but not well known—along with a hundred of his letters. The latter have been tantalizing and little used by scholars, however, because most of them are incompletely dated. Few people know these few Charles Wesley letters well. Fewer still realize the literary and historical treasure lying hidden in the other six hundred extant. On countless occasions, these may add a new dimension to the familiar words of John, or offer a revealing glance at both the cooperation and the rivalry between the two brothers.

Too seldom do people think about Charles Wesley as his own person, though many surmise that he was by no means a pale imitation or echo of his older brother. Too many think that Charles was relatively content to retire into his hymnwriting hermitage a few years after Methodism had reached its full stride, was mildly annoyed at the innovations of his iconoclastic brother, but preferred to remain safely ensconced within the fold of upper class religiosity. Only a minority of scholars have realized the deep divisions of character between the two brothers, divisions which split at least one solid English Methodist family into two rival groups, the

Johnites and the Charlesites. Such was the family of Dr. John S. Simon (1843–1933), major authority on British Methodist law and discipline, and author in his later years of an innovative five-volume biography of John Wesley. One of his Johnite children was Elsie S. Harrison (née 'Grace Elizabeth') best known for *Son to Susanna: The private life of John Wesley* (1937). Describing a literary contretemps in which I was embroiled with her over forty years ago can harm no one now, and may dramatically reveal the contrasts perceived between the two brothers even then.

In the June 1945 issue of the *Proceedings* of the Wesley Historical Society appeared a letter written (apparently) by John Wesley which was clearly of major importance. It was written as he approached the coast of Georgia on his missionary venture, "On board the *Sim[m]onds* off the Island of Tibey in Georgia, February 5, 1736." It began: "God has brought an unhappy unthankful wretch hither, thro' a thousand dangers, to renew his complaints, and loath[e] the life which has been preserved by a series of miracles. . . . In vain have I fled from myself to America; I still groan under the intolerable weight of inherent misery! . . . Go where I will, I carry my Hell about me. . . ." This was no forgery. But was it really penned by John? To Mrs. Elsie Harrison was assigned the task of interpreting this letter, at the cost of some psychological somersaults: "The John Wesley we know," she wrote, "is as steady as a rock, and takes an even pace with God for more than fifty years of life. The nervous turmoil and introspection of this letter seem to belong to a different man altogether from the Wesley of Aldersgate Street."[1]

As soon as possible I visited the Methodist Mission House, to which the letter had been donated—those were not the days when you might hope for a photocopy by return of post! Immediately I saw that the letter's handwriting was not in fact that of John Wesley, but of Charles. In an article for the *Proceedings of the Wesley Historical Society* I explained the major differences in calligraphy and in substance from what I had expected to find in a letter from John.[2] With some timidity I informed Mrs. Harrison of her error. She was delighted, and wrote: "What good news about that letter! It was very puzzling coming from John, and it took a real effort of the mind to make it fit him, but to think that it was my old enemy Charles all the time is in one way a great relief and in another makes me feel that I owe John an apology. . . ."[3]

The two brothers were indeed different people, yet very close. Just over two hundred letters remain of the huge correspondence passing between John and Charles Wesley from 1724 to 1788. Clearly these letters are very important in throwing light on the changing moods of both brothers, their theological convictions, their literary labors, joint and separate, their dreams and problems, their contrasting and sometimes conflicting personalities. This interwoven correspondence is of major significance in its contribution to our understanding of the movement whose leadership they shared, especially as in 1746 John legally named Charles as his successor in charge of Methodism upon his own death, nor ever revoked that decision, in spite of their differences.[4]

Methodists are most fortunate in having rich primary sources to supply them with a documented framework for their early history. They have manuscript or printed records of the deliberations of their annual conferences from 1744. These records are checked and augmented by the autobiographical commentary of John Wesley's own printed *Journal*, and this again is enriched at another level by his thousands of private letters. The literary remains of Charles have been far less readily accessible. His journal was not published until long after his death, and even then it was far more uneven, and petered out in 1756—coincident with major ecclesiastical and theological problems arising between the two brothers. For the major treasure of Charles Wesley's manuscript verse and the minor treasure of his journals and letters we are indebted to the zeal and pertinacity of Thomas Jackson, Connexional Editor in 1824–1842. Jackson had become a close friend of Charles Wesley's family in the declining years of their "genteel poverty," and himself financed the purchase of Charles Wesley's manuscripts for a reluctant Conference in 1829.[5]

Owing mainly to Jackson's zeal there have been preserved for posterity in the Methodist Archives, Manchester, even though disordered and often fragmentary, some five hundred of Charles Wesley's letters. A further hundred holographs are scattered elsewhere in England and America, and a similar number are based on copies printed in various publications old and new. The remarkable thing is that over eighty percent may be studied in Charles Wesley's own handwriting, even if we exclude from these figures the thirty replies which he endorsed in shorthand on letters which he had just received—whose transcription is often treacherous.

It seems desirable to conduct a rapid survey of his early domestic correspondence. His first three surviving letters (1728–29) were written from Christ Church, Oxford, to his older brother John (serving as their father's curate in Epworth and Wroot), and the fourth from the home of their elder brother Samuel in Westminster. Between 1731 and 1735 most of his extant letters were to his brother Samuel, with one to their father. During his few months in Georgia again it was mainly correspondence with John in Georgia or Samuel in Westminster, those to John with passages in Latin, Greek, and Byrom's shorthand as a protection against curious eyes. After John's return to England he and Samuel remained Charles's chief correspondents until Samuel's death in 1739. Other evangelicals had joined the list, including Samuel's former Westminster neighbor, James Hutton, and of course from 1737 onwards, George Whitefield. No letter survives to his mother, who died in 1742, but until 1744 John had taken over as almost his sole correspondent. In 1740 his preaching itinerancy had taken Charles to Wales, in 1742 to Northumberland (which he described as "the rude, populous north"), in 1743 to the Midlands, and later that year to Devon and Cornwall. In general, however, like his brother, Charles moved between the two foci of London and Bristol. As he went he gathered up correspondents, though nothing like as many as did his elder brother John.

On August 8, 1747, William Lunell welcomed John Wesley on an exploratory visit to the infant Methodist society in Dublin, but seeing the great promise—spiced with danger—John speedily sent for his brother Charles to take over. John arranged to meet Charles in Wales on his way out, at Garth, the home of Marmaduke Gwynne, a devout Welsh magistrate converted under Howell Harris. While waiting at their rendezvous Charles fell helplessly in love with the Gwynnes' third daughter, Sally: he was thirty-nine, she twenty. Before he left for Ireland they had made a prayer-pact, and from Dublin on September 17, 1747, Charles wrote the first of some hundreds of letters to Sally, assuring her, "My heart is deeply engaged for you. . . ."[6] He spent a fruitful six months building up the Methodist cause in Dublin, with one week's evangelistic excursion inland to Tyrrellspass and Athlone. In March 1748 John Wesley returned to assist and then take over from Charles, who had laid a firm foundation amid heroic labours and severe persecution. After six months' absence, a physical wreck, Charles Wesley struggled back to Garth on March 25, 1748, when "all ran to nurse me . . . [and] quickly put me to bed"—for a week. A year later, with some difficulty, John managed to assuage the financial fears of Mr. and Mrs. Gwynne about marrying their daughter to an impecunious preacher by standing guarantor for an annual literary income of 100 pounds for the couple. On April 8, 1749, Sally Gwynne and Charles Wesley were married by John Wesley, and set up their home in Bristol.[7]

The courtship letters of Charles Wesley to Sally Gwynne form a saga in themselves, running the gamut of emotions from ecstasy to despair and back again, punctuated by breathless verse, including some poems which were included in the two volumes of *Poems* by which in 1749 Charles sought to prove that his brother's literary confidence was not misplaced. Volume 2 included a poem written to her in a letter from Cork on September 17, 1748—the anniversary of his first letter to Sally from Dublin:

> Breath[e]s as in us both One Soul
>   When most distinct in Place:
> Interposing Oceans roll,
>   Nor hinder our Embrace:
> Each as on *his* Mountain stands,
>   Reach our Hearts across the Flood,
> Join our Hearts, if not our Hands,
>   And sing the Pard'ning God.[8]

My favorite in this category, however, is "Thou God of Truth and Love," a perfect wedding hymn which unfortunately is not easily available to United Methodist congregations, though British Methodists still use it in *Hymns and Psalms*. Charles originally wrote:

> Didst Thou not make us One
>   That Both might One remain,
> Together travel on,
>   And bear each others' Pain,
> Till Both Thine utmost Goodness prove
> And rise renew'd in perfect Love.

In John Wesley's *1780 Collection* "both" was changed to "we" and "all," but that did not destroy its matrimonial suitability. I well remember a visiting guest preacher in my English church vestry telling how he and his wife had used "Thou God of Truth and Love" as their own wedding hymn. I responded that this was most appropriate, because it was in fact a love poem written by Charles Wesley for his future bride—only to be deflated by my wife Nellie on my arrival home, "But don't you remember, *we* used it as *our* wedding hymn!"[9]

The length of time that I take to recount the beginnings of Charles Wesley's major correspondence is by no means disproportionate, for over one-third of all his extant letters were written to Sally Gwynne, fifty-three before their marriage, a hundred and ninety-three after! Indeed, if we add letters to their close relatives, almost four hundred (57%) of Charles Wesley's surviving seven hundred letters may be classified as "family letters"!

And it is, of course, a fascinating family, replete with interesting sidelights. Even more important is the fact that Charles Wesley's family letters introduce us to a largely new cast of characters, and new scenery. It is a tremendous gain to our knowledge of the second largest center of British Methodism that for twenty years Sally Wesley was domiciled in Bristol, and thus brought into daily touch with all its leading members and most of its major themes, which she faithfully relayed to her husband. At the same time, with her own family connections, she moved in a somewhat higher echelon of society, whose members were nevertheless still evangelical in outlook, and learning to live comfortably with the Methodists, though they moved more naturally among the leisurely and well-to-do ranks of the Church of England, with a generous sprinkling of titled people among their visiting acquaintances. In the sample letter of 1760 which we quote later, for example, we meet seven names which are not found in the index to Telford's collection of John Wesley's letters. Another incidental bonus of these family letters is that they help us to extend the chronological framework, enabling us to compile a dated outline of Charles Wesley's life, even after the cessation of his journal, comparable to the invaluable daily *Itinerary* of John Wesley's life as prepared by Richard Green on the basis of John's *Journal* and letters.

As Charles helps us to meet new people on the periphery of Methodism, in a new stratum of society, so it can only make for the enriching of our knowledge of the Methodist movement that through his letters there should come out into the open the tensions between the two brothers. Perhaps it is especially important to realize that there were those who genuinely supported Charles against John in his distrust of the ambitions of the preachers, his differing views of Christian perfection, his even fiercer loyalty to the conventions of the Church of England. Many have too often been inclined almost automatically to align themselves with John, as undoubtedly the greater leader. It is salutary to see more clearly the viewpoint of Charles and his supporters, and to discover in greater detail the actual elements in and the results of the tensions between them.

It is quite impossible, of course, to characterize sufficiently the flavor of the many letters to Sally Gwynne, either during the two hectic years of courtship, or during almost forty years of married life, either during the twenty-two years spent in No. 4 Charles Street, Bristol (while Charles passed much of his time in London), or the closing years from 1771, when they shared the London house leased by friendly Mrs. Gumley, No. 1 Chesterfield Street (off Marylebone Road). They had moved to London both because of Charles's declining health and in order to give their boys the best chance of musical development.

Charles still remained an itinerant preacher of sorts, however, and rare was the year for which no letter to Sally survives—and often there are many. She never knew just how he would address her: "My ever-dearest Sally," "My dear partner," "My beloved friend," or no salutation at all—but the longing for her presence always shows through, even when the dark notes of sorrow are there, or his underlying obsession with death. They are conversational, even gossipy letters, jumping from one point to another like a traveller bubbling over with his varied news and queries. At least one sample should be given (the text is presented with abbreviations extended and words styled in the same format as that of the Bicentennial Edition of *The Works of John Wesley*):

London, Moorfields, January 3, 1760.

My dear Sally's wish has been often mine, to have died in my infancy. I escaped many such thoughts last Saturday, by forgetting it was my birthday till night, when Mr. Fletcher's prayer put me in mind of it. Yesterday I dined alone with my faithful friend and yours, L[ady] H[untingdon], and passed the evening with her in close conference. We could not part till past eleven. I have not had such a time this many a month.

This morning I breakfasted at Lady Piers, and dined at Mrs. Lloyd's with Mrs. Gumley and Miss Derby. The length of the entertainment, and very trifling conversation, tired me to death. I am escaped hither to write to my beloved partner.

Next to feeling Christ present, the most desirable state is *to feel Christ absent*. This we often do: O that we did it always!

You are not too old to be cured of the rheumatism, if you have resolution to use the remedy of constant exercise. I threaten you hard, if we leaven[?, "leave" or "live"] over the winter, and I get a sure horse to carry double or treble.

Can the boy [Charles] walk? It is a question often asked me. You will tell me when his face is well; and how Sally continues. I presume you now begin seriously to think of weaning her.

What says Mr. Hooper to my coming to pray with his wife, before she takes her flight?

How is Mrs. Arthurs?

My love to F. Vigor and all others. You *see* what haste I am in. To the Lord I commend you and yours.

Adieu.

Mr. Caslon told me he had wrote to Mr. Farley that he could not send him the Syriac types till he informed him how many of every letter he wanted.

I must desire you yourself to take 100 of the *Earthquake* hymns out of my study, and give them to Mr. Francis Gilbert to bring me when he returns.[10]

Unfortunately there is a serious problem in utilizing fully Wesley's letters to his wife. They were written for her alone, not for posterity. Therefore he was extremely careless about dating them. In spite of many internal clues, there is some uncertainty even in the actual *order* of a group of twelve provisionally dated forty years ago in the month between December 23, 1748, and January 21, 1749.[11] (During the tightly packed year of 1748 Charles wrote twenty-three courtship letters to Sally, during 1749 a further twenty-seven, with nine to her as his wife. Only in five years do his total extant letters to all correspondents exceed thirty: 1748 (32), 1749 (51), 1750 (33), 1755 (38), and 1760 (32); in only three others do there survive more than twenty, 1756, 1759, and 1785. Even the seemingly more certain dates of some letters within such sequences may eventually turn out to be mistaken, however, as the interlacing of further clues lead to more convincing probabilities. Most dates must therefore remain provisional for as long as possible before publication, and must constantly be checked and rechecked as new evidence becomes available. Near certainty in dating is frequent, absolute certainty rare.

Nor should we downplay the value of the letters written outside the family circle. We have already shown how Charles's pioneer ministry in Ireland was of great historical importance, and more detail about this is reflected in his letters. In general, however, Ireland was left henceforth to John (and later to Thomas Coke), while Charles shuttled backwards and forwards between Bristol and London as second in command for his brother. Occasionally he undertook important expeditions for John elsewhere, both recruiting lay preachers and keeping them under firm discipline. In 1751 John assigned to Charles the specific responsibility of "purging the preachers" in the course of touring the Midlands and the North of England, and his letters reflect his prosecution of this task, with some passages to John disguised in shorthand.[12] He was so enthusiastic—and occasionally impetuous—in his task, that he found himself in trouble through preachers whom he had dismissed, and eventually in hot water with his brother.

Charles was afraid that the clerical ambitions of the lay preachers were edging John to the brink of a separation from the Church of England, and that the only remedy might be to send them back to their worldly trades. He confided these fears to his friend the Countess of Huntingdon, and claimed that to safeguard the Church he wanted to "break [John's] power" and frustrate his "rashness and credulity" from allowing his preachers to inveigle him into forming a separate "sect or religion" within the Church. This letter was intercepted, and a copy handed to John, who chided Charles on December 4, 1751.[13]

Charles continued to undermine John's apparent drift away from the Church of England by fiery letters to clergy otherwise friendly to Methodism, realizing that their advocacy would make a far greater impact upon John than his own. Three letters in rapid succession to Walter Sellon, formerly a master at Wesley's Kingswood School, now in a parish, secured a valuable advocate.[14] John prepared a document to discuss at the 1755 Conference, "Ought we to separate from the Church of England?"[15] This at least deferred the issue, but it remained a nagging problem for years. Charles also enrolled other allies, Samuel Walker of

79

Truro, William Grimshaw of Haworth, and Henry Venn of Huddersfield, to discuss with him and his brother the issue of separation.[16] In a shorthand addition to one of his journal-letters to John, Charles informed him—prophetically—"The short remains of my life are devoted to this very thing, to follow your sons . . . with buckets of water, and quench the flame of strife and division which they have or may kindle."[17]

A goodly proportion of his letters continued to address this theme, especially when in 1760 the threat raised its head in a new form. Many Methodist lay preachers were securing preaching licenses under the Toleration Act, at the cost of sixpence and the legal fiction of declaring themselves to be "Protestants dissenting from the Church of England." On that authority three of them were administering the Lord's Supper in Norwich. Charles sent angry letters to his brother, sarcastic letters to his wife, pastoral letters to Methodist societies in major cities, pleading letters to preachers whose loyalty he doubted, and rousing challenges to leading laymen. His letter to William Grimshaw brought forth a letter threatening to "disown all connection with the Methodists," and Charles's public reading of that letter in the London society "put them in a flame." All this was to such good effect that the Norwich offenders were scolded, Grimshaw remained among the Methodists, and at the ensuing Conference there was "love and unanimity."[18] Undoubtedly Charles Wesley's letters changed the course of Methodist history.

He was unable, however, to prevent John Wesley's major defiance of Church order, no matter how much he brandished the pronouncement of the Lord Chief Justice (his old school friend, William Murray, later Lord Mansfield), "Ordination is Separation." The spiritual needs of the American Methodists in 1784 overrode any legal niceties, and John Wesley remained unrepentant about his ordination of Thomas Coke, Anglican priest already, and his right hand man in Methodism, supplanting even brother Charles as the vicarious provider of Methodist episcopacy for America. John Wesley's secret ordinations in Bristol split the Society there in two, and there was a rash of correspondence between Charles and the protesting "Old Planners," especially Henry Durbin, the publication of whose eight letters to Charles, 1784–85, with Charles's endorsed shorthand replies, will open up an important new sub-chapter in the history of Bristol Methodism, especially supported by related letters to other Bristol Methodists. All this was to little avail, however. John Wesley was unrepentant, and was eventually persuaded—perhaps over-persuaded—to add ordinations for Scotland, and even England.[19]

Although it is impracticable to touch on all the lesser themes which merit attention, it seems clearly desirable to glance at some of them from the years when the journal is no longer available. We will sample different themes to different recipients in chronological order, with the assurance that it would have been simple to multiply these examples many times.

We begin with three extracts from Charles Wesley's thirty letters to his three surviving children, in the order of their seniority. To Charles, aged twenty-four, July 23, 1781:

> I only wish to leave you in the narrow way to life. But what has a man of fashion to do with that? After all, then, you must be content to be a gentleman only. . . . Aspiring, living above themselves, in one word, ambition, is the ruin of the nation. It is natural to us, especially to youth. But what is religion for, if not to conquer our passion? If you and your brother and sister would enter the kingdom of heaven, you must leave ambition, vanity, pride, behind you; and be of the few, not of the many.[20]

To Sally, April 8, 1773, aged fourteen:

> Go to bed at nine; and you may rise at six with ease. It is good for soul, body, and estate to rise early.
>
> I allow you a month longer to get the fourth [of Edward Young's] *Night Thoughts* by heart.
>
> Return our love to M[rs.] Vigor, Jenkins, Farley, and all inquirers.
>
> Can you begin the day better than with prayer and the Scripture? What benefit have you reaped from your band? The knowledge of yourself; or the desire to know Jesus Christ? . . . [21]

To Samuel, March 6, 1773, aged seven:

> Come now, my good friend Samuel, and let us reason together. . . . You should now begin to live by reason and religion. There should be sense even in your play and diversions. Therefore I have furnished you with maps and books and harpsichord. Every day get something by heart—whatever your mother recommends. Every day read one or more chapters in the Bible. I suppose your mother will take you now, in the place of your brother, to be her chaplain, to read the psalms and lessons when your sister does not. Mr. Fry must carry you on in your writing. I don't doubt your improvement both in that, and music. God will raise you up friends when I am in my grave, where I shall be very soon—but your heavenly Father lives for ever: and you *may* live for ever with him; and *will*, I hope, when you die. [22] . . .

To one of their preachers, Thomas Lee, who had labored since 1752 mainly in Yorkshire and Lincolnshire, Charles Wesley wrote on February 12, 1760:

> Few preachers are strong in body. We *live* by the gospel; by waiting upon the Lord we renew our strength. Yet we should use the means of health, strict temperance, and exact regularity.

> I am ready long ago to visit my oldest and dearest friends in the north.
> If it be a work prepared for me to walk in before I have finished my course,
> strength will be given, and my way pointed out. . . .[23]

Described by John Wesley as "one of the best preachers in England," Joseph Cownley frequently labored in Newcastle. To him Charles Wesley wrote July 1, 1764, from London:

> You might have heard of another of my prophecies six years ago: "that a new sect of French Prophets or Ranters would arise, and out of the witnesses of perfection. . . ."
>
> The flood of delusion is much subsided here: and I trust in the Lord he will not suffer the folly and credulity of any man to raise it again. . . .
>
> When I left London last year the number of the witnesses was five hundred. Half of them have since recanted. Those who live another year may expect to see them all convinced of their own great imperfection.
>
> You believe a man perfect because he says, "I am": that's the very reason for which I believe and am sure he is not perfect. How then are you and I exactly of one mind? . . . [24]

Much controversy was raised in Bristol by critics of an organ recital given by Charles Wesley, Jr., aged eleven. His father replied to Eleanor Laroche on February 8, 1769:

> Madam. . . .
>
> I always designed my son for a clergyman. Nature has marked him for a musician, which appeared from his earliest infancy. My friends advised me not to cross his inclination. Indeed, I could not, if I would. There is no way of hindering his being a musician but cutting off his fingers. As he is particularly fond of church music I suppose, if he lives, he will be an organist. In order to this he must be instructed. Instruction implies his playing and hearing the best music both in private and public.
>
> Yet he might not have appeared so soon in the music room . . . had not a person in distress requested it. And believe me, Madam, the boy was better pleased with helping a poor man than with any applauses he might meet there. . . . [25]

James Hutton, a dear evangelical friend of the Wesleys' early years in London, and one of their first publishers, drifted away when he became a leading Moravian. They had come together again in close friendship when Charles Wesley came to live permanently in London. Wesley wrote to him on Christmas Day, 1773:

> God will look to that matter of successors. He buries his workmen, and still carries on his work. Let him send by whom he will send. Rather than they should degenerate into a dead formal sect I pray God the very name of Moravian and Methodist may die together! But I believe with Amos Comenius that God has a special regard to the Church of England;

that, when the oak casts its leaves, the holy seed will be the substance thereof; and that our Lord will have a true church, a living people in this island, till He comes to set up his universal kingdom.[26]

To William Perronet, son of the Rev. Vincent Perronet of Shoreham, a close family friend, written from Bristol, January 23, 1774:

P.S. I have had with me this month or more two very extraordinary scholars and catechumens: two African Princes, carried off from Old Calabar [Nigeria] by a Bristol Captain, after they had seen him and his crew massacre their brother and three hundred of their poor countrymen. They have been six years in slavery, made their escape hither, were thrown into irons, but rescued by Lord Mansfield, and are to be sent honourably back to their brother, King of Calabar. This morning I baptized them. They received both the outward visible sign, and the inward spiritual grace, in a wonderful manner and measure.[27]

On November 12, 1781, John William Fletcher, aged fifty-two, married Mary Bosanquet, aged forty-two. On March 13, 1782, after they had moved from her home, Cross Hall, near Leeds, to his parish, Madeley, in Shropshire, Charles Wesley wrote a letter to them both, with a special note to her:

Yours, I believe, is one of the few marriages that are made in heaven. Better late than never. My friend had thoughts of proposing to you (I am his witness) twenty years ago: but he bare false witness against himself, that he sought not you but yours. . . . I sincerely rejoice that he has at last found out his twin-soul. . . .

My friend's longer or shorter continuance here will depend chiefly on his adviseableness. He is (I know, and he knows) a mule by nature: but is become by grace, and by the Wisdom from above, easy to be entreated. Be a little child yourself, and he will be led by you into all that is right. As to the measure of his labours, we will allow him a vote, and private judgment— but then the last resource must be with you. You have a negative. And while he hearkens to the voice of his wife, he will live, and prosper.[28]

To Samuel Seabury, first bishop of the Protestant Episcopal Church of America, consecrated at Aberdeen 14 November 1784, Charles Wesley wrote on September 12, 1785:

Rt. Revd. Sir,

I rejoice with all the Church of God that He has blessed your going out and your coming in; has been with you in the ship, and brought you safe to the haven where you would be.

The bearer of this, Mr. [Joseph] Pilmore, thinks himself called to America. I think so too, having searched with my best diligence into his character through life. It will bear the severest scrutiny. He seems to me a man of good understanding and sincere piety; has some share of learning;

much prudence as well as zeal; and is in one word (as far as I can judge) a vessel fit for the Master's use.

I cannot help hoping great good from his ministry, if you should count him worthy of Holy Orders. Of all our Preachers in America, he was the most useful and most successful. Beloved and esteemed by the Methodists, he is the most likely man to bring back those deluded sheep into the fold.

The eye cannot say to the foot, I have no need of thee. The great Apostle asked all his flock to pray for him. Your fold and ours make but one and the same flock: therefore you are remembered in all our prayers public and private: and our Lord, we doubt not, lays our burthen upon your heart. Earnestly desiring your faithful prayers, and apostolical blessing, I humbly subscribe myself,

Rt. Revd. Sir,

Your meanest Servant and Son,

Charles Wesley.[29]

We close with an incidental tribute to the Rev. Vincent Perronet, whom Charles Wesley termed "The Archbishop of Methodism," and John Wesley "that venerable saint." He was their most intimate adviser on many problems private and public, their agreed arbitrator on points of tension between them such as the status of the preachers. After fifty-seven years as vicar of Shoreham, Kent, Perronet died May 9, 1785, aged ninety-one, after constant attendance by his granddaughter "Betsy," whose mother, Perronet's daughter Elizabeth, had in 1749 married William Briggs, a customs officer and John Wesley's London steward. Charles Wesley had buried Perronet, and he replies to Betsy's mourning letter a year later, on April 28, 1786:

> "*Sad* anniversary of his *translation*", do you call it, and your "loss irreparable"? The day was the most joyful and happy he ever knew; and your loss is momentary, and reparable in a happy eternity. We ought only to rejoice and give thanks for his having been lent to the world near a century. Therefore from this time, observe, I can allow you to mourn no more.
>
> I am always glad to hear of your affairs. You need take no thought for the morrow, but say, "In all my ways I acknowledge thee; and thou shalt direct my paths." My wife and daughter join in true love for you, with, my dear Betsy, your faithful friend and servant, [C.W.][30]

84

Chapter 5

Charles Wesley's Other Prose Writings

Thomas R. Albin

Charles Wesley is best known for his prodigious poetical output—*but who knows Charles Wesley?* Elsewhere in this volume, Frank Baker has informed us that Charles's personal correspondence numbers more than 600 letters in all. In this essay, I would like to offer a brief review of four other genres of prose writings authored by this youngest son of Samuel and Susanna Wesley. The journals, sermons, tracts, and other miscellaneous writings of Charles Wesley each reveal an important aspect of his multifaceted character. Each distinctive genre of literature provides a unique window of insight into the nature and character of the author, as well as invaluable insights into the history, theology, and ethos of the early days of the Methodist movement.

The Journal

Charles Wesley's practice of keeping a spiritual journal began at Oxford during the time his brother John was serving as their father's curate in Wroot. Charles wrote to John in 1729 requesting advice on how to

> write a diary of my actions . . . . If you would direct me to the same or a like method with your own, I would gladly follow it, for I'm fully convinced of the usefulness of such an undertaking.[1]

Later in 1729 John was recalled to his teaching position in Oxford and together the brothers shared their method of journal keeping with other members of the University who joined the religious study and service group that came to be known as "the Methodists." When the Wesley brothers departed for their mission to the American colony of Georgia in 1735, they continued to keep journals and began to extract portions of it for their family and friends in England. The practice of journal keeping and including extracts within missionary letters continued after their return to Britain and the onset of their itinerant ministries related to the Evangelical Revival.

There are times when the content of Charles's journal and his missionary letters overlapped considerably. In reality, the missionary letters were more journal than letter. Although these documents were generally addressed to his brother, John, or his wife, Sally, they appear to have been a transcription from his journal for that particular period of time with brief personal messages appended. Internal and external evidence make it clear that these letters were written with the express intention that they be shared with the Methodist faithful. Occasionally they were copied by others (including John Wesley) for public reading in the societies and on "letter days."[2]

Unlike his brother, Charles did not intend to publish his journal for the broader view of the public. He had a more particular audience in mind, the faithful adherents and supporters of the Methodist movement. Thus the language and style of his journal was less guarded in its portrayal of events. In them one finds Charles's preaching to a variety of audiences, large and small, friendly and hostile. Often the response of the hearers and the pastoral needs within the individual Methodist Societies or villages is recorded, along with valuable insights into the social and religious context of the significant events.

The journal of Charles Wesley is the best source for subsequent generations to know him as pastor, evangelist, and Methodist leader. One finds insight into the personal religious experience, reading, family life, friends, social life, and general physical health of Charles Wesley (who was frequently ill). There are humorous accounts of early folk remedies, such as his attempt to cure a toothache by smoking tobacco on February 24, 1738, an event of which he said, "it set me to vomiting, and took away my senses and pain together," and moving accounts of his pastoral care in prisons, among the poor and the infirm. The journal is a primary source for Charles's practices in preaching, praying, and singing—alone, in private homes, in the societies, and in the open air. It provides insight into the way he composed and used hymns, both in public and private settings. When used rightly and interpreted with due caution, the journal is a treasure house of information about the Methodist movement. It describes the interaction between Charles Wesley and the early Methodist people, the early opponents of the movement, the dialogue with other Anglican clergy, and personal encounters with a bishop from time to time. For example, in February of 1739, Charles Wesley and his brother John had personal conversations with the Archbishop of Canterbury and the Bishop of London. According to Charles, both leaders were kind, concerned, and offered an open door for further conversation. Therefore in October he dutifully wrote a request to the Bishop of Bristol naming those seeking adult baptism as converts from the Quaker and Baptist traditions.[3]

The story of Charles Wesley's manuscript journal is interesting in its own right. According to Frank Baker, in the latter years of his life Charles had collected much of his manuscript material and recorded it in a thick octavo volume which was bequeathed to his widow with the charge to keep it in her personal possession.[4] This volume was used by John Whitehead when he published his life of Charles Wesley, and later found its way into the hands of Charles, Jr., who lost it for a time. After it was recovered from the loose straw in the public warehouse where his furniture had been stored, the journal was eventually purchased from the young Charles Wesley by the Wesleyan Methodist Conference. This volume is the basic text for the printed journal. Along the way, it had sustained serious damage: several leaves had been cut away from the binding, some had been removed and others were loose but still within the volume.

The manuscript journal covers the period from the eve of the brothers' departure for Georgia in 1736 to the latter months of 1756 when Charles was in the north of England recovering backsliders and solidifying the Methodist loyalty to the Church of England. Unfortunately, neither the printed journal nor its primary manuscript source contains a full and complete account of even this limited period of Charles's life. There are nine gaps varying in size from two weeks to two years. The combined time lost in these omissions amounts to approximately seven years of the twenty possible. In reality, the gaps in the material after August 31, 1751, are so significant that for all practical purposes the journal ends on this date. From August 1751 to November 1756 there are only occasional fragments covering a few days at a time.

The nature of the journal entries undergoes significant change as well over the period. Early entries are comparatively full of details about people, places, and events. One finds the author's inward struggle and reflection more thoroughly documented. After the pivotal year of 1738, journal entries become progressively more terse and focus increasingly on the spread of the gospel across England, Ireland, and Wales. The content shifts from the inner self-reflection of the early years to a more narrative description of itinerant activity. However, as we shall see, the more austere form of the text is not always a result of Charles's own pen.

In the nineteenth century Thomas Jackson used the manuscript journal extensively in his two-volume *Life of Charles Wesley* (1841). Then in 1849 Jackson published *The Journal of the Rev. Charles Wesley, M.A.* in two additional volumes which remain the standard edition to this day, having been reprinted in 1980 by Baker Book House. In the twentieth century, Nehemiah Curnock began working on Charles's journal to provide Methodists with an authoritative edition similar to that of John Wesley. John Telford joined in the task and in 1910 the first of the three projected volumes of the new edition was published. It was a significant improvement over the Jackson edition which had transcribed none of the shorthand passages and omitted other prose sections for reasons known only to Jackson. This first volume of the new *Journal of Charles Wesley* covered the period from March 9, 1736, to August 27, 1739. Fortunately, Telford's edition of the early journal has been subsequently distributed by the Methodist Reprint Society. It is unfortunate that Telford's other volumes were never completed, and although Leslie Church did some work toward producing a complete edition of Charles's journal which was properly collated and annotated—this work too, has failed to reach either a printing press or the people called Methodists.

What would be the benefit of a new edition of Charles Wesley's journal? Would anyone beside the modern day adherents of the Methodist movement be interested in such a work? First of all, in addition to those within the Wesleyan tradition who lack access to the journal, historians from a variety of disciplines would welcome such a publication. Historians of eighteenth-century Britain, historians of music, poetry and religious verse could provide a market for an accurate scholarly edition of Charles Wesley's journal. In addition, one might expect sociologists of religion to be interested in Charles's description of his audiences in London, Bristol, and Newcastle. Those interested in literacy, evangelism, prison conditions, and Christian spirituality in this period would also find such a resource of value for their work, particularly if it were properly indexed and reasonable in price.

The Sermons

The sermons of Charles Wesley, with two exceptions, are even less available to Wesleyan scholars and historians than the journal discussed above. Charles Wesley's well-known sermon, "Awake Thou That Sleepest" was first published in 1742 and later included by John in the 1746 edition of his *Sermons on Several Occasions*. The only other sermon by Charles Wesley published during his lifetime was *The Cause and Cure of Earthquakes*, first published anonymously in 1750 and later with an identification of the author in the 1756 edition. Thomas Jackson included both sermon texts in his 1825 edition of John Wesley's *Sermons* and also in the third edition of John's *Works* without any indication of the actual authorship. Because the Jackson edition has been frequently reprinted in the twentieth century, students and scholars have had relatively easy access to two of Charles's sermons, if they knew where to look. The same cannot be said for the other sermon texts printed for the only time in the 1816 volume entitled *Sermons by the Late Rev. Charles Wesley*. Research by Richard Heitzenrater proved that at least six of the twelve sermons attributed to Charles in this volume were actually written by John Wesley. It would appear that neither the nineteenth-century editor nor the publisher could understand Charles's shorthand notation which clearly stated that these sermons were "transcribed from my brother's copies;" therefore, they assumed that all sermons in Charles's handwriting were of his own composition.[5] It is now clear that the 1816 volume of Charles Wesley's Sermons actually contains, at very most, five authentic sermons:

> No. 3, Luke 16:10, Faithfulness in Little Things (1736)
>
> No. 4, Matthew 5:20, Except Your Righteousness Exceed (January 5, 1735)[6]
>
> No. 7, Psalm 126:6, Go Forth Weeping and Return Rejoicing (1736)
>
> No. 11, Philippians 3:13–14, Press on Toward the Mark (October 21, 1735)
>
> No. 12, 1 Kings 18:21, How Long Halt Ye (preached November 30, 1735)

It is beyond the scope of this chapter to take a firm position on the exact number of homilies from this 1816 volume that are authentic Charles Wesley sermons. One might argue that all five sermons not clearly attributable to John ought to be considered the work of Charles. However, the case for identifying the homilies from Matthew 5:20, Philippians 3:13–14, and I Kings 18:21 as Charles Wesley sermons is exceedingly weak. At present, there is no evidence to support this claim other than the fact that the extant manuscript documents are in Charles's own hand. There is no clear evidence to determine whether the sermons were original compositions or simply copied by Charles from other sources. In the case of the homily on Matthew 5:20, it is likely that this is a John Wesley sermon. John's sermon register indicates that he preached a sermon on this very text on the same day, January 5, 1735. Since Charles was not ordained at this time (not until late September 1735) it seems probable that this is John's sermon and that Charles omitted a notation to this effect when he copied the document on the way to Georgia.

One might go even further and question the origin of the two sermons of the 1816 volume yet to be discussed. If one did not accept the authenticity of the sermons from Luke 16:10 and Psalm 126:6, this would certainly avoid a number of difficulties for defining the parameters of the Charles Wesley sermon material. By limiting the corpus to the six shorthand manuscript sermons and the two sermons published during his lifetime, one could be certain that all these texts were composed by Charles. On the other hand, to exclude the five questionable texts from a future published volume would deny historians, scholars, and other readers access to texts that were preached by at least one of the Wesley brothers during the period prior to their evangelical experiences in 1738.

In 1987, the British Wesley Historical Society published for the first time six Charles Wesley shorthand sermons transcribed from eight shorthand documents totaling more than 100 manuscript pages.[7] The earliest of these sermons was written and preached within two months of Charles's evangelical experience on May 21, 1738, and the latest one appears to have been preached by August 14, 1743. All of these sermons are valuable and merit careful study. Perhaps the two most interesting sermons would be those taken from John 8:1 (on the woman taken in adultery) and the sermon Charles preached before the University of Oxford, July 1, 1739, "On Justification." In the sermon about the woman, Charles raised a question rarely asked, namely, "Why the woman [alone], since the man's offence was equal if not greater?"[8]

In the Oxford sermon on justification, Charles made a clear statement aimed at Samuel Clarke (1675–1757) and others who subscribed to the thirty-nine Articles of the Church of England in "a sense altogether repugnant to the true intended one." Charles referred to these priests as modern Arians and heretics who denied the doctrine of the Trinity— who preached a gospel of faith and works contrary to the true position of Church. In opposition to this false teaching, Charles asserted the Reformation doctrine of justification by faith alone, clearly present in the Articles and Homilies of the Established Church. He suggested that this foundation for true Christian faith had been abandoned by the Anglican clergy "from the time of the Grand Rebellion," when Puritan doctrine came to be identified with political anarchy.[9]

There can be little doubt about the need for a new edition of Charles Wesley's sermons with an adequate introduction to each text and scholarly annotations similar to the recent volumes of John Wesley's *Sermons* edited by the late Albert Outler. There is a special power in Charles

Wesley's preaching acknowledged by his older brother when John wrote: "You were *made*, as it were, for this very thing. Just here you are in your element. In connexion I beat you; but in strong, pointed *sentences* you beat me."[10]

Contemporary preachers will be no less interested in a new edition of Charles Wesley's sermons than the historians of eighteenth-century preaching and doctrine. Sermons are a very different genre of literature than journals, letters, or tracts. Unlike John's published sermons, Charles's sermons retain more of the form and language in which they were delivered.[11]

Tracts, Essays, and Fragments

Without a doubt, the only prose tract published by Charles Wesley during his lifetime was a resounding success. His eight page pamphlet entitled *A Short Account of the Death of Mrs. Hannah Richardson* sold for one penny when it was first printed in 1741. It was reprinted four times within the first two years and subsequently reissued throughout the remainder of the eighteenth century and into the next. Thomas Jackson appended the document to the second volume of his *Life of Charles Wesley* (1841) with the comment that it "ought never to be out of print." What was the significance of this tract for the Methodist movement then? And what value, if any, might there be for us today? The first part of this question has been answered for us by Thomas Jackson who observed that this publication, in April of 1741, was "one of the most striking and effective antidotes to the peculiarities which were taught by [Philip Henry] Molther"—the Moravian "stillness" doctrine which condemned the Wesleys' understanding of the means of grace as useless for the unconverted and unnecessary for the believer.[12] In poignant prose, Charles described the religious experience of Mrs. Richardson, who had been justified under his ministry and then later "gave place to the reasoning devil" who tore away "all the comfort of faith, all her peace and joy in believing." To her credit, Hannah "waited in a constant Use of all the Means of Grace" and "persisted in glorious obstinacy," never neglecting to speak to others about God and always "tender-hearted towards the sick, whether in body or soul." It was not until she lay on her deathbed that God "took away the veil from her heart and revealed himself in her in a manner the world knoweth not of." Hannah died "without any agony, or sigh, or groan. She only rested; and sweetly fell asleep in the arms of Jesus."[13]

91

The testimony of Mrs. Richardson's life and death vindicated the Wesleys' teaching concerning the means of grace and validated the experience of abandonment (known in classic Christian spirituality as the "dark night of the soul") as an acceptable part of the spiritual journey for Methodists. It was the first uniquely Methodist model for Christian experience. Up to this time, the Wesleys had published extracts of the lives of Thomas Haliburton in 1739[14] and Monsieur de Renty in 1741[15] but Hannah was the first woman and the first Methodist.

Is there value for contemporary adherents to the Methodist tradition in this *Short Account of the Death of Mrs. Hannah Richardson?* I think so. In addition to the intrinsic historical value, this Charles Wesley tract opens the way for contemporary Christians to explore our own spiritual pilgrimage, our own experiences of the absence of God (or abandonment), and our own concerns about death. The document's clear statement that God brought Hannah into the wilderness and intentionally withdrew from her puts Charles at odds with the understanding John advocated in his sermon on "The Wilderness State."[16] Therefore, this tract adds important primary source data for the discussion of the differences between the Wesley brothers begun anew in John Tyson's volume on *Charles Wesley on Sanctification.*[17]

There are other prose writings by Charles Wesley that deserve mention—some published and others unpublished. The first published document was printed in 1781 by the Honorable Daines Barrington. It contains Charles Wesley's account of his two sons and their unusual musical talents. These descriptions of Charles Jr. and young Samuel were printed in the *Philosophical Transactions* and Barrington's *Miscellanies.* Thomas Jackson reprinted these documents and included them at the end of volume two in his edition of *Charles Wesley's Journal.*[18] Interspersed in the accounts of these two child prodigies, one finds the picture of a father in awe of God's musical gift to each son. At the same time one can see a concerned parent struggling to provide the best direction and training possible for the proper development of extraordinary musical talent.

Most scholars would agree with Frank Baker's suggestion that Charles was perhaps the author of the anonymous *Strictures on the Substance of a Sermon, preached at Baltimore, in the State of Maryland,* by Thomas Coke in December 1784. There is no doubt that Charles strongly disagreed with his older brother on this point and had no qualms about expressing his opposition; e.g. his extended poem against the ordinations. Other manuscript documents by Charles Wesley name the lay preachers to be laid aside in 1752 and show how important the whole issue of episcopal ordination for itinerant preachers was for him.[19]

Students of liturgy and worship would be very interested in the ninety-eight page manuscript volume which concludes "Finished July 12, 1779 / in a fortnight / by C[harles] W[esley] aged 70." This volume contains prayers for morning and evening as well as collects and thanksgivings.[20] There is also a manuscript fragment of a bound volume with three pages of Charles's personal Psalter.[21]

Any discussion of Charles Wesley's eucharistic theology and hymnology would be enriched by a careful reading of his eight page manuscript treatise "On the Weekly Sacrament" which begins with a quotation of Acts 20:7 (in both Greek and English) along with an extended quotation from Justin Martyr, followed by two selections from the Apostolic Constitutions (also in Greek). This short tract concludes:

> The sum of the matter is this. We have the testimony of St. Luke in several passages of his Acts of the Apostles, of St. Paul in his first Epistle to the Corinthians, of Tertullian, St. Justin the Martyr, the Apostolic Constitutions and lastly of the Roman, Pliny, to prove that the Holy Eucharist is to be celebrated every Lord's Day at the least. More authorities might have been added, both from the ancient Fathers and from the oracles of God, but those I think are abundantly sufficient to demonstrate what I undertook, namely, that both Scripture and tradition do give plain evidence for the necessity of making at least a weekly oblation of the Christian sacrifice and of honouring every Lord's Day with a solemn public celebration of the Lord's Supper.[22]

There are numerous other items of interest that will be added to the list of manuscript and printed sources that Dr. Kimbrough is developing from the basic bibliographies of Frank Baker.[23] Let me mention a few of the more interesting manuscript documents in the hand of Charles Wesley:

- The manuscript sermon on the nature of religion based on John 4:41, 16 pages, unfinished.[24]

- The manuscript source for the biographical sketches of his two musical sons discussed above, Lamplough 352.

- Three separate volumes of subscription lists to works published by the Wesley brothers. These volumes also contain attendance lists for concerts given by Charles's sons. An analysis of the 1,274 names subscribed prior to the publication of the 1749 volume of *Hymns and Sacred Poems* would provide an interesting insight into the degree to which Charles Wesley's religious verse was known and accepted by Londoners in the first decade of the revival.[25]

- A journal extract containing additional information for the period from November 29 to December 11, 1753.[26] This would help fill a gap in the printed journal from December 6, 1753 to July 8, 1754.

- Several account books of the Wesley household give interesting insights into family life, income sources, and expenses.[27]

Conclusion

There is a very real need for a scholarly edition of Charles Wesley's prose works. One would hope that such a project might be undertaken soon and that there be wide publicity about the project. This should include an invitation for all libraries, archives, and individuals aware of Charles Wesley manuscript materials to contribute copies of additional texts for inclusion. It may well be that other journal fragments exist like the shorthand fragment stored in the vestry safe of Wesley's Chapel in London[28] or the document housed in the Leicester Record Office which has recently come to light.[29] One might even hope that additional segments of the journal, original letters, hymns, and poems may be found.[30] It is time to produce a critical edition of Charles Wesley's prose writings in order to allow this great Christian poet to come to life for current and future generations.

PART II

Charles Wesley's Theology

Chapter 6

CHARLES WESLEY AS THEOLOGIAN

Thomas A. Langford

I am pleased to address myself to the topic of "Charles Wesley as Theologian" because of my love of Charles Wesley's hymns and because I needed to know more about this matter. In doing so, I must acknowledge my indebtedness to J. Ernest Rattenbury and Frank Baker, both of whom have worked to clarify and interpret the primary sources, and to Teresa Berger, who has attempted to expound Charles Wesley's theology.[1] My work on Charles Wesley is largely derivative and my main contribution is to reflect on his writing as it has bearing on my specific topic.

Hymns and Theology

E. H. Sugden has claimed that, "The real embodiment of Methodist theology is the Methodist Hymnbook and especially Charles Wesley's hymns."[2] This suggestive, although partial, claim sets a stage for our discussion.

"Methodism was born in song." This was the introductory sentence in the 1933 British Methodist Hymnbook: and it is an appropriate introduction to Charles Wesley and his role in the Methodist movement. It also is an appropriate introduction to Charles Wesley's theology. To understand Charles Wesley's theology it is necessary to understand that it is theology-as-hymn, that is, it is theology expressed by, limited by, enlivened by its hymn form. Charles Wesley's theology is "a theology one can sing." In this sense it is a theology with which one can praise; it is a theology with which one can pray, a theology with which one can teach; it is a theology which one can use to initiate, to guide, and to envision the final hope of Christian existence.

As hymn, theology is memorable, emphases are made clear as central issues are held in focus. As hymn, theology is memorable, it possesses an instructional form for newborn and even illiterate Christians. It might be claimed that hymns were to eighteenth-century England what stained glass windows were to medieval Europe—a medium for teaching. Theology-as-hymn arises from a praxis setting, it is in the context of worship that hymn-theology is expressed and for life transformation that theology is developed.

Given the fact that theology is hymn-formed, how may a hermeneutic for interpretation be established? First a series of questions: can one bring an established theological pattern to the interpretation of the hymns? Or does such an approach distort the intention and use of the hymns and the theology in the hymns? Again, can one insist on completeness, balance, or systematic form in such a theology or must the character of Wesley's theology be made evident precisely through its concretely embodied form? Finally, can one insist on questions or arguments which a hymn form does not yield?

How does one proceed to interpretation? It is possible to see how the *1780 Collection*, for instance, was intended to be theologically shaped by the arrangement of the hymns or in an indexed consideration of topics. Or, might we survey the material to find consistent emphases as determined by the frequency of use of themes, scripture passages, or key words? Lastly, can we attempt to determine the actual use of the hymns in the Methodist revival movement and develop a theological statement on the basis of that praxis?

We hold these options open as we concentrate on the content of the hymns. Teresa Berger has raised the interesting question of whether or not hymns are the most adequate medium for Methodist theological expression? I shall return to this question.

To read or sing and study Charles Wesley's hymns is a rich and enriching experience, especially for one who has been nurtured in the Methodist evangelistic tradition. These hymns lead one back to basic themes and emotions of the formative faith: the soteriological center, the emphasis on God's grace and human appropriation, the challenge for growth and missional responsibility. Whatever one may say in a more formal way about the theological aspects of Charles Wesley's work, the comments are made recognizing past and current indebtedness to this hymnwriter who presents the heart of the Methodist movement.

Theology in Charles Wesley's Hymns

I want to begin in a traditional way and comment on the content of Charles Wesley's hymns. Charles Wesley is certainly a theologian in the same sense that anyone who thinks, sings, paints, or dances about God is a theologian; namely, every expression about God, every interpretation of Divine presence possesses implicit and inescapable theological beliefs and commitments.

Wesley is also a theologian in the sense that his convictions are organized and exhibit determined priorities, emphases, and arrangements. These structural characteristics, however, are not idiosyncratic or creative constructs of his own fashioning. Rather, they are the received and developing emphases of the revival movement in which he was a participant. In spite of J. E. Rattenbury's claim, "It is certainly true that his, Charles's and not John's, was the most effective and comprehensive statement of Methodist doctrine,"[3] there is, I think, little evidence for giving him a primary, creative role in the general movement. A claim can be made that Charles Wesley gave expression to and helped to disseminate the revival themes, and this was no small accomplishment. One can take the corpus of Charles Wesley's sermons[4] and hymns and establish the doctrinal themes which were central revival emphases. But these are not unique to Charles. Indeed, what usually happens is that the more sharply honed emphases of John Wesley are used to provide the frame of Charles Wesley's more amorphous—even prodigal—production of hymns. Nevertheless, Rattenbury is correct when he states that John treated the Methodist hymns (as he edited and arranged them) as doctrinal documents.

It is, perhaps, at this juncture that the critical issues in regard to Charles Wesley being a creative theologian must be joined. Namely, within the larger revival movement of the eighteenth century, there is a definite Methodist Wesleyan stream, a stream which emphasized God's universal love, assurance of faith and sanctification, and the necessary interconnection of faith and works. The question is, to what extent did Charles play a formative role in developing and guiding this stream? It is clear that there was mutual influence between John and Charles, for they discussed issues, agreeing on the soteriological focus and universal love, on justification and the faith-works relation, but differing on the relation to the Moravians, the instantaneous realization of sanctification, and on the Methodist movement's relation to the Anglican Church.

Can it be determined what Charles's role and contribution were in regard to the basic theological commitments of the Methodist revival movement? It cannot with clarity, but because of John's role as editor of Charles's hymns, because of John's leadership in conference theological discussions, because of the normative role of John's sermons and his New Testament *Notes*, and because of John's personal style and character, it seems safe to attribute to John the primary role as theologian of the

Methodist movement.[5] Charles served a supportive, encouraging, and propagandizing role to and for John.[6]

Franz Hildebrandt might have offered help in assessing this conclusion in his part of the introduction to the *1780 Collection*. The joint editors had already quoted Bernard Manning who states that John Wesley "arranged his hymn-book as a spiritual biography of the sort of person whom he called in the Preface a real Christian."[7] But in his presentation Hildebrandt is ambiguous. He says the hymnbook is "Wesley's doctrine," presumably meaning Charles, then he calls this "an unavoidable abbreviation of a complex relation which underlies the joint editorship of John and Charles."[8] This is a complexity he does not attempt to clarify.

Frank Baker has told me (and here we rely upon oral history) that Hildebrandt was convinced that Charles Wesley was the main theologian of the two brothers and that it was only through pressure that he [Hildebrandt] included John at all. Further, Hildebrandt believed that Charles's importance was as the poet who put theology into verse, and at times the virtue of his use of language was the quality which Hildebrandt most valued. If this is so, it is incumbent upon Hildebrandt to make such a case. The substance of the teaching of the hymns, Hildebrandt argues, can be found in the biblical texts most frequently used by Charles. He does not attempt to summarize this material and since he lists over one hundred texts the number is too large to provide a sharply defined center or outline. I have reviewed these texts but can discern only the general revival pattern of God's universal love and the necessity of human response. The list certainly does not provide, as Hildebrandt claims, "a basis for the *summa* of Charles Wesley's theology."[9] The theological content is embedded in the hymns and Hildebrandt asserts that "If any one hymn may be singled out as the epitome of Charles Wesley's thought it would be 124 ["For Mourners brought to the Birth"]."[10] Note especially the absence of distinctly Wesleyan/Methodist themes in this hymn:

> With glorious clouds encompassed round,
>   Whom angels dimly see,
> Will the Unsearchable be found,
>   Or God appear to me?

> Will he forsake his throne above,
>   Himself to worms impart?
> Answer, thou Man of grief and love,
>   And speak it to my Heart!

In manifested love explain
  Thy wonderful design:
What meant the suffering Son of man,
  The streaming blood divine?

Didst thou not in our flesh appear,
  And live and die below
That I may now perceive thee near,
  And my Redeemer know?

Come then, and to my soul reveal
  The heights and depths of grace,
The wounds which all my sorrows heal,
  That dear disfigured face.

Before my eyes of faith confessed
  Stand forth a slaughtered Lamb,
And wrap me in thy crimson vest,
  And tell me all thy name.

Jehovah in thy person show,
  Jehovah crucified;
And then the pard'ning God I know,
  And feel the blood applied.

I view the Lamb in his own light
  Whom angels dimly see,
And gaze, transported at the sight,
  To all eternity.[11]

Hildebrandt's commentary is instructive in terms of his satisfaction with the theology in this hymn. For interpretation he simply puts phrases together.[12]

> 'With glorious clouds encompassed round.' Here is the waiting with bated breath for the revelation of the mystery ('Will the Unsearchable be found?'), the 'wonderful design' that made him 'forsake his throne above' so that he might 'in our flesh appear, and live and die below,' the 'man of grief and love,' 'that dear disfigured face,' 'Jehovah crucified'; and all for me ('that I may now perceive thee near,' 'the wounds which all my sorrows heal'), so that 'the pardoning God I know,' being wrapped 'in his crimson vest,' and can 'view the Lamb in his own light.' Again the vista of 'the heights and depths of grace,' the persistent quest 'And tell me all thy name,' the plea 'And speak it to my heart'—which, in characteristic fashion, other hymns take up and lead to the climax: 'And speak me at last to the throne of thy love.'

These are emphases of the revival movement, but not especially of the Wesleyan stream of that movement. Consequently, we are left with little help by Hildebrandt in specifying Charles Wesley's role as a distinctive theologian; and certainly not with the primacy of Charles as the theologian of the Wesleyan revival movement.

If this interpretation is correct, Charles is not a theologian in the sense of one who explores new interpretation, who adds fresh ways of understanding the gospel or who cuts new paths of theological explication. Rather, Charles Wesley is a conservator and conveyor of doctrine, he is not a creator of theological interpretation. His role as a conveyor is itself a creative achievement—and a very distinctive one to be praised and honored—but it is the achievement of an artist, not that of a thinker.

Charles Wesley's Theology-as-Hymn

In dealing with Charles Wesley it is necessary to allow his hymns to retain their distinctive theological form so as to emphasize the dynamic relation he was attempting to convey. Too much reduction to order tends to delete the life which the hymns actually present.

At this point I want to return to Teresa Berger's question: are hymns the most appropriate form for expressing Methodist-Christian experience and therefore a necessary—or the most adequate mode—for its theological expression? Certainly the hymns capture affective as well as cognitive dimensions of Methodist spirituality. But what does one do with this in relation to a hermeneutical principle? Let me explore this by beginning with the Wesleys' emphasis on "personal" experience.

It is customary to speak of the theology of Charles and John Wesley as experimental, experiential, scriptural, and personal in character (all of the terms may be taken as synonymous although "scriptural" at times can be separated out). J. E. Rattenbury insists that we can only understand Charles Wesley if this is clearly and centrally recognized; and Robert E. Cushman in his new book *John Wesley's Experimental Divinity*[13] makes the same assertion. Obviously this is true, but it is often more difficult to analyze the obvious than the recondite. What, precisely, does it mean to make experience central? What sort of experience is intended? "Experience" is an exceedingly elusive word and defies quick definition. For the Wesleys it referred to human acknowledgment, reception, and transformation. But the human response is to an explicit and concrete call and challenge: it is experience of Jesus Christ. Human response is not an inchoate experience of God or of the Holy Spirit, nor is it "religious" experience or experience defined by social location, ethnicity, or gender. These latter modes may be shaping channels for human reception, but the experience with which the Wesleys began is of God's action in Jesus Christ.

Yet, the Wesleys do emphasize human response and do so to such an extent that there is, at times, a trespassing across the line toward excessive subjective or introspective evaluation. This, I am convinced, is evident in the discussions of assurance, backsliding, and sanctification. The Wesleys were correct in their primary placement of emphasis on the experience of God's saving presence in Jesus Christ, and the secondary, but necessary, human acknowledgment of God's acts. They were, nevertheless, tempted, and at times yielded to the temptation, to refocus their attention upon human reception which obfuscated the clear priority they originally affirmed. (It is confusing in this connection to differentiate too sharply between "objectivity" and "subjectivity" as dimensions of human experience; the two are inseparably tied together, each requires the other; the two come in holistic fashion. But a priority can be set and this the Wesleys do.)

Now we turn to the hermeneutical issue. Charles Wesley's hymns—filled as they are with an enormous range of human affection—from penance to praise, from honest self-judgment to exaltation in God—are, at their base and at their best, acknowledgments of what God has done, is doing, and will do. In this sense, Wesley's was a personal religion, it was reception of God and the finding of life in Jesus Christ. It is this personally engaged aspect of life in Christ which his hymns express and the question we want to ask is: how does this personal religion find expression in his theology?

With such an emphasis on personal experience, there is the need in his hymns for recognition, response, commitment—indeed all of the dimensions of loving relationship—and all of this has theological implications; in such a setting theology cannot be treated as an end in itself, as an abstract discussion of intellectual problems, or as treatises for uninvolved discussion. Again, theology is not a use of signifying words which point to that which is beyond human experience and human knowing. Rather, theology is itself an involved and involving activity which is immediate talking to God even as it talks about God. Arthur S. Gregory's title, *Praises with Understanding*, is suggestive in the right direction and Teresa Berger's discussion of soteriological concentration of Wesley's hymns with her culminating exploration of the composite emphasis upon "to feel-to know-to prove" sets the theological position firmly.[14]

In the history of Christian thought, there are a variety of genres of theology. There is theology as prayer—i.e., doxological theology (in distinction from a theology of prayer) which is classically embodied in Augustine's *Confessions* and Anselm's *Proslogium*. There is theology as psalm, which one finds both in Scripture and in the musical traditions of the church. And there is, among others, theology-as-hymn. That is, a theology through which hearts and voices are lifted to God even as there is affirmation of belief in and about God. To ask of this theology that it function as an essay or a *summa* is to ask it to change character. But this it cannot do and still retain its most authentic expression of engaged affection/reasoning/willing relation to God.

In this sense, Charles Wesley is important not because he added new thoughts or insights to theological discourse, but because he creatively provided for the Methodist revival a theological character suited to its self-understanding. He added a distinctive theological dimension; or, perhaps better, he helped provide a new dimension to theological expression for the Methodist revival; that is, he kept theology immediately and ineluctibly related to the worship and service of God. This is a close kin to theology as doxology, as Teresa Berger suggests. And it provides a significant—unexpungeable—character to Methodist theology.

The Wesleyan tradition is characterized by praxis theology. Praxis theology, as distinguished from a theological method which establishes a theory and then applies it in practice, holds practice/theory, theory/practice in inseparable unity. Theory arises from the concrete situation of life even as it also informs the manner of living. Theory is not developed prior to and independent of active engagement in life-situations; rather one comes to know the truth by doing the truth. The split of theory and practice is a commonly recognized problem in contemporary philosophical and theological discussions, but resistance to this split has been an enduring characteristic of the Wesleyan movement. Christian understanding has, in this tradition, been rooted in the ways concretely actual communities of persons characteristically relate to God and the world. Charles Wesley's hymns represent a central expression of such praxis theology.

Jacques Barzun, in a recent article on creativity, discusses the changing uses of the word "genius." He makes the historical point, "By the 1750s *genius* was defined by the poet Edward Young as 'the power of accomplishing great things without the means generally reputed necessary to that end.'"[15] In an interesting way this definition fits Charles Wesley. His accomplishment as a theologian was along a different route from that which was historically thought necessary for significant theological work. He was not a formidable intellect, his contribution was not that of new rational insight, exegetical perception, or an engagement with the regnant philosophy of the age. Rather, he set theological expression within a special context; he tied theology inseparably to the worship of God; he welded theory and praxis together; he made theology an inseparable part of the holistic love of God.

For the Methodist tradition, theology is never an end in itself; it is always a means to the transformation of life. As such, theology is developed to underwrite proclamation and the renewal of personal and corporate life. It possesses no independent existence. One does not do theology then apply it; the doing of theology is itself transformative. In Charles Wesley's hymns—both the hymn form, which requires participation, and the hymn context, namely worship—theology is given its proper instrumental role. In this sense Charles Wesley's theology is a most appropriate medium for Methodist theology.

It is not, however, the only appropriate medium for Methodist theology. For there remains a function for biblical theology, for historical theology, for critical and constructive theology. But all of these, in so far as they represent the tradition which Charles Wesley helped form, are also only instrumental to the transformation of life in its entirety and the transformation of the entire life. To embody this, I think, is Charles Wesley's achievement.

Frank Baker has written the appreciation Charles Wesley deserves:

> To later generations, naturally enough, Charles Wesley's hymns have been hailed as his greatest contribution to the Methodist revival, and on them securely rests his fame. The 'sweet singer' of Methodism provided in his robust scriptural song both spiritual education and an inspiring means of giving expression to the richly varying experiences of those pressing along the highway of personal religion.[16]

It is perhaps appropriate to conclude this essay with lines from one of Charles Wesley's hymns:

"O heavenly King, look down from above,
Assist us to sing Thy mercy and love."

Chapter 7

CHARLES WESLEY AND BIBLICAL INTERPRETATION

S T Kimbrough, Jr.

Introduction

In 1905 George H. Gilbert summarized the landmarks for biblical interpretation in the eighteenth century in which Charles Wesley lived in these words:

> The eighteenth century was distinguished by its work for a purer text of the New Testament, by the beginning of a formal science of interpretation, by the production of one of the few great commentaries, by the establishment of the documentary hypothesis to explain the origin of Genesis, by the weakening of the traditional doctrine of inspiration, by general progress in the rationalization and humanization of Scripture, and, last of all, by the discovery that the Bible is not only a divine guide for the heart and will, but is also a thesaurus of immortal poetry, which fascinates and up-lifts the imagination.[1]

Charles Wesley's biblical interpretation reflects the imprint of some of the above enumerated developments in biblical interpretation in the eighteenth century. Therefore, a brief overview of these developments is requisite to understanding him in the context of his time. It is not necessary to treat in detail the extensive subject of the biblical interpretation of the Church Fathers, which continues to be scrutinized carefully by specialists in patristics. However, where certain of its aspects are reflected in Wesley's biblical interpretation, they will be noted in the discussion. The medieval period is not of great importance to the analysis here, since rabbinical exegesis actually had little influence upon Christian exegetes *until* the seventeenth century. Like Christian exegetes of the medieval period, Charles Wesley saw Christ in the Old Testament. Unlike them he was not ignorant of Greek. As they did, he also used allegorical interpretation but was not enslaved by it. He did not find Jesus becoming Moses' mouth to utter the decalogue. To be sure, there is some mystical interpretation in Charles Wesley but he generally applied it to himself. His use of allegory and mystical interpretation does not tend to obscure the biblical text as it did in John Wyclif's fourteenth-century interpretation.

Biblical Languages

There were some limited attempts at more pragmatically oriented exegesis which sought to illumine the spirit rather than the letter of the text. But the most important development for future biblical interpretation was perhaps the growing interest in the value of biblical languages. Already at the end of the fifteenth century courses in Greek and St. Paul's letters were offered at Oxford University. Biblical interpreters began to work intensively with grammars and lexicons as they explored the biblical text. Luther fostered the rediscovery of Hebrew and Greek, as well as the sciences. In spite of the fact that humanism in England at the beginning of the sixteenth century was particularly religious and embraced considerable hope for the study of Scripture, "There was no strong inner force in the English Church proceeding from a fresh contact with the truth of Scripture."[2] While one cannot overlook the importance of Miles Coverdale's (1488–1569) translation of the Bible in 1535 and the circulation of the Bible, the impetus for interpretation came largely from the continent. Tyndale (1484–1536) studied at Wittenberg, and the preface and notes of John Rogers's *Matthew's Bible* in 1537 were based on Luther's work. Furthermore, his reproduction of many of Luther's errors indicates the dominance of continental interpretation and the lack of a driving force in English biblical interpretation. Nevertheless, William Whitaker (1547–95) was already pleading the case of Greek and Hebrew knowledge as the companion to prayer in discovering the meaning of the Bible in the eighteenth century. One of the significant contributions in this period was the collation and comparison of biblical manuscripts, and one of the most important breakthroughs of the seventeenth century was the introduction of rabbinical writings to the arena of Christian exegetes by John Lightfoot (1602–75). The breakthrough was in the value of rabbinical interpretation and the Jewish parallels to Scriptural statements, not in Lightfoot's arbitrary method and his devotion to traditional theology. There is little evidence that this breakthrough, however, influenced Charles Wesley.

Interpretative Approaches

Certain views and approaches to Scripture which developed on the continent and in England are important for understanding Wesley's interpretation.

(1) *Literalism.* The move of the Reformers toward a more literal interpretation of Scripture was in large measure not only a reaction against Papal infallibility but also against the excesses of allegorical and esoteric interpretations of Scripture. Luther essentially rejected allegorical interpretation but was not able to escape it completely and his christologizing of the Old Testament often blocked the possibility of discovering the truth of Scripture. For example, Luther claimed that Ps. 3:5

> I laid me down and slept,
> I awakened, for Jehovah sustaineth me,

referred to the resurrection of Christ, not sleep of the human body.

Calvin also rejected allegorical interpretation but his overreaction stressed literalness and in reading biblical poetry as prose, he simply missed completely the character of the text. For Calvin the gospel writers were the Holy Spirit's stenographers. There were no contradictions in the gospels, and Scripture was appropriated by means of traditional, orthodox doctrines. It is indeed interesting how a passion for the infallibility of Scripture among the Reformers, particularly as the counterpoint to papal infallibility, resulted in a dual literalism: (a) literalism bound to the doctrines produced by the theology of the early church, and (b) literalism bound to the scriptural text. Yet, the former dominated the latter and in general the Reformers were never willing to be wholly vulnerable in faith to the Scripture alone. *Sola scriptura* reads like what it was not, namely, trusting oneself to the Scriptures alone without any priorities of doctrine.

In seventeenth-century England the seeds of an extreme literalism were sown by George Fox, the founder of the Quakers. In the century following, Charles Wesley broke on the British ecclesiastical scene with a high regard for the authority of Scripture.

> Doctrines, experiences to try,
> We to the sacred standard fly,
> Assur'd the Spirit of our Lord
> Can never contradict his word:

> Whate'er his Spirit speaks in me,
> Must with the written word agree;
> If not: I cast it all aside,
> As Satan's voice, or nature's pride.[3]

Wesley, however, moved back and forth between a literalistic and non-literalistic view of biblical interpretation, although the latter seems to be more dominant than the former. Note the following statements from volume II of *Short Hymns on Select Passages of the Holy Scriptures* (1762). In the first he apparently anticipates the actual return of Christ based on a literal reading of the biblical text:

> Trusting in the literal word,
> We look for Christ on earth again:
> Come, our everlasting Lord,
> With all thy saints to reign.[4]

In the second poem he distinguishes between three levels of textual meaning: a literal sense, a spiritual sense, and an experiential sense. There is meaning imparted by Scripture which literalism cannot release:

> Thy word in the bare *literal* sense,
> Tho' read ten thousand times, and read,
> Can never of itself dispense
> The saving power which wakes the dead;
> The meaning *spiritual* and true
> The learn'd expositor may give,
> But cannot give the virtue too,
> Or bid his own dead spirit live.[5]

There is little slavish, biblical literalism in Wesley which would impute words with power which God alone possesses, or rob human beings of the experience and apprehension of truth which lies beneath the words.

(2) *Mysticism.* Meanwhile another approach to Scripture had been flowering—mystical interpretation. Emmanuel Swedenborg (1688–1772), who placed no value on biblical languages, grammar, and language dictionaries, pursued a mystical interpretation of Scripture which supposedly through some inner light unlocked its truth. Even Blaise Pascal (1623–62) viewed Jesus and the apostles as decipherers of the Hebrew Scriptures which were supposedly written in code or cipher.

A champion of mystical interpretation, which was often inseparable from allegorical interpretation of his work, was Jonathan Edwards (1693–1758), who believed there was a mystical purpose in Scripture placed there by God for the human edification of wisdom and exploration. Hence, Edwards saw the feast of Ahasuerus in the Book of Esther unequivocally as the gospel feast.

On the whole it must be said, however, that allegorical interpretation was generally rejected in the sixteenth and seventeenth centuries and biblical interpreters began to view the Scriptures as intelligible. Neither Edwards nor Tyndale may be considered the norm of interpretation at this time.

As this author has stated in another article, for Charles Wesley "Allegory is . . . primarily a means of translating biblical reality rather than stretching its veracity."[6] It is perhaps his personalization of allegory which saves it from the pitfalls of Edwards and Tyndale. For him allegory was a means of integrating the metaphors, similes, figures of speech, names, etc. in Scripture into the universal experience of human beings, but primarily seen through his own eyes. There are hints in Charles Wesley's poetry also of mystical biblical interpretation, but it is probably fairer to say that there are occasional indications of the influence of mysticism in his interpretation.

Neither of the above mentioned hermeneutical approaches, however, could be categorically identified as *the* approach for Wesley.

Wesley's Classical Heritage

Charles Wesley stood within a classical tradition, largely inherited from his father, an astute classical scholar, and from the rich classical education of the Westminster School in London and Oxford University. He inherited a classical tradition which came to view biblical interpretation as having integrity when it was grounded securely in a mastery of biblical languages and saw the Scriptures as being intelligible. He also shared Luther's perspective that the Holy Spirit must be a guide in scriptural interpretation. It is not possible, however, to place him in the camp of those before him and in his time, who claimed that all biblical truths are very clear and the Bible itself is the only infallible rule for the interpretation of Scripture. Wesley stood outside that tradition, for he interpreted Scripture with and through poetry. Indeed, his poetry is laced with the use of Scripture interpreting Scripture, but it is the art form of poetry which is the cloak of his hermenuetic. The poetical elements of which he is master such as rhetoric, metre, rhyme, assonance, alliteration, and many others become the warp and woof of the hermeneutical cloak.

Unquestionably the exegesis of the sixteenth, seventeenth, and eighteenth centuries placed a high value on the doctrines of the church. As already indicated, however, this often resulted in searching the Bible not for what it actually taught, but for what one assumed it was teaching. Wesley cannot be absolved of this pitfall. The *tête à tête* with his brother John over the doctrines of holiness and perfection, as well as with the London group which claimed to have achieved full perfection, exposes Charles's enthusiasm to find a view of gradual holiness and perfection in the Scriptures as descriptive of the Christian's life-pilgrimage. He devoted many poems to this subject in his 1762 volumes of *Short Hymns on Select Passages of the Holy Scriptures*. John's notes in his own copies of these volumes, which Charles did not let him edit, show that he came to the biblical text with a different set of presuppositions at a number of points as regards these ideas than did Charles.

It is a fair assessment that the dominant element in Charles Wesley's biblical interpretation in *not* merely an effort to seek support in Scripture for the traditionally orthodox doctrines of the church. He generally moved beyond this endeavor to the genuine quest for the teaching of Scripture from within. This quest was grounded in a superb command of biblical languages and a keen pastoral and social sense.

Like Spinoza, Charles Wesley sought the sense of words and depended upon reason as a means of illuminating Scripture. No doubt he parted ways with Spinoza as to the value of the Holy Spirit's role in the illumination of Scripture. Nevertheless, both scholars mistrusted supernatural illumination as the *only* means of scriptural interpretation. Unquestionably Spinoza's *Traité théologico-politique* (1670) anticipated aspects of historical method which Spinoza himself was not able to carry out with consistency.

Charles Wesley lived in a time which gave birth to historical criticism and while he mastered the linguistic tools which would have given him access to a careful appropriation of its beginnings, they (i.e. the beginnings) were not a force in his biblical interpretation. Nevertheless, Wesley stood firmly on the newly established ground that exegesis is a facet of human learning, not merely the result of supernatural will.

Biblical Studies in England

The England of Charles Wesley's day was by no means devoid of the dynamic beginnings of historical criticism. Richard Simon's *Histoire du critique du texte, des versions, et des commentateurs du Vieux Testament*, in which he questioned the Mosaic authorship of the Pentateuch and suggested multiple authors for it on the basis of repetitious passages, was published in 1678 and translated not long thereafter into English by John Hampden. Dom Augustin Calmet's *Dictionary of the Bible* published in Paris from 1722-28 was translated into English in 1732. The work is a strange collection of sometimes rather esoteric ideas but as the mentor of François Marie Arouet (Voltaire) it is understandable that his work would be perused as biblical science and the humanities developed.

There was unquestionably more activity on the continent than in England in this period as regards the birth of historical criticism: in France—Jean Astruc[7] (1684-1751), in Germany—J. A. Bengel[8] (1687-1752), J. S. Semler[9] (d. 1791) and J. A. Ernesti[10] (1707-1781), and G. E. Lessing[11] (1729-81).

An important English contribution of the time was Bishop Lowth's (1710-1787) *De sacra poesi Hebraeorum praelectiones academicae* (1753) in which he viewed Hebrew poetry as divine revelation but claimed it as beautiful literature.[12] Charles Wesley surely exemplified Herder's later averment in *Vom Geist der Ebräischen Poesie* (2 vols. 1782-3) that the Bible is a garden, not a prison, and must be read on human and spiritual terms, for it enriches and expands the human mind and heart.

Summary

In summary Charles Wesley shared the spirit of the progress in biblical interpretation in his time without participating in the full spectrum of its discoveries. (1) He was keenly interested in establishing the proper text of the Bible, as his use of various translations from the original languages, including his own, indicates. (2) He benefitted greatly from the rationalization and humanization of Scripture as the general freedom of his interpretation from the tyranny of dogma reveals. (3) He did not appropriate the movement toward the documentary hypothesis, and (4) there is little evidence that the exploration of rabbinical literature influenced him. Here he might have found a resource that would have enriched his poetry and interpretative awareness. (5) Wesley's work exemplifies the "discovery that the Bible is not only a divine guide for the heart and will, but it is also a thesaurus of immortal poetry and uplifts the imagination."[13]

The eighteenth-century vacuum in the English Church of no inner driving force to wed the powers of intellect to the interpretation of Scripture was filled in large measure by the Wesley brothers.

It is to the discovery of Scripture as a thesaurus of immortal poetry and an enhancer of imagination that I wish to turn in exploring Charles

Wesley's biblical interpretation. The study of Scripture for him was an unending discovery of the spontaneous, the sacred, and the mysterious. These three, however, are inevitably bound to language as an imperative avenue to unlocking imagination. Charles Wesley understood already in his time what Amos Wilder has succinctly articulated in our own: "While theology properly takes the form of clear thinking about God, faith, and the world, it has a basic substratum of imaginative grasp on reality and experience."[14] While Wesley's poetry is not devoid of attempts to clarify ideas of theology, he also sounds the depths of human experience, and these soundings have a profound resonance in the human heart.

What about the world of reality to which Charles Wesley's imagination responded in interpreting Scripture and faith? What governed his perceptions? What ruled his senses? For whatever else he is about, he is unquestionably about the business of exposing naked humanity to Being itself, to the primal mystery. "Being itself," should be understood as written with a capital "B" and a small "b." However, this should not be misconstrued as an invention either of who the Being (God) is or who the beings (mortals) are.

A Hermeneutic of Imagination

Imagination is used here "as a modern category that speaks of the capacity of the whole person to penetrate the mystery of reality and to express creatively what has been encountered."[15]

There is an interesting tension in Charles Wesley's hermeneutic imagination: while he is extremely faithful to traditional authorities and worlds of meaning which he has inherited as an eighteenth-century English Anglican, he is, and perhaps through his art, open to new categories of meaning. For example, while he gives no conscious attention in his writings to "emptiness" as a revelatory category as in Zen, the attention is there. He said, "Next to feeling Christ present, the most desirable state is *to feel Christ absent*. This we often do. O that we did it always."[16] He was somewhat preoccupied in his poetry with emptiness evoked intermittently by the absence of Christ throughout his Christian pilgrimage.

What Charles Wesley consciously or unconsciously asked in the study of Scripture was—Is there a new vision? Biblical interpreters, especially in our time, tend to be suspicious of imagination as aesthetically separable and irresponsible, and with such suspicion it is easy to approach Wesley's work as though his poetry consists of the crafting of a predetermined object. Yet, the "deepest apprehensions of the world and the gods

113

or of God . . . have always been poetic in the sense of symbolical and metaphorical."[17] Nevertheless, biblical interpretation has not traditionally or in our time generally allowed imagination, especially poetical imagination, much integrity in the hermeneutical process. Indeed, it is suspicious of the full play of the aesthetic or psychological. However, Charles Wesley through his poetical interpretation of Scripture has shown how the dramatic mythology of the Bible comes alive, just as the contemporary black church continues to do through its spirituals.

(1) *Charles Wesley reenacts the initial experience of Scripture and penetrates ancient categories.* He does this in many ways.

(a) He personalizes the text so that the experience of the text becomes his own. Wesley responds to Jesus' words, "Lazarus come forth" (Jn. 11:43) in this way:

> Jesus, quickning spirit, come,
> Call my soul out of its tomb;
> Dead in sins and trespasses,
> Thou art able to release
> Canst the life of grace restore,
> Raise me up to sin no more.[18]

Lazarus' death is his own death and he becomes the Lazarus who must be called forth.

(b) He changes narrative into dramatic monologue and dialogue so that the original event transforms reality. Notice this at work in a series of unpublished poems by Wesley based on the story of the "Good Samaritan" in Luke 10.

Lk. 10:30, *A certain man went down from Jerusalem to Jericho and fell among thieves, etc.*

> 1. How desperate is the state of man!
>   My misery will his case explain
>   Who among robbers fell:
>   Pure from the hands of God I came;
>   Now in the cruel hands I am
>   Of sin, the world, and hell.

> 2. That city of the living God
>   Was built to be my soul's abode;
>   My soul from thence came down,
>   Down to this Jericho beneath,
>   This place accurst of sin and death,
>   And endless pains unknown.

3. Far from the new Jerusalem,
   Deeper and deeper still I seem
       Implung'd in guilt and woe,
   Lower, and lower still I sink,
   And trembling hang as on the brink
       Of the dark gulph below.

4. The thieves have torn away my dress,
   That robe of spotless righteousness
       I did in Eden wear:
   Spoil'd of my immortality,
   Naked of God, my shame I see,
       And Satan's image bear.

5. The thieves have rob'd, and stript, and bound,
   And mangled me with many a wound,
       And bruis'd in every part:
   My putrid wounds stand open wide,
   My head is faint, and sick of pride,
       And all corrupt my heart.

6. Too long insensible I lay,
   The ruffians had secur'd their prey,
       And left my spirit dead:
   Or if one spark of life remains,
   It makes me feel my mortal pains,
       And feebly gasp for aid.[19]

Lk. 10:31, *And by chance there came down a certain priest that way, etc.*

1. The prophets, saints, and patriarchs old
   Could man's most helpless case behold,
       But not his fall repair;
   They saw, but pass'd the sinner by,
   They left as at the point to die
       The wounded traveller.

2. The venerable priest may see
My wounds, but cannot succour me,
   But cannot heal his own;
Not all the righteousness of man
Will mitigate my grief and pain,
   Or for my sins atone.[20]

Lk. 10:32, *Likewise a Levite, when he was at the place, came and looked on him, etc.*

1. The Levite stern approaches nigh,
Observes with unrelenting eye,
   And shows my desperate case,
Commands, but brings me no relief,
But aggravates my sin and grief
And all my wounds displays.

2. The Law commands, Do this and live,
But power and grace it cannot give,
   It cannot justify,
It leaves the miserable man
To bleed, and languish, and complain,
   Till in my sins I die.[21]

Lk. 10:33, *But a certain Samaritan, as he journeyed, came where he was, etc.*

1. But Life I see in death appear!
The good Samaritan is near,
   From heaven to earth he comes,
His country he for me forsakes
Upon himself my nature takes
And all my sins assumes.

2. Attach'd to earth he sees me lie,
He marks me with a pitying eye,
   And all my wounds surveys:
Ev'n now his yearning bowels move,
His heart or'eflows with softest love,
   And heaven is in his face.[22]

Lk. 10:34, *He went to him, and bound up his wounds, pouring in oil and wine, etc.*

1. Stranger unknown, Thou art my God!
    From me, while weltring in my blood,
    Thou canst not farther go:
    Pour in thy Spirit's wine and oil,
    Revive me by a gracious smile,
    Thy pardning mercy show.

2. Bind up my wounds by opening thine,
    Apply the balm of blood Divine
    To save a sinner poor;
    To life, and joy, and gospel-peace
    (Sure pledge of perfect holiness)
    My gasping soul restore.

3. The bitterness of death is past,
    And lo, I on thy mercy cast,
    Into thy church convey'd
    Most surely feel my cure begun;
    And still I trust thy love alone
    And hang upon thine aid.[23]

Lk. 10:35, *On the morrow when he departed, he took out two pence, etc.*

1. Thy patient in thy hands I lie,
    All helplessness, all weakness I,
    But thy almighty skill
    On sinners to the utmost shew'd,
    Shall thro' the virtue of thy blood
    My soul compleatly heal.

2. Thou didst, ascending up on high,
    Pour down thy blessings from the sky,
    And gifts on man bestow,
    Gifts to supply thy people's wants,
    Gifts for the perfecting the saints
    In thy great inn below.

3. Thou bidst the ministerial host
Dispense thy med'cines at thy cost;
   And with thy sympathy
My wounds he carefully attends,
Talents, and gifts, and grace expends,
   And life itself on me.

4. Sure from his dear returning Lord,
To gain the hundred-fold reward,
   The steward of thy grace
Laborious in the strength divine,
Saves his own soul, in saving mine,
   And dies to see thy face.[24]

Each poem is a dramatic monologue in which the reality of an ancient story converses with Charles Wesley's world of reality and that of the reader. The ancient categories of suffering and alienation are penetrated as one becomes robbed and left for dead. Even the overarching *dénouement* of biblical history which lays bare the human condition is transformed with telescopic vision into present reality. As the abandoned, suffering person, one sees the helplessness of history pass before one's eyes—the helplessness of the prophets, saints, patriarchs, priests, the law. Suddenly the myth of the unknown compassionate stranger becomes a reality. In Wesley's interpretation the story of the "Good Samaritan" is not only aesthetic, it animates, engages, and the social imagination of the New Testament is transformed into that of the present.

It seems self-evident for Wesley that the drama of Scripture and of life anticipates and requires the wedding of faith and imagination through which a sense of the unknown comes.

(2) *Wesley often transforms the imagery of Scripture into categories of contemporaneous experience.* This is a hazardous interpretative principle for Holy Scripture. While the transformation often results in powerful imagery, it sometimes has little or nothing to do with the text. An example of this is found in Wesley's poem based on Luke 5:3, He entered into one of the ships, etc. Wesley writes:

1. That apostolic ship,
      That church where Christ abides,
   Loosed from the earth, while in the deep,
      Above the deep it rides.

Of unity the school
Of truth the sacred chair!
Jesus delights to sit and rule,
And teach his people there.

2.   He at the helm appears,
Directs by his command,
Cooperates with his ministers,
And bids them leave the land,
Themselves from sin secure,
From worldly things remove,
And keep their life and conscience pure,
And work for Him they love.[25]

Wesley transforms the ship of Luke 5 into the metaphor of the church, to which he often referred as "the old ship," and paints a powerful picture of the apostolic ship at sea with Jesus at the helm, but his transformed metaphor has only a faint relationship, if that, to the text.

At other times his transformation of biblical imagery moves directly to the heart of the text's meaning. It is often effective, when the inanimate becomes animate. On the parable of the figtree in Luke 13, Wesley pens these lines:

I the barren figtree am
Planted here in sacred ground:
Oft to me my Planter came,
Fruit he sought, but none he found,
Void of vital piety,
No good works were wrought by me.[26]

As a parable of fruitlessness and penitence, Wesley is right on target. Those listening knew Jesus was making clear that Israel had borne no fruit and had only a short time for repentance and renewal. Wesley treated only one aspect of the story, namely, barrenness, fruitlessness. He himself and those who read his poem become the figtree articulating the powerful awareness of their own emptiness. Here the art of poetic speech raises the question of the meaning of the parable and bridges the following levels of awareness: awareness of what the parable meant in the world in which it was told, in the world in which it is now told, and in one's own private world. The telescoping and focusing of human experience at these levels is part of the genius of poetic imagination, generally left by theologians and biblical interpreters to the task of the homiletician who may be excused for "spiritualizing" the text. However, there is perhaps a parable for biblical interpretation that may already have come of age in Wesley's poetry in something Rudolf Bultmann's wife once related about her husband. She said that whenever he preached in his Marburg parish church at Christmas time "he forgot all about his demythologizing and invoked the poetry of the birth narratives without any reserve."[27]

Focusing on the meaning of a text is the endless task of exegesis and interpretation, but blending this focus with transforming awareness is the interpretative genius of Wesley's poetic art.

(3) *Wesley's biblical interpretation is one of metamorphosis.* He is changed, redirected, healed, or utterly devastated by what he reads in Scripture. This transpires in part because of the nature of the biblical text to appropriate itself to diverse human situations. It is here that Wesley's poetic art provides the creative tension in biblical interpretation which allows the symbols, metaphors, similes, and figures of speech of Holy Scripture to impact various interpretations. Indeed, his poetic art becomes a vehicle of the Bible's self-appropriating quality or power.

He creates the biblical moment in the present by painting word pictures which convey not only the meaning but the mood of the text. Consider two poems based on Luke 18:11-13, the encounter with the Publican and the Pharisee.

Lk. 18:11-12, *God, I thank thee, that I am not as other men are, etc.*

> The modern Pharisee is bold
> In boasting to surpass the old:
> Triumphant in himself, he stands
> Conspicuous with extended hands,
> With hideous screams and outcries loud
> Proclaims his goodness to the croud,
> Glories in his own perfect grace,
> And blasphemies presents for praise!
> "Again I thank thee, and again,
> "That I am not as other men,
> "But holy as thyself, and pure,
> "And must, O God, like thee indure:
> "Thyself I now to witness call,
> "That I am good, and cannot fall,
> "Thee to exalt, repeat the word,
> "And thus I glory—in the Lord!"[28]

Lk. 18:13, *The publican standing afar off, would not lift up so much as his eyes to heaven, etc.*

<blockquote>

1. A penitent indeed
    Has nothing good to plead,
  Guilt confesses with his eyes,
    Dares not lift them up to heaven,
  Not so much in words, as sighs
    Prays, and begs to be forgiven.

2. O'rewhelm'd with conscious fear
    He trembles to draw near;
  Far from the most holy place;
    Far from God his distance keeps,
  Feels his whole unworthiness,
    Feels—but shame has seal'd his lips.

4. Labours his strugling soul
    With indignation full;
  With unutter'd grief opprest,
    Grief too big for life to bear,
  Self-condemn'd he smites his breast,
    Smites his breast—and God is there!

5. Loos'd by the power of grace,
    Behold, at last he prays!
  Pleads th'atoning sacrifice
    For meer sin and misery,
  Humbly in the Spirit cries,
    "God be merciful to me!"[29]

</blockquote>

Is this not an amplification of the text? Of course, but it is more like synthetic parallelism of Hebrew poetry in which the second line of the couplet fleshes out, accentuates, stresses what is said in the first line. How poignantly and dynamically Wesley juxtaposes the Pharisee's pompous verbosity with the Publican's humble economy of words. The Pharisee proclaims, "Again I thank thee, and again, etc." The Publican says only, "God be merciful to me."

"A text is enriched by the Bible when an author skillfully integrates into a text the religious wisdom and literary craft of the Bible."[30] This is precisely what Wesley does here and elsewhere generally with discretion and restraint. He creates theological modules in which there is a metamorphosis of the text as well as of the poet and reader/singer.

There are times when Wesley makes the text say something it is not saying, particularly when he contextualizes it by the projection of eighteenth-century imagery, metaphors, etc. upon the text. Nevertheless, at times his telescopic overview of what the Scripture is constantly saying at various levels in the Old and New Testaments is an eloquent digestion of biblical theology and ideas. He responds to the simple description of Acts 4:34-5 with a penetrating summary of the New Testament understanding of stewardship, which through its opening question is a call to metamorphosis.

Acts 4:34-5, *Neither was there any among them that lacked: for as many as were possessors of lands or houses sold them, and brought the prices of the things that were sold, and laid them down at the apostles' feet: and distribution was made unto every man according as he had need.*

> 1. Which of the Christians now
>   Would his possessions sell?
>   The fact ye scarce allow,
>   The truth incredible
>   That men of old so weak should prove,
>   And as themselves their neighbour love.
>
> 2. Of your redundant store
>   Ye may a few relieve,
>   But all to feed the poor
>   Ye cannot, cannot give,
>   Houses & lands for Christ forego,
>   Or live as Jesus liv'd below.
>
> 3. Jesus, thy church inspire
>   With Apostolic love,
>   Infuse with one desire
>   T'insure our wealth above,
>   Freely with earthly goods to part,
>   And joyfully sell all in heart.
>
> 4. With thy pure Spirit fill'd,
>   And loving Thee alone,
>   We shall our substance yield,
>   Call nothing here our own,
>   Whate'er we have or are submit
>   And lie, as beggars, at thy feet.[31]

At times Wesley amplified biblical ideas, images, metaphors, symbols, similes, etc. in a "spiritualized" manner which has little or nothing to do with the text itself. Examples of this kind of textual metamorphosis are found in two poems which are a response to Jesus' words from the cross, "I thirst." (John 19:28)

1. Expiring in the Sinners' stead,
    "I thirst," the Friend of Sinners cries,
    And feebly lifts his languid Head
    And breathes his Wishes to the Skies.

2. Not for the Vinegar they gave,
    For Life, or Liberty, or Ease,
    He thirsted—all the world to save,
    He only thirsted after this.

3. He thirsted for this Soul of mine,
    That I might His Salvation see,
    That I might in his Image shine;
    Dear Wounded Lamb, he long'd for me.

4. Willing that All his Truth should know,
    And feel the Virtue in his Blood,
    He thirsted to redeem his Foe,
    And reconcile a World to GOD.

5. And shall not we the same require,
    And languish to be sav'd from Sin!
    Yes, Lord, 'tis all our Soul's Desire;
    O wash, & make us pure within.

6. We thirst to drink thy healing blood,
    To wash us in the cleansing Tide,
    We only long for Thee our God,
    Our Jesus, and Thee crucified.

7. Be satisfied; We long for Thee,
    We add our strong Desires to Thine,
    See then, thy Soul's hard Travail see,
    And die, to make us all Divine.[32]

On the same verse of Scripture he also wrote:

> He thirsted, to redeem his foe,
> And reconcile a world to God,
> He long'd that all his love might know,
> Sav'd by the virtue of his blood!

123

> Be satisfied; we thirst for thee,
> We add our strong desires to thine:
> See then, thy soul's hard travail see,
> And die, to make us all divine.[33]

Interestingly even the silence of the biblical text can become the context of metamorphosis in Wesley's biblical interpretation, as a poem on a Lukan passage illustrates.

Lk. 3:23, *Jesus . . . began to be about thirty years of age.*

> Jesus, my long-sequester'd God,
> The lesson of thy life I hear;
> It bids me shun the noisy croud,
> And Thee in solitude revere:
> Important far above our thought
> Was thy conceal'd humility:
> Silence for thirty years it taught;
> Thy other truths were taught in three.[34]

Even the biblical text's thirty years of silence regarding Jesus' life before his ministry are didactic for Wesley.

There are two aspects of metamorphosis in Wesley's biblical interpretation which have to do with the dynamics of the interrelationship of the Old and New Testaments. Both aspects find expression in his poetic imagination.

(a) The New Testament *determines* Old Testament interpretation. Wesley's paraphrases of many Hebrew Psalms provide numerous examples of this facet of his biblical interpretation. While his poetry frequently captures the sense of the Psalms and embodies their spirit, there is no question that he reads them christologically. The complaints, afflictions, penitential pleas, praise, and thanksgiving of the Psalter are Christ's and Wesley's. He finds Christ and himself there. He does not sing the Psalter as a Jew but as a believing recipient of the Old and New Testaments which testify to a messianic hope for humankind expressed in Jesus Christ. The Psalms sing the glory of creation and nature and God's concern for both, the dignity of being human, the indignation of sin, God's atoning love, and the power of God's Spirit, all of which for Charles Wesley culminate and are fulfilled in Jesus Christ. The Psalms, therefore, are Christ's and Wesley's, as Christ's follower.

Christologizing the Psalter presents problems, for there is the danger of imposing the theology of a later period on a theological literature of an earlier one. Charles's brother Samuel cautioned about this in the following poem entitled "On altering the Psalms, to apply them to a Christian State":

> Has David *Christ to come* foreshow'd?
>   Can Christians then aspire
> To mend the harmony that flow'd
>   From his prophetic lyre?
>
> How curious are their wits and vain,
>   Their erring zeal, how bold,
> Who durst with meaner dross profane
>   His purity of gold!
>
> His Psalms unchanged the saints employ,
>   Unchanged our God applies:
> They suit th' apostles in their joy,
>   The Saviour when he dies.
>
> Let David's pure, unalter'd lays
>   Transmit through ages down
> To thee, O David's Lord, our praise!
>   To thee, O David's Son!—
>
> Till judgment calls the seraph throng
>   To join the human choir,
> And God, who gave the ancient son,
>   The new one shall inspire.[35]

There is, however, also danger of assuming that there is only one proper interpretation of the Psalms and that it is a pre-Christian one. Both Jews and Christians claim the Psalms as their hymnbook. Christians sing them as ones who have moved beyond the Mosaic law, therefore, they sing them differently. They see in Christ the new cornerstone and fulfillment of the law, therefore, they sing the Psalms from an enlarged perspective. Does this then justify Christian paraphrases of the Psalms?— or are they "flights of fancy" as the distinguished Reverend William Romaine once claimed of Isaac Watts's Psalm poetry?[36] A key consideration is to what extent a paraphrase through a particular theological perspective nullifies or alters the self-appropriating quality of the Psalms themselves—their ability to find people where they are and speak to them and their needs, be they Jew or Christian.

Unquestionably the New Testament interprets the Psalms from time to time in relation to the incarnation of Jesus, so that they have an expanded contextuality and enlarged historical meaning. Christians view the God of the Psalms and the New Testament as one and the same.

Hence, the New Testament is an extension of the Old Testament expression of that God. Even Samuel Wesley says in the poem above:

> They suit th' apostles in their joy,
> The Saviour when he dies.

In part, however, the point he is making is the one against which he argues. On the other hand, he points specifically to the Psalms' self-appropriating power. Christ and the apostles find that they suit their needs in joy and sorrow.

When Christians read Psalm 22 on Good Friday, they read it differently from Jews. For them its meaning encompasses Christ. It expresses his own agony and struggle in moments of crisis and impending death. Christians read it within the context of the Christ-event. While it need not be christologized *per se*, it is contextualized. Like Christ, Christians at times also may feel forsaken by God, yet they know that in their most desperate moments God has not forsaken or abandoned them, rather has drawn them into an eternal, divine fellowship.

Charles Wesley's christologized version of Psalm 23 specifically understands the tetragrammaton YHWH to be personified in Jesus Christ. In other words, he is the embodiment of the God whom Israel designated by the four Hebrew consonants YHWH, the unpronounceable name for God. Such an interpretation means that Psalm 23 is to be grasped entirely in terms of the incarnation, as Wesley's following poem makes clear.

Psalm 23[37]

> Jesus the good Shepherd is
>   Jesus died the sheep to save;
> He is mine and I am his
>   All I want in him I have:
> Life, and health, and rest, and food,
> All the plenitude of God.
>
> Jesus loves and guards his own;
>   Me in verdant pastures feeds,
> Makes me quietly lie down,
>   By the streams of comfort leads:
> Following him where'er he goes,
> Silent joy my heart o'erflows.

He in sickness makes me whole,
  Guides into the paths of peace;
He revives my fainting soul,
  Stablishes in righteousness;
Who for me vouchsafed to die,
Loves me still—I know not why!

Love divine shall still embrace,
  Love shall keep me to the end;
Surely all my happy days
  I shall in thy temple spend
Till I to thy house remove,
Thy eternal house above.

Without question the New Testament understands Jesus as the Good Shepherd who lays down his life for the sheep, the shepherd who goes in search of lost sheep at all costs. He is the one who directs the paths of his sheep, brings comfort, refreshes them with the water of life, is the author of peace, and gives life sustained continuity. These are all primary themes emphasized by the psalmist and Wesley has paraphrased most of them. The character of the psalm, however, has been radically transformed through Wesley's paraphrase.

(1) In the second line of verse one the death of Jesus, his sacrifice at Calvary, is the key to fullness and completeness in life. It is because he lays down his life that nothing is lacking in the lives of those who follow him. All human needs are fulfilled in him and through his death. (2) In verse three there is a radical shift in the character of the psalm. The psalmist's confidence and faith in God's sustenance amid life's darkest moments shifts to an emphasis upon Jesus' suffering and death. One moves from the suffering psalmist to the suffering Jesus:

Who for me vouchsafed to die.

The overwhelming awe with which one faces the wonder of God's love in the sacrifice of Jesus, so often a theme in Wesley's hymns and poems, is made the climax of verse three:

Loves me still—I know not why!

(3) In the psalm it is God's goodness and mercy which give lasting sustenance. In Wesley's paraphrase, however, this emphasis is transformed into divine love.

Love divine shall still embrace
Love shall keep me to the end.

127

Certainly the New Testament understands that which the Old Testament affirms about God's nature as a shepherd and the care and concern for the sheep to be fulfilled in Jesus. Indeed, these aspects of God's care and sustaining power culminate in the incarnation. In this sense, Wesley's paraphrase of Psalm 23 is true to a New Testament understanding of the Old Testament. Nevertheless, it places a theological cloak around the psalm which changes its character and is not necessary for the Christian's understanding of it. A unique aspect of the Word of God is its self-appropriating power: its ability to find people where they are and speak to them and their needs. The church and its interpreters, however, often have found it difficult to rely on such a power and have set themselves to the task of appropriating the Word so that it will speak to people where they are.

Wesley's paraphrase of Psalm 23 is a valid summary of the New Testament understanding of God's sustaining and shepherding concern for the living. It is less satisfying as an expression of the psalmist's own affirmation of faith that in the midst of life's darkest gloom there is a God who sustains. Wesley's verse requires a psychological and theological shift from a deep inward look at the bleakest moments in one's life to the bleakest moment in Christ's life. Hence, two important questions arise for the interpretation of the psalm. (1) Does removing the inner despair and suffering of the psalmist enhance the grasp of God's sustaining concern? (2) Does viewing one's own despair and suffering serve a better understanding of that concern? To be sure, the latter question is a primary matter in Psalm 23 and it is minimized, if not excized, by Wesley. Indeed, he is concerned with an inward journey, but from the standpoint of the Christ-event.

(b) The Old Testament *informs* New Testament interpretation. There are other psalm paraphrases of Wesley in which he is more faithful to the spirit of the psalm in its Old Testament context. Among the hitherto unpublished poems and hymns of Charles Wesley another paraphrase of Psalm 23 is to be found. It is entitled "Ps,23rd as a prayer." Throughout the poem Wesley remains in the first person and captures more appropriately the sense of the psalmist's deep inward pilgrimage than in the previously cited paraphrase.

> O gentle Shepherd, hear my cry,
> And hearken as thou passest by
> To a poor wand'ring sheep;
> Relieve me with thy tender care,
> Behold my want of help; draw near
> And save me from the deep.

Come, lead me forth to pastures green;
To fertile meads, where all serene
   Invites to peace and rest;
Near the still waters let me lie,
To view them gently murmur by,
   Then bless the Ever-blest.

O God, thy promis'd aid impart,
Convert my soul and change my heart,
   And make my nature pure;
Come, change my nature into thine;
Still lead me in the path divine,
   And make my footsteps sure.

When thro' the gloomy shade I roam,
Pale death's dark vale, to endless home,
   O save me then from fear;
Vouchsafe with love my soul to fill,
That I in death may fear no ill,
   And only praise declare.

Tho' foes surround, before their face
Prepare a table deck'd with grace,
   Thy food, O Lord, impart;
With sacred oil anoint my head,
And let thy mighty love o'erspread
   With joy my willing heart.

A pilgrim whilst on earth I rove,
O let me all thy goodness prove;
   Let mercy end my days;
Admit, at last, my wand'ring feet
Thy courts to enter, Thee to greet
   With everlasting praise.[38]

There is no attempt here to christologize the psalm. Indeed, the psalmist's affirmations are transformed into prayerful pleas. Ps. 23:3b, He leads me in paths of righteousness for his name's sake, becomes:

O God, thy promis'd aid impart,
Convert my soul and change my heart,
   And make my nature pure;
Come, change my nature into thine;
Still lead me in the path divine,
   And make my footsteps sure.

129

The psalmist's affirmation becomes a plea for personal transformation, or metamorphosis, and purity. Of primary importance, however, is that personal despair and suffering are not shifted to Christ but remain focused on God's sustenance amid human need, which is true to the spirit and thrust of the psalm.

Wesley's paraphrase of Psalm 104, "Author of every work divine," is also an example of an interpretation which is faithful to the spirit of the psalm in the its Old Testament context. Psalm 104 is often designated as a psalm of nature. In the paraphrase, as in the psalm, one's soul effervesces with praise of God the Creator. Both express a theology of renewal of all creation by God's continuing creative process. The earth *and* its creatures are renewed.

Psalm 104[39]

Author of every Work Divine,
Who dost thro' both Creations shine,
　　The God of Nature and of Grace,
Thy glorious Steps in all we see,
And Wisdom attribute to thee,
　　And power, and Majesty, and Praise.

Thou didst thy mighty Wings outspread,
And, brooding o'er the Chaos, shed
　　Thy life into th'impregn'd Abyss,
The Vital Principle infuse,
And out of Nothing's Womb produce
　　The Earth, and Heaven, and all that Is.

That All-informing Breath Thou art,
Who dost Continued Life impart,
　　And bidst the World persist to Be:
Garnish'd by Thee yon azure Sky,
And all those beautous Orbs on high
　　Depend in Golden Chains from Thee.

Thou dost create the Earth anew,
(Its Maker and Preserver too)
　　By thine Almighty Arm sustain:
Nature *perceives* thy secret Force,
And still holds on her even course,
　　And owns thy Providential Reign.

> Thou art the *Universal* Soul,
> The Plastick Power that fills the whole,
>   And governs Earth, Air, Sea, and Sky:
> The Creatures all thy Breath receive;
> And who by thy Inspiring live,
>   Without thy Inspiration die.

> Spirit immense, Eternal Mind,
> Thou on the Souls of lost Mankind
>   Dost with the benignest Influence move:
> Pleas'd to restore the ruin'd Race,
> And new-create a World of Grace
>   In all the Image of thy Love.

What does Wesley mean in verse one by "God of nature *and* of grace?" Does he mean that God is the God of heavens *and* the earth? or the God of nature *and* human relationships? That is difficult to determine, but his intention is clear; namely, God does not bestow grace upon human beings and withhold it from the rest of creation. *All* creation receives God's grace!

With the words "Thy glorious steps in all we see" Wesley affirms no shallow pantheism, nor does the psalm, rather he declares with the psalmist that God's imprint is everywhere to be found in creation. This is a primary emphasis throughout the entire psalm. The concluding line of verse one "And power, and majesty, and praise" is reminiscent of verse one of the psalm.

Verse two of the poem does contain the element of *creatio ex nihilo* which is not found in Psalm 104, but it is often attributed to the Genesis creation story.

> And out of Nothing's Womb produce
> The Earth, and Heaven, and all that Is.

Wesley's main emphasis, however, is on God's imparting of life.

> Thy life into th'impregn'd Abyss,
> The Vital Principle infuse,

Verses 8–23 of the psalm are a proclamation of the Creator's setting life in motion. God creates life out of lifelessness, and plants and animals begin their cycles of nourishment, growth, and survival. Human beings begin their cycles of labor (vs. 23). Wesley's use of the word "abyss" should not be understood as referring to some primeval deep but to the emptiness and lifelessness which are infused with life.

Interestingly Wesley captures the spirit of the psalmist's use of participles, which may indicate God's ongoing and sustaining, creative action, by his use of verbs in the present tense which infer the continuity of God's support and action.

Wesley refers to the Creator in verse three as the "all-informing Breath," which recalls verse 30a of the psalm. Creation expires without God. It lives from God's ongoing creative action. God is creation's life and breath:

> When thou sendest forth thy breath,
> they are created.

Psalm 104 declares in verses two through four that God has created the world of the heavens by self-will. Wesley responds,

> And bidst the World persist to Be.

This is the one idea which dominates Psalm 104 from beginning to end: God has created by self-will, and the celestial world is dependent upon that Will and bears testimony to its power and wisdom.[40]

Verse four of Wesley's psalm paraphrase proclaims the affirmation of Psalm 104:5–9: The earth like the heavens is the result of divine creative action. In verse 30 the psalmist avers, "Thus thou renewest the face of the earth." Not only is God its Creator but its renewer as well. Wesley paraphrases,

> Thou dost create the Earth anew,
> (Its Maker and Preserver too)
> By thine Almighty Arm sustain:

Even the inanimate earth and its mountains respond to God:[41]

> Nature *perceives* thy secret Force,
> And still holds on her even course,

Wesley's poetry is characterized by names for God which grow out of the Scripture, scriptural contexts, and life situations. As he views the inclusive nature of God as perceived by the psalmist in, through, over, above, and beyond creation, he sings a hymn of praise to God, the Universal Soul, in verse five. Since all which exists issues from this Universal Soul, God is for Wesley "The Plastick Power which fills the whole." God moulds life and fills creation with life in every form. Such is the plasticity of God's power. It moulds itself to every need in creation.

Wesley's poem reviews the arenas of God's provenance: the earth (Psalm 104:10–18), sea (104:25–6), air and sky (104:2–4, 19–23). Of the seven wonders of creation mentioned in the psalm: (1) sky (verses 2–4),

132

(2) earth (verses 5–9), (3) water (verses 10–13), (4) vegetation (verses 14–18), (5) moon and sun (verses 19–23), (6) sea (verses 24–6), (7) life (verses 27–30)—Wesley omits (3), (4), and (5). Nonetheless, he claims boldly that *all creation* hinges upon God's life-giving and sustaining breath:

> The Creatures all thy Breath receive;

The absence of God's life-principle means death:[42]

> And who by thy Inspiring live,
> Without thy Inspiration die.

Verse six of the poem is a prayer which moves beyond the psalmist's emphasis upon the origin of life and the world expressed in Psalm 104. Wesley reflects upon the world as a Christian. He views its inhabitants as lost:

> Thou on the Souls of lost Mankind
> Dost with benignest Influence move.

To connect this emphasis with the psalmist's confidence in God's renewal of creation is appropriate for Wesley and by no means does an injustice to the psalm. New creation and renewal are themselves acts of God's grace and he concludes his prayer with the plea:

> And new-create a World of Grace
> In all the Image of thy Love.

The idea of a new creation fulfilled by the image of love throughout the world is certainly a New Testament emphasis.

However, Wesley has not used the idea to appropriate the psalm. Rather, he has let the psalm make its own declaration without imposing a New Testament christology on the psalm. When he concludes the psalm paraphrase with a prayer for the creation of a "world of grace" marked by the image of love, he does so within the context of Psalm 104's affirmation that it is God and God alone who renews creation. This is the foundation of biblical faith, Old and New Testament. Hence, Wesley understands the New Testament perception of love based on the psalmist's faith, not vice versa. Thus the Old Testament informs New Testament interpretation.

Wesley is usually at his best in interpreting the Old Testament, when he seeks to capture the spirit of the text without the imposition of a New Testament theological and linguistic cloak which may deny the Scripture its own self-appropriating power to find people where they are and speak to them through the Word's own power.

Scriptural and Theological Method

Is this not too ambitious a topic for Charles Wesley of whom it has been said elsewhere in this volume that he may not be regarded as a theologian in the "classical" sense? It is clear that he never wrote a treatise on this subject nor spelled out his Scriptural and theological method. But, if one moves from within his biblical interpretation outward, one discovers convergencies and divergencies with a contemporary approach to Scripture and theology such as narrative theology. It should be emphasized, however, that some of the best examples of Wesley's relevant biblical and theological interpretation for such an analysis are found in his long narrative hymns/poems,[43] which were probably never intended to be sung in their entirety.

There follows a brief overview of some congruencies and divergencies in Charles Wesley's biblical interpretation with some aspects of narrative theology. The narrative/canonical approach has proved helpful in responding to the challenges of historical criticism and this overview will highlight certain facets of Wesley's interpretation which similarly may have come of age in responding to such challenges. They will require further in-depth exploration and study, to which space cannot be devoted here.

(1) *The Bible as literature.* Unlike some narrative and canonical approaches, Charles Wesley does not pursue the meaning of the text as determined by an understanding of its peculiar shape and literary function. Yet, he has an amazing sense of Scripture as literature in the way he is able to bring biblical characters and the *dénouement* of the stories to life. He does not juxtapose the Bible as literature over against the view of it as a sourcebook for the early church. Wesley has a concern for the original text but not in terms of a historically, critically reconstructed text. Unequivocally for him the canonical text is authoritative.

(2) *The nature of the Bible.* While Wesley does not openly claim, as do many narrative theologians, that the historicity of the biblical accounts is secondary to narrative interpretation, in his poetry he often avers that the nature of Scripture is based on the Bible's actual content and that, if one reads it with common sense, Jesus Christ will be discovered as its central focus. Thus he shares the view of those narrative theologians who view the entire Bible as a commentary on God's redemptive work in Christ. For Wesley the biblical witness has a christocentric center.

(3) *Interpreting the biblical narrative.* When Charles Wesley interprets a narrative, does he read it literally? Does the text mean what it says? Does he see only one, inflexible, descriptive meaning of a Bible passage? Reading but a few of his narrative poems on biblical texts reveals not

only that he often sought a deeper meaning "behind" a text but some-times "beyond" it.[44] It is here that one might do an interesting study of the role of the interpreter's perspective in the interpretation of a text,[45] especially in the light of the claim of Paul Ricoeur and Gabriel Fackre that the meaning of biblical accounts is related to the interpreter's response to them.

It is difficult to bring Charles Wesley into the arena of a discussion of opposing views wherein Ricoeur maintains that the meaning of the text is given afresh in each new context and Brevard Childs maintains that scriptural texts may indeed have determinative and plain meaning. What is relevant to this discussion in Wesley's interpretation, however, is that he generally does not foreclose on the meaning of the biblical text.

It is not Wesley's purpose or intention to explicate the various stages of biblical interpretation as might be done by Hans Frei, but he does attempt to retell the story so that it may be comprehended by all interpreters.

One sees levels or stages within Wesley's interpretation and hence often a single, descriptive interpretation is generally not an option for him, nor even desirable. When he appropriates or applies the text christocentrically, the text functions for Wesley to render Christ present to readers so that they will identify themselves with the world depicted in Scripture, acknowledge and affirm its truth.

In addition, Wesley applies Scripture differently in different con-texts. Nevertheless, generally he does not reduce Scripture to his own life perspective. Here he is very close to Luther, and perhaps greatly influenced by him, in viewing the Word of God as having its own power as the Word of God regardless of its effects or interpreters.

Wesley interprets Scripture very much as a diamond reflects light. The one common source of light (God) may be reflected and refracted in many ways as one turns the diamond in the light source. Hence, it is not unusual to find diverse interpretations of the same passage of Scripture within his poetry, as the discussion of Psalm 23 above illus-trates.

(4) *The biblical world view.* Wesley stands very close to narrative theology in understanding the biblical world to be the norm by which Christians orient themselves and their experiences. He sees the primary biblical characters as Jesus and God Almighty and he is a master at disclosing how they are made present by the text. How? They are made present as believers identify with other characters in the biblical narra-tive. It is Wesley's poetical genius which often enables this identification.

For Charles Wesley the world of the Bible supplies the structure for interpreting reality. He has no mere propositional view of Scripture, rather once again in convergence with narrative theology he underscores the value of biblical language in shaping Christian response. Nevertheless, the study of Scripture and the quest to understand it are not ends in themselves, that is, to obtain mere intellectual knowledge. Rather, both supply transforming perception and experience(s). The reality of Scripture transforms present reality. Charles Wesley assumes the reality of the biblical world and like some interpreters of narrative theology understands the Christian's reality to be defined by the scriptural accounts. Therefore, Scripture *is* a living Word.

Conclusion

Charles Wesley's imaginative poetic art sets Holy Scripture and theology in a symphonic language of numerous keys. It creates modulations of the course of humankind: the way of mortals with God and God's way with them. It paints the course and goals of the world-process, the trials, the suffering, and the fulfillment of life.

Wesley cultivates the aesthetic in interpretation. He understands that images condition spirituality. He exemplifies that symbol, liturgy, and theology can be nurtured by imagination. He illustrates that there is a poetic relationship between earth and heaven. He personifies the reality that "no age can exist without poetry, without imagination, creating song, the dance, the poetic vision of life."[46]

Chapter 8

CHARLES WESLEY, MENTOR AND CONTRIBUTOR TO LITURGICAL RENEWAL

Laurence Hull Stookey

It seems on the face of it foolhardy to suggest that someone who died two centuries ago could be a mentor for or a contributor to current efforts at liturgical renewal. That renewal has looked back much farther for its sources, primarily to the patristic era, and largely has been in rebellion against influences and practices of the past several centuries. Yet in many ways the Wesleyan revival was both a profound exception to eighteenth-century liturgical piety and practice (or lack thereof)—and an anticipation of the future, the fullness of which could not be grasped until now.

Central Issues in Liturgical Renewal

One crucial development of the contemporary liturgical renewal movement is the joining again of scripture-sermon and sacrament. For most Protestants this means above all a recovery of both eucharistic theology and frequency, as for Roman Catholics it means a re-examination of the role of Scripture in the Sunday liturgy and implications for preaching. But while Protestants have never had any lapse of *frequency* in preaching, and for the most part have not lacked theological justifications for it, they also are having to reexamine the use of Scripture in preaching.

Another primary interest for both Catholics and Protestants, in the United states at least, is ecclesiology: What it means to have *corporate* worship, as distinct from having essentially private devotions conducted in public.

In all of these areas, Charles Wesley has both interest and insight, and we shall look now at his potential contribution to liturgical renewal under three major heads: Ecclesiology, Biblical Preaching, and Eucharistic Theology.

Ecclesiology

It has become a cliché within the liturgical movement to say that liturgy is "the work of the people." Understood at too shallow a level this becomes devastatingly horizontal, such that liturgical reform is understood as simply getting everybody present in the place of worship involved in the action. The current catchword for worship is "the assembly."

Because a theology of assembly *is* important, the term needs to be defined fully. We need to say at least three things more clearly than they have sometimes been stated:

A. the liturgical assembly is constituted by Christ, who is present in the midst of the worshipers by the power of the Holy Spirit;

B. the liturgical assembly is not to be equated with the local congregation gathered for worship, but is to include the church catholic, both past and present; and

C. the liturgical assembly is eschatologically oriented; it lives into the future.

These three assertions are needed, if the definition of assembly is to imply more than sociological or psychological understandings of worship.

To these concerns Wesley speaks eloquently. He is clear first that it is Christ who constitutes the worshiping assembly. In the hymns "for the society on meeting" he asserts:

> Called together by his grace,
>   We are met in Jesu's name,
> See with joy each other's face,
>   Followers of the bleeding Lamb.[1]

And again:

> Appointed by thee, We meet in thy name,
> And meekly agree To follow the Lamb.[2]

And while our mortal eyes may see Christ dimly, he is in our midst according to the promise of Matthew 18:20; we need not invoke his presence in the assembly but only ask that the reality of it be experienced more fully by us:

> Jesu, we look to thee,
> Thy promised presence claim,
> Thou in the midst of us shalt be,
> Assembled in thy name.
>
> Thy name salvation is,
> Which here we come to prove;[3]
> Thy name is life, and health, and peace,
> And everlasting love.
>
> . . . .
>
> Present we know thou art;
> But Oh! thyself reveal!
> Now, Lord, let every bounding heart
> The mighty comfort feel![4]

And again:

> See, Jesu, thy disciples see,
> The promised blessing give!
> Met in thy name, we look to thee,
> Expecting to receive.
>
> . . . .
>
> With us thou art assembled here,
> But Oh! thyself reveal!
> Son of the living God, appear!
> Let us thy presence feel.
>
> Breathe on us, Lord, in this our day,
> And these dry bones shall live;
> Speak peace into our hearts, and say,
> "The Holy Ghost receive!"[5]

Wesley is clear about the nature of the liturgical assembly; it is constituted by the risen Lord who is present in the power of the Holy Spirit. He is also clear that there is a distinction to be made between the objective presence of Christ and our subjective experience of him. Wesley's insight would illumine many a comment by persons who sup-

139

pose God is not present in worship apart from their clear apprehension of that presence.

Wesley rejects the notion that the assembly consists only of those present in the house of worship. The communion of saints is for him an ever present reality:

> The church triumphant in thy love,
>   Their mighty joys we know;
> They sing the Lamb in hymns above;
>   And we in hymns below.
>
> Thee in thy glorious realm they praise,
>   And bow before thy throne!
> We in the kingdom of thy grace:
>   The kingdoms are but one.[6]

Nor are those "in the kingdom of thy grace" divided by "parties and sects," as Charles notes in his poem "Catholic Love," appended to John's sermon on the "Catholic Spirit"; of the whole company of believers he says,

> For these, howe'er in flesh disjoin'd,
>   Where'er dispers'd o'er earth abroad,
> Unfeign'd, unbounded love I find,
>   And constant as the life of God.[7]

Finally, in Wesley's ecclesiology the church ever tends toward the eschatological hope. As someone has said, "Though Wesley's hymns may begin on earth, they end in heaven." Typical is a hymn concerning a meeting for worship which concluded with this prayer:

> Thou, who hast kept us in this hour,
>   O keep us faithful to the end!
> When, robed with majesty and power,
>   Our Jesus shall from heaven descend,
> His friends and confessors to own,
> And seat us on his glorious throne.[8]

Those who seek a more adequate liturgical ecclesiology than is sometimes evident can look to Charles Wesley for assistance.

Biblical Preaching

Much has been said in the past several decades about the recovery of biblical preaching. Usually the emphasis has been on preaching: its form and content as derived from the Scriptures. But more needs to be said about Scripture itself. Certain hermeneutical assumptions are made by the compilers of the astonishingly popular three-year lectionary; but in hearing "lectionary-based sermons," one has to wonder whether the preachers know how to use or even understand the concepts of *sensus plenior* and typology. To back up even further: What kind of authority does Scripture have, and how does this relate to preaching?

For Charles Wesley Scripture has clear authority; but it is not in the book as such. The same Spirit who inspired the authors must apply the truth of their words to our hearts, to be received by faith. Scripture does not reveal; it is God who reveals through Scripture:

> While in thy Word we search for thee
> (We search with trembling awe!)
> Open our eyes, and let us see
> The wonders of thy law.
>
> Now let our darkness comprehend
> The light that shines so clear;
> Now the revealing Spirit send,
> And give us ears to hear.[9]

And also:

> Come, Holy Ghost (for moved by thee
> The prophets wrote and spoke);
> Unlock the truth, thyself the key,
> Unseal the sacred book.
>
> . . . .
>
> God through himself we then shall know,
> If thou within us shine;
> And sound, with all thy saints below,
> The depths of love divine.[10]

In a poem based on I Corinthians 1:21, Wesley begins with this admonition:

> "The foolishness of preaching hear,
> Sinners the strange report believe."[11]

The Spirit working through faith applies the truth to us when the Scriptures are read and expounded; without that there is nothing profitable:

> Whether the Word be preached or read,
>   No saving benefit I gain
> From empty sounds or letters dead;
>   Unprofitable all and vain,
> Unless by faith thy word I hear
> And see its heavenly character.
>
> Unmixed with faith, the Scripture gives
>   No comfort, life, or light to see,
> But me in darker darkness leaves,
>   Implunged in deeper misery,
> O'erwhelmed with nature's sorest ills.
> The spirit saves, the letter kills.[12]

It is a mark of the relevance of Wesley that the poem just cited was included with four stanzas, not two, in *The United Methodist Hymnal* of 1989; it is there not as a hymn but as poetry to be studied, in the section on Holy Scriptures, in an attempt to teach a sound theology of Scripture and preaching. It is also a mark of Wesley's relevance that any number of his stanzas can function as Prayers for Illumination before the reading of Scripture in the worship service.

Wesley is a good antidote for those who know the history of biblical interpretation in the short term but not in the long term. During the fundamentalist-modernist controversy, the conservatives proclaimed themselves the keepers of the true tradition—the worthy successors of both the ancient commentators and of the reformers. Many of their opponents came to believe that, until the mid-nineteenth century or so, all Christians held to a mechanistic understanding of Scripture; this assumption lingers today to the detriment of sound biblical understanding. Wesley's theology of Scripture is a corrective to such an inaccurate reading of history.

Another result of the fundamentalist-modernist controversy was at least a suspicion and usually a rejection on the part of progressives of any christological interpretation of the Old Testament and certainly of typology, which C. I. Scofield plunged into understandable disrepute.

Then comes the three-year lectionary which, in its pairing of Old Testament and gospel passages assumes a rigorous theology of *sensus plenior* and at least some tolerance for typology. Not only have seminaries ill prepared their graduates for such developments, but in Old Testament courses students may have feared failure for suggesting such hermeneutical approaches. Charles Wesley to the rescue!

It is clear that Wesley believed in *sensus plenior*; he was always seeing a fuller sense to the Old Testament than its writers could have intended.

In a poem based on Exodus 24:5-6, he sets Old and New Testament names in apposition in the baldest manner:

> Great God! to me the sight afford
> To him of old allowed;
> And let my faith behold its Lord,
> Descending in a cloud

. . . .

> Jehovah Christ I thee adore
> Who gav'st my soul to be!
> Fountain of being, and of power,
> And great in majesty.[13]

Wesley is never averse to finding Christ in the Old Testament, though frequently he is more subtle than in the example just noted: Instead of naming Christ, he will use the ambiguous terms "Lord" and "Savior"; but a careful study of the text will reveal that he has moved well beyond the Jewish understanding of those terms.

Nor does he fear typology: finding in the Old Testament a person or event in which Christ can be seen in a shadowy way or which Christ brings to a higher level of meaning. Two examples, finding types in Gideon (based on Isaiah 9:2-5, which alludes to the conflict with Midian) and in Zerubbabel (based on Zechariah 4:7):

> Thou hast our bonds in sunder broke,
> Took all our load of guilt away!
> From sin, the world, and Satan's yoke
> (Like Israel saved in Midian's day),
> Redeemed us by our conqu'ring Lord,
> Our Gideon, and his Spirit's sword.[14]

> O great mountain, who art thou,
> Immense, immovable?
> High as heaven aspires thy brow,
> Thy foot sinks deep as hell.
> Thee, alas, I long have known,
> Long have felt thee fixed within;
> Still beneath thy weight I groan—
> Thou art indwelling sin.

. . . .

143

Not by human might or power
  Canst thou be moved from hence,
But thou shalt flow down before
  Divine omnipotence;
My Zerubbabel is near,
  I have not believed in vain;
Thou, when Jesus doth appear
  Shalt sink into a plain.[15]

It is more difficult than might be supposed to find a Charles Wesley poem on the Old Testament that can be readily aligned with a lectionary reading. But one that is excellent for our purposes is his poem based on Isaiah 61:1-3, beginning:

The Spirit of the Lord our God
  (Spirit of power, and health, and love)
The Father hath on Christ bestowed,
  And sent him from his throne above;

Prophet, and Priest, and King of peace,
  Anointed to declare his will,
To minister his pardoning grace,
  And every sin-sick soul to heal.[16]

Isaiah 61:1-4 appears twice in the lectionary. In Year C on the Sunday of the Baptism of the Lord it is paired with Luke's baptismal narrative; and in Year B on the third Sunday of Advent (with verses 8-11 added) it is paired with John 1:6-8, 19-28. The christological interpretation of Isaiah is clearer in the first instance perhaps, but by no means absent in the second. And while Wesley's poem is not a direct paraphrase of the passage, any preacher using the lectionary on these occasions could take courage in approaching Isaiah christologically by observing Wesley's interpretation.

Further, it must be said that Wesley's use of the Old Testament accords well and even corrects aberrations in the currently popular idea of "sermon as story." The degeneration of this idea into a preoccupation with stories of human interest to the neglect of Scripture has produced one written protest entitled "God Has a Story, Too."[17] Indeed so, and Wesley does a lot to teach us that we do not have to look outside of Scripture to find our story; instead if we will read carefully we will find ourselves there in the biblical accounts. This we have seen above. Christ is "our Gideon" and "my Zerubbabel."

The premier example, of course, is "Wrestling Jacob," which in fact I use when teaching seminarians the principle of *sensus plenior*. But since we have dealt thus far so exclusively with the Old Testament, here Wesley may better be illustrated from his New Testament poems. In "Come, Sinners to the Gospel Feast" the poet himself is in Jesus' story, playing the role of the servant sent out to invite the guests; and we are the excuse-makers to whom the messenger is sent. So Wesley addresses us:

> Sent by my Lord, on you I call,
> The invitation is to all:
> Come all the world: come, sinner, thou!
> All things in Christ are ready now.
>
> . . . .
>
> Do not begin to make excuse,
> Ah! do not you his grace refuse;
> Your worldly cares and pleasures leave,
> And take what Jesus hath to give.[18]

In another instance, we find ourselves not in one gospel story but in an entire complex of them:

> Jesu, if still thou art today
>   As yesterday the same,
> Present to heal, in me display
>   The virtue of thy name!
>
> If still thou goest about to do
>   Thy needy creatures good,
> On me, that I thy praise may show,
>   Be all thy wonders showed.
>
> Now, Lord, to whom for help I call,
>   Thy miracles repeat;
> With pitying eyes behold me fall
>   A leper at thy feet.
>
> Loathsome, and foul, and self-abhorred,
>   I sink beneath my sin;
> But if thou wilt, a gracious word
>   Of thine can make me clean.
>
> Thou seest me deaf to thy command;
>   Open, O Lord, my ear;
> Bid me stretch out my withered hand,
>   And lift it up in prayer.

Silent (alas! thou know'st how long),
   My voice I cannot raise;
But Oh! when thou shalt loose my tongue
   The dumb shall sing thy praise.

Lame at the pool I still am found;
   Give, and my strength employ;
Light as a hart I then shall bound—
   The lame shall leap for joy.

Blind from my birth to guilt and thee,
   And dark I am within;
The love of God I cannot see,
   The sinfulness of sin.

But thou, they say, art passing by;
   O let me find thee near;
Jesus, in mercy hear my cry;
   Thou Son of David, hear!

Long have I waited in the way
   For thee, the heavenly Light;
Command me to be brought, and say,
   Sinner, receive thy sight![19]

As I read or sing the text, sequentially I am the leper Jesus heals (Matthew 8:2-3 and parallels); the one who was deaf and mute (Mark 7:32-37 and parallels); the man with the withered hand (Luke 6:6-10); the paralytic at the Pool of Bethsaida (John 5:2-9), and blind Bartimaeus (Mark 10:46-52 and parallels). God's story *is* my story! In an age duly sensitized to the feelings of persons with handicapping conditions, the preacher may want to use other instances; but Wesley serves well as a model of how we can be drawn into any number of biblical stories—not as spectators but as participants.

Finally with respect to Wesley and preaching, we note what should be obvious but apparently is not: that he can be used for sermon content as well as theological and hermeneutical assumptions. A revulsion against the "three points and a poem" stereotype of preaching has made many shy of ever using any poetry in the pulpit. But it is commendable to quote Wesley when poetry is germane to the sermon rather than being an extraneous flourish at the end. Using liturgical poetry of Wesley (or others) does several things.

First, if the poetry is used as a hymn or other act in the service, citation in the sermon helps provide continuity throughout the liturgy;

it illustrates the liturgical character of preaching and helps establish the fact that hymns have substance and are not sung in worship because we like the tunes. Second, even if the poetry is not used elsewhere that day, inclusion in a sermon can establish the role of such verse as an aid to piety rather than as something to be analyzed aesthetically or under the canons of literary criticism. Third, quoting poetry helps inbed key passages into the memory of the Christian, from whence they can be called in times of need.

Probably Charles Wesley's least contribution to contemporary preaching is his own sermons; eighteenth-century preaching generally does not serve as a helpful homiletical model for the twentieth century. Fortunately Wesley has left us a much more extensive legacy, and one from which we can learn a great deal.

Eucharistic Theology

Until recently, the Lord's Supper among Protestants was a dreary matter to be observed infrequently by the unworthy—except that those who were too unworthy ought not to engage in it at all! And among Catholics until recently, the Mass was more a weekly duty to be done than a feast of grace to be devoured. Protestants were not sure they had a theology of the presence of Christ in the Eucharist—or wanted one; this, largely out of over-reaction to a Catholic theology of presence perceived as so mechanical or magical as to be repugnant.

Reconsideration of the meaning of the sacrament and appropriate frequency is becoming widespread. But that does not mean all is well theologically; and since current theology often consists of rebellion against whatever preceded it, various types of problems occur all at once. Among Protestants who have had dreary rites, almost to the point of being funereal, "celebration," superficially defined, seems in danger of casting out any sense that death on a cross is intimately bound up with resurrection. Among Catholics, who have had a strong vertical emphasis in the past, the Eucharist in some quarters has become distressingly horizontal—a congregational fellowship meal. Each group is in danger of discovering what has been missing in its tradition and then elevating that to the status of an exclusive absolute.

For such problems, Charles Wesley can offer help. Aside from the sheer bulk of hymns he contributed, possibly Charles Wesley's greatest gift to hymnody was precisely in the area of the Eucharist. The appearance in 1745 of *Hymns on the Lord's Supper* was a signal event; how many other poets in the history of the church have published 166 eucharistic hymns in a single collection—to say nothing of those he published in the remaining forty-three years of his life!

Quantity, of course, counts for little in itself. But the Wesley corpus of eucharistic hymns is distinguished by its breadth of content. Both Lutheran and Calvinian strains of Anglican eucharistic thought coalesce with patristic and medieval sources. And there is a balance of forces that brings together theological emphases often considered to be antagonistic if not mutually exclusive. Almost any contemporary church that senses an imbalance in its thought can find in Wesley a helpful counterweight.

With sarcasm and impatience, Wesley rejects anti-sacramentalism:

> Ah, tell us no more
> The Spirit and Power
> Of Jesus our God
> Is not to be found in this Life-giving Food!
>
> Did Jesus ordain
> His Supper in vain,
> And furnish a Feast
> For none but His earliest servants to taste?
>
> Nay, but this is his Will,
> (We know it and feel,)
> That *we* should partake
> The Banquet for All He so freely did make.
>
> In rapturous Bliss
> He bids us do This,
> The Joy it imparts
> Hath witness'd his gracious Design in our hearts.[20]

For Wesley, the Supper is an evidence of the goodness of God, an experience of joy and grace. He made the following entry in his journal on January 13, 1739: "Pierced with the prayers of Hester Hobson, I expected a fresh manifestation of Christ continually; which I found the next day at the sacrament."[21] As Christ is both present objectively and experienced subjectively when two or three are gathered in his name, so much more is he both represented and experienced in the Eucharist. This Wesley summarizes in a two-stanza prayer:

Jesu, my Lord and God, bestow
All which thy Sacrament doth show,
   And make the real Sign
A sure effectual Means of Grace;
Then sanctify my Heart, and bless,
   And make it all like thine.

Great is thy Faithfulness and Love,
Thine Ordinance can never prove
   Of none Effect and vain;
Only do Thou my Heart prepare
To find thy Real Presence there,
   And all Thy Fulness gain.[22]

Wesley espouses an understanding of Real Presence that is useful both to those trapped in a bare memorialism and to those who have a theology of Presence so rational and articulated that it stifles mystery and joy:

O the Depth of Love Divine,
   Th' Unfathomable Grace!
Who shall say how Bread and Wine
   God into Man conveys!
How the bread His flesh imparts,
How the wine transmits his blood,
   Fills His Faithful People's Hearts
   With all the Life of God!

Let the wisest Mortal shew
   How we the Grace receive,
Feeble elements bestow
   A Power not theirs to give.
Who explains the wondrous Way,
How thro' these The virtue came?
   These the Virtue did convey,
   Yet still remain the same.

How can heavenly Spirits rise,
   By earthly Matter fed,
Drink herewith Divine Supplies,
   And eat immortal Bread?

Ask the Father's Wisdom *how*;
Him that did the Means ordain!
Angels round our Altars bow
To search it out in vain.

Sure and real is the Grace,
The Manner be unknown;
Only meet us in Thy Ways,
And perfect us in one.
Let us taste the heavenly Powers;
Lord, we ask for Nothing more:
Thine to bless, 'Tis only Ours
To wonder and adore.[23]

While the manner of the Presence is not to be explained, but rather enjoyed, yet it can be described. There is to it a sacrificial character through which the offering on the cross is made present by the action of the Spirit. In the process there is a transmutation of time; note the present tense of the verb in the final line of this hymn:

O Thou eternal Victim, slain
A sacrifice for guilty man,
By the Eternal Spirit made
An Offering in the Sinner's stead,
Our everlasting Priest art Thou,
And plead'st thy Death for Sinners now.

Thy Offering still continues New,
Thy Vesture keeps its Bloody Hue,
Thou stand'st the ever-slaughter'd Lamb,
Thy Priesthood still remains the same,
Thy Years, O God, can never fail,
Thy Goodness is unchangeable.

O that our Faith may never move,
But stand unshaken as thy Love,
Sure Evidence of Things unseen,
Now let it pass the years between,
And view Thee bleeding on the Tree,
My God, who dies for Me, for Me![24]

The following hymn continues the motif of the transmutation of time but includes also other themes familiar to us: *sensus plenior*, typology, and eschatology:

Our Passover for us is slain,
The Tokens of his Death remain,
  On these Authentic Signs imprest:
By Jesus out of *Egypt* led,
Still on the Paschal Lamb we feed,
  And keep the Sacramental Feast.

That Arm that smote the parting Sea
Is still stretch'd out for us, for me,
  The Angel-God is still our Guide,
And, lest we in the Desert faint,
We find our Spirits' every Want
  By constant Miracle supplyed.

Thy Flesh for our Support is given,
Thou art the Bread sent down from Heaven,
  That all Mankind by Thee might live;
O that we evermore may prove
The Manna of thy quickening Love,
  And all thy Life of Grace receive!

Nourish us to that awful day
When Types and Veils shall pass away,
  And perfect Grace in Glory end;
Us for the Marriage-feast prepare,
Unfurl thy Banner in the Air,
  And bid thy Saints to Heaven ascend![25]

For Wesley there is in the sacrament intense joy; but it is not
"celebration" devoid of agony. The two aspects are viewed together, and
at times the *anamnesis* of Calvary can be almost too graphic to bear:

Victim Divine, thy Grace we claim
  While thus thy precious death we shew;
Once offer'd up, a spotless Lamb,
  In thy great Temple here below,
Thou didst for All Mankind atone,
And standest now before the Throne.

Thou standest in the Holiest Place,
  As now for guilty Sinners Slain;
Thy Blood of Sprinkling speaks, and prays,
  All-prevalent for helpless Man;
Thy Blood is still our Ransom found,
And spreads Salvation all around.

151

> The Smoke of thy Atonement here
>   Darken'd the Sun, and rent the Vail,
> Made the New Way to Heaven appear,
>   And show'd the great Invisible:
> Well pleased in Thee our God look'd down,
> And call'd his Rebels to a Crown.
>
> He still respects thy sacrifice,
>   Its Savour Sweet doth always please;
> The Offering smokes thro' Earth and Skies,
>   Diffusing Life and Joy and Peace;
> To these thy lower Courts it comes,
> And fills them with Divine Perfumes.
>
> We need not now go up to Heaven,
>   To bring the long-sought Saviour down;
> Thou art to All already given:
>   Thou dost even Now thy Banquet crown,
> To every faithful Soul appear,
> And shew thy Real Presence here![26]

For Wesley, the Eucharist is not only a means of grace; it is the crowning means of grace:

> The Prayer, the fast, the Word conveys,
>   When mixed with Faith, thy life to me,
> In all the Channels of thy Grace
>   I still have Fellowship with Thee,
> But chiefly here my Soul is fed
> With Fulness of Immortal Bread.
>
> Communion closer far I feel,
>   And deeper drink th' Atoning Blood,
> The Joy is more unspeakable,
>   And yields me larger Draughts of God,
> Till Nature faints beneath the Power,
> And Faith fill'd up can hold no more.[27]

Nor are these joys for the selfish benefit of the believer; they are to effect sanctification; the believer who through the sacrament shares in the sacrifice of Christ is to become thereby a living sacrifice to God:

> Amazing Love to mortals shew'd!
> The Sinless Body of our God
>   Was fasten'd to the Tree.
> And shall our sinful Members live?
> No, Lord, they shall not Thee survive,
>   They all shall die with Thee.
>
> The Feet which did to Evil run,
> The Hands which violent Acts have done,
>   The greedy Heart and Eyes,
> Base Weapons of Iniquity,
> We offer up to Death with Thee,
>   A whole burnt Sacrifice.[28]

And again:

> God of all-redeeming Grace,
>   By thy pardoning Love compell'd,
> Up to Thee our Souls we raise,
>   Up to Thee our Bodies yield.
>
> Thou our Sacrifice receive,
>   Acceptable thro' Thy Son,
> While to Thee alone we live,
>   While we die to Thee alone.
>
> Just it is, and Good, and right
>   That we should be wholly Thine,
> In thy only Will delight,
>   In thy blessed Service join.
>
> O that every Thought and Word
>   Might proclaim how Good Thou art,
> HOLINESS UNTO THE LORD
>   Still be written on our Heart.[29]

It is, of course, impossible in a paper of this brevity to show the full sweep of Wesley's eucharistic piety. But surely it is already evident that he achieved impressive balances between objective and subjective, personal and cosmic, historical and eschatological, individual and corporate, theoretical and experiential, death and resurrection, justification and sanctification. Without adopting his eucharistic theology in its detailed points, we can learn from his ability to hold in tension things that all too readily are broken apart and scattered if they are deemed theological opposites rather than theological complements.

Time fails to tell of Wesley's potential contribution to other key interests in liturgical renewal: baptism and other aspects of Christian initiation; the liturgical calendar; reform of the wedding and funeral; and the like. But even a limited examination reveals the way in which in our age Charles Wesley can serve as one of our mentors for, and contributors to, the reform and renewal of the church's worship.

PART III

Charles Wesley and the Church

Chapter 9

CHARLES WESLEY AND ANGLICANISM

Robin A. Leaver

Concerning John Wesley, Frank Baker has written:

> It would be impossible to write an adequate history of the Church of England without devoting a chapter to John Wesley and the movement of which he was the centre. Nor can Wesley himself be understood apart from the Established Church. . . . In thought and affection, in habit and atmosphere, his whole being was inextricably interwoven with that of the church. . . .[1]

The same words can be applied with equal force to Charles Wesley, indeed, perhaps, more so, since Charles did not step outside the discipline of the Church of England as John eventually did, an action that the younger brother strenuously opposed.

In attending Westminster School Charles grew up within the shadow of Westminster Abbey and its daily Prayer Book services—it must, therefore, have been a poignant occasion for him to preach in the Abbey just a few months after his "awakening."[2] Similarly, his time as a student at Christ Church, Oxford, was marked by Prayer Book services each day in the college chapel, which also served as the cathedral church for the Diocese of Oxford, a unique double function in the Church of England.[3] Thus after the sequence of ordination (September 1735), the trials of Georgia, and the return to England in a state of spiritual unrest, he wrote in his journal just a few weeks before his "awakening" in 1738: "I got abroad to the evening prayers at Christ-church; and received comfort from the lessons and anthem."[4] Throughout his life, witnessed in journal entries and letters, he would "strongly avow" again and again his "inviolable attachment to the Church of England,"[5] its formularies of faith and patterns of worship, and the comfort he received from them.

The experience of "awakening," "assurance," or "conversion," depending on one's perspective, that occurred in the life of Charles Wesley in May 1738 was certainly as dramatic a turning point for him, as it was for his brother John just a few days later. It began with the discovery of Luther and justification by faith. Significantly, Charles Wesley relates his experience of Christ to the doctrinal formulations of the Church of England:

> *Wed., May 17th [1738].* I experienced the power of Christ rescuing me from temptation. To-day I first saw Luther on the Galatians . . . and found him full of faith. . . . Who would believe our Church had been founded on this important article of justification by faith alone? I am astonished I should ever think this a new doctrine; especially while our Articles and Homilies stand unrepealed, and the key of knowledge is not yet taken away.[6]

The touchstone of Charles's thinking and action in the wake of these few days of spiritual illumination was the doctrine of justification, "my favourite subject," as he wrote in his journal under the date September 6, 1739.[7] In the weeks and months that followed his "experience of justification," he preached often on the doctrine, and frequently did so against the background of the Articles and Homilies of the Church of England.[8] Indeed, both Wesley brothers preached on justification during this period. John Wesley effectively took the doctrine as the subject of the sermon he preached before Oxford University, in St. Mary's, the University Church, on June 18, 1738. It was issued in print some weeks later, John Wesley's first publication following his experience of justification.[9] Of the six shorthand manuscript sermons of Charles Wesley, which have recently been deciphered and published,[10] the first five originated between July 1738 and July 1739, and all of them deal in some way with the doctrine of justification and its implications.

The fifth of these sermons was preached in London on February 20, 1739, "The Woman Taken in Adultery" (John 8:1ff.).[11] It includes the following passage:

> You that go out of the Church, and yet call yourselves Christians, to you I speak, and set before you the things you have done. You are they that cannot endure sound doctrine. Well do you Pharisees reject the counsel of God against yourselves, even His counsel to justify them freely when they deserve to be damned . . . you will not accept of Christ upon His own easy terms. . . . When I speak as the oracles of God, and tell you the truth as it is in Jesus, it is a small thing, think you, not to receive my testimony. Nay but in not receiving it, in not embracing these offers of salvation by grace, you have trodden under foot the Son of God, and counted the blood of the covenant an unholy thing, and done despite unto the Spirit of grace. Ye stiffnecked and uncircumcised in heart and ears, ye do always resist the Holy Ghost. . . . I warn you of the dreadful consequences of your having so denied the Lord that bought you. . . . Repent therefore of this your wickedness, and pray God if perhaps it may be forgiven you. . . . Till you

do confess it you are in a state of damnation still, as surely as God is true. And the man that dares tell you otherwise . . . I myself shall rise up in judgment against that man: and . . . whosoever does not from his heart confess he deserves to be damned, is in a state of damnation at this very hour![12]

These were strong words and clearly caused offence, particularly among other clergy. Indeed, the two Wesley brothers stirred up significant opposition, and complaints began to be made against them. Thus on February 21, 1739, that is, the day after Charles had preached the sermon cited above, the two brothers were interviewed by the Archbishop of Canterbury, Dr. John Potter, who, as Bishop of Oxford, had ordained both men. Charles recorded in his journal:

With my brother I waited on the Archbishop. He showed us great affection . . . cautioned us to give no more umbrage than was necessary for our own defence; to forbear exceptional phrases; to keep the doctrines of the Church. We told him we expected persecution; would abide by the Church till her Articles and Homilies were repealed.[13]

This focus upon "Articles and Homilies," found in the writings of both Wesley brothers, as well as their concern for the doctrine of justification, has its roots in Article 11 of the Thirty-Nine Articles of Religion found in every edition of the Book of Common Prayer:

We are accounted righteous before God, only for the Merit of our Lord and Saviour Jesus Christ by Faith; and not for our own Works or Deservings. Wherefore, that we are justified by Faith only, is a most wholesome doctrine, and very full of comfort, as more largely expressed in the Homily of Justification.

The reference in the final sentence is to the Homily "Of Salvation," written by Thomas Cranmer and first published in *Certayne sermons, or homilies, appoynted by the kynges maiestie, to be redde by all persones[,] vicars, or curates, euery Sondaye in their churches, where thei haue cure* (1547). The book was issued as part of the Edwardian Reformation and provided clergy with sermon material on biblical doctrines. A second part was published during the early Elizabethan years, *The seconde tome of homelyes* (1563), and, from 1623, the two books were brought together to form the Book of Homilies of the Church of England. The doctrinal formularies of the Church of England are, therefore, Scripture (Art. 4), the Thirty-Nine Articles (to which every ordinand must subscribe), the Homilies (referred to in Art. 11), and the Book of Common Prayer, sources from which Charles Wesley drew inspiration, as is witnessed in his various writings and especially in his hymns.

Between the last few days of 1738 and July 1, 1739, Charles Wesley prepared and preached at least three sermons on justification which include substantial *verbatim* quotations from the homilies. The first sermon, "Faith and Good Works,"[14] preached initially on December 21, 1738, makes much use of the homilies on "Almsdeeds," "Faith," and "Good Works." One month later, January 21, 1739, he preached on "Justification by Faith," and made substantial use of the homily on "Salvation," and on "Almsdeeds,"[15] as well as Articles 11–13. In it he is critical of those churchmen who, when subscribing to the Thirty-Nine Articles, do so with mental reservations and thus betray both Scripture and the Established Church to which they nominally belonged. In particular he singled out the fashionable Arians of the day, Rationalists who denied the divinity of Christ, effectively theological Unitarians within the Trinitarian church. Many of Charles Wesley's hymns, therefore, were understandably written from a strongly Trinitarian perspective, and his two collections of hymns on the Trinity are considerably more than just anthologies of doxological verse to be appended to other hymns or to the end of worship.[16]

Some months later Charles Wesley had the opportunity to preach before the University of Oxford, as his brother had done the previous year. He chose justification as his subject and produced what amounts to a re-working of the January 21, 1739, sermon on the doctrine.[17] His text was Romans 3:23–25: "All have sinned and come short of the glory of God, being justified freely by His grace, through the redemption that is in Jesus Christ; whom God hath set forth to be a propitiation through faith in His blood." After his exposition of the text Wesley announced: "I shall deliver this offending doctrine of justification by faith only, in the words of our own excellent church as they are plainly set forth in the homilies."[18] Thereafter follow eleven consecutive paragraphs taken virtually verbatim and in sequence from the homily on "Salvation." There are some omissions, principally quotations from such early Fathers as Basil and Ambrose, some emendations, such as substitutions for archaic vocabulary, and the scriptural quotations are changed to conform to the Authorized Version (KJV). Following this substantial quotation Wesley again refers to Articles 11–13, those that deal with faith and justification. Then, after quoting the homily on "Faith," and referring to the witness of Scripture, Wesley continues:

> Thus mighty are these men in the Scriptures; and as deeply skilled are they in the doctrines of our own church. Tell me, you that are of the church, do ye not hear the church? I know ye do; and to you I therefore appeal. Judge you, which are the schismatics, we who maintain, or they who deny, justification by faith only? Indeed they are worse than schismatics who

deny; for if they have ever subscribed our Articles, they are perjured schismatics. God forbid that I, or any of my brethren, should preach another gospel; for we have so declared upon oath our belief of justification by faith only, and for us to hold another doctrine would be widely felt [as] inexcusable perjury. . . .[19] Let not those therefore who deny this doctrine any longer call themselves of the Church of England. . . . In short, they may call themselves anything but Church of England men and Christians; for such we can never allow them to be; since, to repeat the words of our own church, "Whosoever denieth this doctrine, is not to be counted for a Christian man, nor a setter-forth of Christ's gospel, but for a setter-forth of man's vain glory, an adversary to Christ and His gospel."[20]

Wesley made his position abundantly clear: the doctrine of justification that he preached was not a "new" doctrine invented by "schismatics," but the teaching of Scripture and of the Church of England. Both Charles and John Wesley frequently complained that whereas they were indeed faithful to the doctrinal standards of the Church of England, and were criticized for it, the clergy who opposed them were often openly at variance with the discipline and formularies of faith of the Established Church. In order to remind the church of its doctrinal heritage, before the end of the year 1739, the Wesley brothers published *The Doctrine of Salvation, Faith, and Good Works: Extracted from the Homilies of the Church of England* (London: Hutton, 1739), and John Wesley issued *Two Treatises: The First, on Justification by Faith only, according to the Doctrine of the Eleventh Article of the Church of England: The Second, On the Sinfulness of Man's Natural Will . . . according to the Ninth, Tenth, Twelfth, and Thirteenth Articles* (London: Lewis, 1739). For this latter title John Wesley extracted material from Foxe's *Book of Martyrs*, originally written by Robert Barnes (1495–1540), considered one of the founding fathers of the Church of England. About the same time as these publications appeared Charles wrote in his journal:

I took occasion to show the degeneracy of our modern Pharisees. . . . None of them regard [Friday], though enjoined [in the Church of England], as a fast. As to prayer and sacrament, their neglect is equally notorious. And yet these men cry out, "The Church, the Church!" when they will not hear the Church themselves; but despise her authority, trample upon her orders, teach contrary to her Articles and Homilies, and break her Canons. . . .[21]

In the 1740s and 1750s there were various stresses and strains from within the "Methodist" societies and from the Church at large over the question of their loyalty to the Church of England. Part of the problem was the term "Methodist." Charles felt that John's use of it was somewhat ambiguous and capable of misinterpretation. In early 1744, a time when rebellion and civil war were in the air, John had sent a loyal address to the King in the name of "Methodists." Charles took John to task for giving the wrong impression:

> My objection to your address in the name of the Methodists is, that it would constitute us as a sect; at least it would *seem to allow* that we are a body distinct from the national Church. Guard against this.[22]

The Wesley brothers were frequently accused by other clergy of creating sectarian assemblies, hotbeds of "enthusiasm," that were not really part of the Established Church. The accusations were intensified after the first Methodist Conference of 1744. Both John and Charles Wesley insisted again and again that their societies were not set up in opposition to the Church of England but rather in order to revive the spiritual life of the members of the national Church. Even though some individuals within the Methodist societies did become impatient with the Church of England and separated themselves from it, both Wesley brothers exhorted them to return and to remain members of the "old Church." Thus at the thirteenth Methodist Conference, held in Bristol in August 1756, the question of loyalty to the Church of England was a principal issue. John Wesley's account was transcribed by Charles in a letter to a friend:

> We afterwards spoke largely of keeping united to the Church; and there was no dissenting voice, but all were knit together in one mind and one judgement. The subject was resumed on the second and third days; my brother and I ended the conference with a strong declaration of our resolution to live and die in the communion of the Church of England. We all unanimously agreed, that whilst it is lawful or possible to continue in it, it is unlawful for us to leave it.[23]

A few months later, Charles Wesley included in his journal transcriptions of two letters he had written, under the date October 29, 1756. The first was to William Grimshaw, vicar of Haworth, Yorkshire, in which he reported on the "poor shattered Society" in Manchester: "I have once more persuaded them to go to church and sacrament, and [I intend to] stay to carry them thither the next Lord's day. . . ."[24] The second letter was addressed to the society in Leeds, Yorkshire. Wesley exhorted them: "Continue in the old ship. Jesus hath a favour for our church; and is wonderfully visiting and reviving his work in her. . . . Let nothing hinder your going constantly to church and sacrament."[25]

Charles, however, remained uneasy about what he saw as ambivalence in his brother John. He wrote to a friend: "My soul abhors the thought of separating from the Church of England. You, and all the preachers know, if my brother should ever leave it, *I should leave him*—or rather *he me.*"[26] The fateful action of separation occurred at the beginning of September 1784, when John Wesley surreptitiously ordained three men to serve the needs of American Methodists. Charles was unaware of the action until someone wrote and told him. To another friend Charles wrote in an excusing manner:

> He is the dupe of his own cunning. . . . [He said] 'that he would never separate from the Church without my consent.' Set this then to his age [John was then aged 81]: his memory fails him. . . .[27]

But to John himself he wrote more caustically:

> What foul slanderers those [enthusiasts?] are! How they for three score years said [John Wesley was?] . . . a Papist: and lo he turns out at last a Presbyterian![28]

Somewhat later, Charles wrote to John:

> Dear Brother,—I have been reading over again & again your *Reasons Against Separation* . . . and entreat you, in the name of God, and for Christ's sake, to read them again yourself, with previous prayer, and stop, proceed no farther, till you receive an answer to your inquiry, "Lord, what wouldest *thou* have me to do?" . . . Every word of your eleven pages deserve the deepest consideration: not to mention my testimony and hymns. Only the seventh I could wish you to read,—a prophecy which I pray God may never come to pass.[29]

The work in question is John Wesley's *Reasons Against Separation from the Church of England . . . With Hymns for the Preachers among the Methodists (so called), by Charles Wesley* (London: Strahan, 1758). The seventh "Reason," to which Charles Wesley refers specifically in the letter cited above, can be taken as the younger Wesley brother's fundamental and unwavering position on the issue:

> Because, whereas controversy is now asleep, and we in great measure live peaceably with all men, so that we are strangely at leisure to spend our whole time and strength in enforcing plain, practical, vital religion . . . this would utterly banish peace from among us, and that without hope of its return. It would engage me, for one, in a thousand controversies, both in public and private; (for I should be in conscience obliged to give the reasons of my conduct, and to defend those reasons against all opposers); and so take me off from those more useful labours which might otherwise employ the short remainder of my life.[30]

In Charles's view, his brother John, by these unlawful ordinations, had separated himself not only from the Church of England but also from his younger brother. The pain of that separation is evident from Charles's letter to John, August 14, 1785, cited above. It continues:

> *Go to your grave in peace*: at least, suffer me to go first, before this ruin is
> under your hand . . . I am on the brink of the grave. Do not push me in,
> or embitter my last moments.[31]

There was bitterness when Charles died some three years later,
March 29, 1788. He was buried, not in the common tomb John had
prepared for the two brothers in the burial ground attached to the City
Road chapel, but in the churchyard of his local parish church, St.
Marylebone. At his funeral, on April 5, the pallbearers were eight
clergymen of the Church of England.[32] Thus Charles fulfilled his de-
clared resolution "to live and die in the communion of the Church of
England."

Charles Wesley's Anglicanism is perhaps best seen in his eucharistic
devotion. Although there are significant periods of his life in which he
either did not keep a journal or the documents have subsequently been
lost, the witness of his extant journal entries to his regular attendance at
the Eucharist is impressive. For much of his life it seems that he was
accustomed to receive the sacrament weekly. During some periods of his
life, for example, in June 1738, the month following his "awakening," his
attendance at the Eucharist was almost daily.[33] When in London, he took
the opportunity to attend the eucharist at St. Paul's Cathedral,[34] and on
his travels he either attended or, if invited, ministered the Eucharist. The
following are fairly typical Sunday journal entries:

> I began the sacrament with fervent prayer and many tears, which almost
> hindered my reading the service. . . . It was a solemn season of love; and
> yet more so at the sacrament. . . . In the sacrament I was constrained to
> pray again and again, with strong cryings and prayers. So it was every day
> of this *great and holy week*. . . .[35]

The Methodist societies were essentially meetings for prayer, song,
preaching, and encouragement. They were additional to the public
worship of the local parish churches of the Church of England. In that
the meetings of the societies included preaching and hymnody some
members might have been tempted to view them as substitute services,
replacing the Prayer Book orders of Morning and Evening Prayer.
Similarly, others might think that the love feast among the Methodists
removed the necessity of attending the Eucharist at the local parish
church. Such views were anathema to Charles Wesley. For example, in
the months that followed the Bristol conference in 1756, at which
non-separation from the Church of England was unequivocally concluded, Charles's journal entries demonstrate that he regarded the sign
of non-separation was not simply that members of the societies attend
their parish church, but that they specifically attend the sacrament. In

October 1756 Charles Wesley visited various Methodist societies in and around York.

> Through God's blessing on my week's stay among them, I hope, 1. Peace and love are restored; 2. They will recover their rising at five; 3. They are brought back again to church, and sacrament, and family prayer . . . I strongly exhorted them to continue steadfast in fellowship with each other, and the whole Church of England . . . I earnestly pressed the duties of constant communicating, of hearing, reading, practising the word, of fasting,[36] of private, family, and public prayer.[37]

At Haworth the fruits of this "churchly" Methodism were plainly apparent:

> I preached a second time at Haworth, (Mr. Grimshaw [the vicar] reading prayers). . . . The church, which had been lately enlarged, could scarce contain the congregation . . . we had a blessed number of communicants, and the Master of the feast in the midst.[38]

Wesley would use the incidence of growing attendance at communion in a particular church as evidence that the Methodists were not sectarian but rather effectively strengthening the Established Church. Some two years earlier, August 1754, Charles Wesley, after communicating in Norwich cathedral, wrote in his journal:

> The number of communicants begins to increase: a sign we do not make for separation, as a zealous advocate for the Church charged me in going home. I set him right, and he was in good measure appeased.[39]

Participation in the Prayer Book order of the Lord's Supper was, therefore, at the center of spiritual life for Charles Wesley, as well as being the outward sign of loyalty to the worship and discipline of the Church of England.[40]

Charles Wesley's specific eucharistic devotion is found enshrined in many of his hymns, especially the *Hymns on the Lord's Supper* (Bristol: Farley, 1745).[41] Some of these hymns appear to be straightforward metrical versions of the Prayer Book eucharistic rite, such as "Lord and God of heavenly power," a versification of the Preface and Sanctus, and "Glory be to God on high," based on the Gloria in Excelsis Deo.[42] But a closer examination will usually reveal some subtlety or development of thought that profoundly goes beyond the Prayer Book text. A good example is another paraphrase of the Preface and Sanctus:

1. Meet and right it is to sing
    At every Time and Place
    Glory to our Heavenly King,
    The God of Truth and Grace:

> Join we then with sweet accord,
>   All in one Thanksgiving join,
> Holy, holy, holy, Lord,
>   Eternal Praise be Thine!

2. Thee the first-born Sons of Light
      In choral Symphonies
    Praise by Day, Day without Night,
      And never, never cease:
    Angels, and archangels all
      Sing the Mystic Three in One,
    Sing, and stop, and gaze, and fall
      O'erwhelm'd before thy Throne.

3. Vyeing with that happy Quire
      Who chaunt thy Praise above,
    We on Eagles Wings aspire,
      The Wings of Faith and Love:
    Thee they sing with Glory crown'd
      We extol the slaughter'd Lamb,
    Lower if our Voices sound,
      Our Subject is the same.

5. Father, God, thy Love we praise,
      Which gave thy Son to die,
    Jesus full of Truth and Grace
      Alike we glorify,
    Spirit, Comforter Divine,
      Praise by All to Thee be given,
    'Till we in full Chorus join,
      And Earth is turn'd to Heaven.[43]

The first two stanzas are closely based on the Prayer Book text,[44] but even here there are expansions of thought, such as "the first-born Sons of Light" who, "in choral Symphonies," never cease to sing praise day and night. The last two stanzas almost literally take flight on their "Eagles' Wings" in a paean of praise to "the slaughter'd Lamb," the focus of the Eucharist.

Charles Wesley's creative use of the Prayer Book is of much the same order as his use of Scripture. The language of the Bible abounds in his hymns, so much so that J. Ernest Rattenbury made the much-quoted claim that "a skilful man, if the Bible were lost, might extract much of it from Wesley's hymns."[45] But this is a simplistic view that suggests that Wesley had a "cut and paste" approach to the text of Scripture. On the contrary, his use of Biblical imagery is much more complex and profound. J. R. Watson concludes:

> Charles Wesley's verse shows an impressive sense of literary craftsmanship and a feeling for metaphor: in some of his hymns, such as "Come, Holy Ghost, our hearts inspire," the metaphors tumble over one another in profusion to make an intricate pattern, not of biblical texts (as has so often been assumed) but of witty and shaped variations on literary texts. He revives the metaphors, makes them new, gives them a shape which makes us feel their force, defamiliarizes them.[46]

In the same way, therefore, Charles Wesley's many allusions to the Book of Common Prayer are not mere quotation but rather sophisticated recreations of Prayer Book imagery, theologically understood and poetically expressed. It is witness to a man who was not only aware of the verbal content of the Anglican book of worship but who had also imbibed its basic thought-forms and images to form an essential part of his creative genius.[47]

Charles Wesley's dependence on the Prayer Book was not restricted to his hymns. In a sermon he could remind his hearers of words they were familiar with, such as the general confession in the service of Holy Communion: "Which of you, my brethren, will . . . suffer God to save him in His own way? You have often told him in the words of the church, that the remembrance of your sins was grievous unto you, the burden intolerable."[48] In his journal of 1749 he recorded his birthday with a parody on the *Venite* (Psalm 95), the invitatory psalm at Morning Prayer: "Forty years long have I now grieved and tempted God, proved him, and seen his works."[49]

Although a convinced and an unalterable Anglican, Charles Wesley recognized that the message of salvation he preached and lived by had ecumenical implications. For example, he observed in his journal: "The Presbyterians say I am a Presbyterian; the church-goers [i.e. Anglicans], that I am a Minister of theirs; and the Catholics are sure I am a good Catholic at heart."[50] The legacy of his hymns has been claimed by all denominations in succeeding generations. Anglicans, however, were, as a whole, somewhat slow in adopting his hymns.

The Church of England at large was somewhat suspicious of the evangelical revival of the eighteenth century, especially the Methodist societies, which together, though they ostensibly avowed a loyalty to the Church of England, took on the appearance of a sect. Indeed, in some areas they did become so, even before the fateful ordinations of 1784. Anglicanism at the time had a Rationalist face; the workings of the church were to be "reasonable" and not subject to the whims of untrammeled "enthusiasm." Methodism was therefore suspect to a majority of Anglicans. Added to this suspicion was the fact that it was the common view that the Church of England permitted only metrical psalms to be sung with Prayer Book services. Thus the congregations in most Anglican parishes were restricted to singing either the Old Version psalms of Sternhold and Hopkins, or the New Version of Tate and Brady, together with a few freely-composed hymns found appendixed to the Old or New Version psalms.

But the "Methodism" of the evangelical movement did find a place within the Church of England. The growing number of evangelical men who had been ordained found great difficulty in securing ministerial positions: bishops could be found to ordain them, but it was almost impossible to persuade patrons to appoint them to parishes. Thus titled people, kindly disposed to the new movement, such as the Countess of Huntingdon, had chapels built on their own property. These were then licensed by the respective bishops; and the Countess, or whoever, was then free to appoint ordained evangelicals to serve as chaplains in these proprietary chapels. Other evangelical clergy were appointed to charitable institutions to serve their semi-private chapels. The worship of all these extra-parochial chapels conformed in every way to Prayer Book forms, the principal difference being that "Methodist" hymnody, in addition to metrical psalmody, was sung. Thus it was the Anglican evangelicals who were the first to sing regularly the hymns of Charles Wesley.

The hymnal collections of these Anglican evangelicals remain largely under-researched: their detailed contents and interrelationships are imperfectly known. The hymn collections of the Wesley brothers, on the other hand, have been the subject of continued and sustained research. What has generally gone unnoticed is the fact that the hymn collections of these other Anglican evangelicals—largely, though not exclusively, Calvinist in their theology—constitute a sequence of hymnal publication that parallels the "Methodist" collections of John and Charles Wesley.

At least three Anglican evangelical collections proved to be widely influential. The first was the hymnal edited by George Whitefield for use, first, at his chapel in Moorfields, London, then later at the Countess of Huntingdon's chapel in Tottenham Court Road, London: *A Collection of Hymns for Social Worship, more particularly design'd for the use of the Tabernacle Congregation in London* (London: Strahan, 1753). Within a few years a small supplement of hymns was added and the hymnal went through an enormous number of editions and reprints, far into the nineteenth century. It was also quarried by other hymnal editors, one notable example being, *A Collection of Psalms and Hymns for Social Worship*

(London: [s.n.], 1767), edited by the "Rev'd Mr. Dyer, late of Plymouth, Devon," which was heavily dependent on Whitefield's collection. The second was the hymnal edited by Martin Madan, chaplain to the Lock Hospital, London, for use in the institution's chapel: *A Collection of Psalms and Hymns, Extracted from Various Authors* (London: [s.n.], 1760). Madan also made substantial use of Whitefield's collection and his hymnal was in turn used by the editors of other hymnals. The third was Augustus Toplady's hymnal, which was dependent on both Whitefield's and Madan's collections, and, like them, was widely used: *Psalms and Hymns for Public and Private Worship* (London: Dilly, 1776).

All three hymnals contained the hymns of Charles Wesley. For example, of the 132 hymns in the original edition of Whitefield's collection, around seventy are by Watts and the following twenty-four are by Charles Wesley. They are given here in chronological order according to their earliest sources:

Hymns and Sacred Poems (London: Strahan, 1739).

> "Glory be to God on high"
> "Hail the Day that sees him rise"
> "Hark! the herald Angels sing"
> "Lord and God of heav'nly Powers"

Hymns and Sacred Poems (London: Strahan, 1740).

> "Christ, from whom all Blessings flow"
> "Christ whose Glory fills the Skies"
> "Come and let us sweetly join"
> "Come, Holy Ghost, our hearts inspire"
> "Father, Son and Spirit, hear"
> "Giver of Concord, Prince of Peace"
> "Partners of a glorious Hope"

Hymns and Sacred Poems (Bristol: Farley, 1742).

> "Blest be the dear uniting love"
> "Try us, O God, and search the Ground"
> "Ye that pass by behold the Man"

A Collection of Psalms and Hymns, 2nd ed. (London: Strahan, 1743).

> "Clap your Hands, ye People all"

Hymns for the Nativity of our Lord ([London: Strahan, 1744]).

> "Father, our hearts we lift"

169

Hymns for Times of Trouble and Persecution (London: [Strahan], 1744).

"Ye servants of God"

Hymns for Times of Trouble: for the Year 1745 ([London: Strahan], 1745).

"Head of the Church triumphant"

Hymns for Our Lord's Resurrection (London: Strahan, 1746).

"Rejoice, the Lord is King"

Hymns and Sacred Poems in Two Volumes: By Charles Wesley (Bristol: Farley, 1749).

"Come, divine Emmanuel, come"
"Meet and right it is to sing"
"O Love divine, how sweet thou art"
"Sinners, obey the Gospel Word"
"The Lord of Earth and Sky"

The above listing is based on preliminary research. There may well be other Wesley centos to be identified in Whitefield's collection.

Another hymn included by Whitefield illustrates something of the interdependence of these later eighteenth-century Anglican hymnals, and also gives some insight into the way in which Charles Wesley's verse could be inspired by the work of others.

The hymn in question was written by the elder brother of John and Charles, Samuel Wesley, Jr., first published in 1736 and beginning "Hail! Holy, Holy, Holy Lord!" (Fig. 1.A)—the same first line of two Charles Wesley hymns dating from 1746 and 1767 respectively (Fig. 1.B and 1.C). All three hymns have the same metrical structure—Common Metre (CM), although there is some variation in the arrangement of the stanzas—and also share a commonality of imagery, complete lines, rhyming schemes, and vocabulary.

The first, by Samuel Wesley, Jr., (Fig. 1.A), was included in John Wesley's Charlestown collection of 1737, with stanza 3 omitted, some changes in punctuation and capitalization, and the alteration of line 6 from "E'er Time its Race began" to "E'er Time its Round began." This version was also included in the Wesleys' *Hymns on the Great Festivals, and other occasions* (London: [s.n.], 1747), but in three stanzas of CMD. Whitefield, for his 1753 collection, appears to have used John Wesley's Charlestown hymnal as his source, since the four stanzas he includes (1, 2, 6 and 7 of the original) are left in CM (Whitefield also follows John Wesley's modification of "Round" for "Race" in line 6). Dyer's collection of 1767 repeats Whitefield's four-stanza version but Madan's hymnal of

Fig. 1. Three Trinitarian Hymns

A
Samuel Wesley [Jr.], *Poems on Several Occasions*, (Cambridge: Bentham, 1736), pp. 6–7.

1. Hail! Holy, Holy, Holy Lord!
   Be endless Praise to Thee!
   Supreme, Essential One, ador'd
   In Co-eternal Three!

2. Enthron'd in everlasting State, 5
   E'er Time its Race began!
   Who join'd in Council to create
   The Dignity of Man!

3. Thou Father, Son, and Holy-Ghost 10
   Empow'ring to Baptize,
   Restor'st, for earthly *Eden* lost,
   An heav'nly *Paradise.*

4. To whom Isaiah's Vision show'd,
   The Seraphs veil their Wings;
   While Thee, Jehovah! Lord and God, 15
   Th' Angelick Army sings.

5. To Thee, by mystick Powers on high,
   Were humble praises giv'n
   When *John* beheld with favour'd Eye
   Th' Inhabitants of Heav'n. 20

6. All that the Name of *Creature* owns
   To Thee in Hymns aspire;
   May we as Angels on our Thrones
   For ever join the Quire!

7. Hail! Holy, Holy, Holy Lord! 25
   Be endless Praise to Thee!
   Supreme, Essential One, ador'd
   In Co-eternal Three!

B
Gloria Patri, &c. Or Hymns to the Trinity [issued anonymously]. (London: Strahan, 1746), p. 7.

1. Hail holy, holy, holy Lord,
   Thrice Blessed Trinity,
   By all thy Heavenly Hosts ador'd,
   E'er Man began to be;
   Worship'd by all thy Saints below, 5
   The God of Truth and Grace,
   Thro' Faith, the great Three-One they know,
   And triumph in thy Praise

2. The upper and the lower Quire
   Shall soon be join'd in One, 10
   And both triumphantly conspire
   To worship round thy Throne:
   Angels and Saints, when Time shall end,
   Shall all thy Love display,
   And in thy glorious Praises spend 15
   An everlasting Day.

C
Hymns on the Trinity [issued anonymously]. (Bristol: Pine, 1767), pp. 69–70.

1. Hail holy, holy, holy Lord,
   Whom One in Three we Know,
   By all thy heavenly host ador'd
   By all thy church below!
   One undivided Trinity 5
   With triumph we proclaim:
   Thy universe is full of Thee,
   And speaks thy glorious name.

2. Thee, holy Father, we confess,
   Thee, the holy Son, adore, 10
   Thee, Spirit of true holiness,
   We worship evermore:
   Thine incommunicable right,
   Almighty God, receive,
   Which angel-quires and saints in light 15
   And saints embodied give.

3. Three Persons equally Divine
   We magnify and love;
   And both the quires e'er long shall join
   To sing thy praise above: 20
   Hail holy, holy, holy Lord,
   (Our heavenly song shall be).
   Supreme, Essential One ador'd
   In co-eternal Three.

1760 follows the six-stanza version found in the Charlestown collection of 1737. Toplady apparently had at least two sources in front of him when editing the text for his hymnal, since he accepts the "Round" for "Race" modification of John Wesley but also includes all seven stanzas of Samuel Wesley's original hymn, albeit in a modified sequence and with varying levels of rewriting.[51]

The second hymn (Fig. 1.B) appeared in Charles Wesley's collection *Gloria Patri, &c. Or Hymns to the Trinity* (London: Strahan, 1746). This second hymn is clearly related to the first. It has the same metre, except that whereas A is in CM, B is in four stanzas of CMD. The opening line of both hymns is identical, and the rhyming scheme of the first four lines of each is the same: *Lord/ador'd and Thee/Three* in A; *Lord/ador'd and Trinity/be* in B. Lines 3–4 of B appear to be a contraction of the thoughts expressed in A, lines 5–8; and B lines 9–12 and A lines 21–24 are related in terms of the imagery of singers in heaven and on earth, and in the similar rhyming scheme: *Quire/conspire* and *One/Throne* in B; *owns/Thrones* and *aspire/Quire* in A. It is perhaps a measure of the overlooked poetic ability of the elder Wesley brother that his perfect rhyme *Owns/Thrones*, is superior to Charles Wesley's assonance of *One/Throne*!

The third hymn, also by Charles Wesley (Fig. 1.C), is the one that entered into common usage throughout the following centuries, and appears, for example, in the current British Methodist hymnal, *Hymns and Psalms* (London: Methodist Publishing House, 1983; no. 6). Hymn C is related to both hymns A and B in its utilization of the same first line; it also employs the same basic metre and shares similar imagery.

Lines 1 and 3 of C are identical with lines 1 and 3 of B—except that "Hosts" has become singular—and the rhyme of these lines, *Lord/ador'd* is the same in all three hymns. There is also some correspondence between vocabulary and imagery in C, lines 4–8, and B, lines 5–8. Similarly, the specific Trinitarian expression in C lines 9–16 parallels that of A lines 9–16. Further, lines 21 and 23–24 of C are identical with lines 25, 27–28 of B, in addition to being related to the opening four lines of both A and B. Lines 25–26 of A could not have been taken over without modification because line 26, "Be endless praise to thee," would have been repetitious if it were employed after C, line 20, "To sing thy praise above." Therefore Charles Wesley substituted the new, parenthetical line: "Our heavenly song shall be."

This evidence of Charles Wesley "borrowing" and reworking his brother's verse is illuminating for a variety of reasons. First, it underlines Charles Wesley's respect for his brother Samuel's poetry, a respect that continued for more than a generation, long after Samuel's death in 1739. Second, it reveals that the poetry of others could exercise a significant influence on Charles's poetic creativity. Third, it offers some insight into the way in which the poet reworked his own material over a period of some twenty years. Fourth, it underscores the orthodox Anglicanism of Charles—in common with the other Wesley brothers—in his concern to enunciate a fundamental Trinitarian theology against the Unitarian tendencies of the later eighteenth century. All these are areas that need further research, which should be undertaken alongside a detailed analysis of the contents of the many "Anglican" hymnals of the second half of the eighteenth century that parallel the development of the better-known "Methodist" collections.

It was from the collections of Whitefield, Madan, Toplady, and other similar hymnals, that Anglicans first sang the hymns of Charles Wesley. Indeed, it was the particular use of some of his hymns by these Anglican evangelicals that established their common forms in later Church of England—and wider—usage, as the following case history demonstrates.

In *Hymns and Sacred Poems* (1739), Charles Wesley's "Hymn for Christmas Day" appeared thus (10 stanzas, 7.7.7.7):

> 1. Hark how all the Welkin rings
>   "Glory to the Kings[52] of Kings,
>   "Peace on Earth, and Mercy mild,
>   "God and Sinners reconcil'd!
>
> 2. Joyful all ye Nations rise,
>   Join the Triumph of the Skies,
>   Universal Nature say
>   "Christ the Lord is born to Day!

Whitefield abbreviated the hymn for his collection and altered the opening couplet to:

> "Hark! the Herald Angels sing
> Glory to the new-born King!"

and lines 6–8 to:

> Join the Triumphs of the Skies,
> Nature rise and worship him,
> Who is born at Bethlehem.

as well as other changes. Madan accepted the opening couplet of Whitefield, and some of his other emendations, but changed lines 7–8 to:

> With th'angelic Host proclaim,
> Christ is born in *Bethlehem*!

Thereafter Wesley's Christmas hymn, substantially in the Whitefield-Madan form, passed into many different collections used by Anglican evangelicals.

The singing of the now-famous Christmas hymn by the wider Church of England dates from 1782 when it appeared in the brief appendix of the Cambridge University Press edition of Tate and Brady's New Version of the psalms. It was, of course, issued without indication of authorship, and the text was abbreviated and modified so that the opening couplet was repeated at the end of each of the six, eight-line stanzas.

It was this Anglican source that changed Wesley's "Pleased as man with men to appear" to "man with man." Another Anglican source, John Kempthorne's *Select Portions of Psalms: From Various Translations and Paraphrases and Hymns from Various Authors, Many of Them Considerably Altered, in Order to Fit Them for the Use of Congregations of the Church of England, and the Whole Arranged According to Her Yearly Seasons* ([Bristol?: Albion?], 1810), made a further modification so that the lines now read:

> Pleased as Man with man to dwell,
> Jesus, our Emmanuel.

The basic text was now fixed and, after its appearance in this form in the first edition of *Hymns Ancient and Modern* (1861), its future was assured as part of the basic corpus of Anglican hymnody—notwithstanding the abortive attempt in the 1904 edition of *Hymns Ancient and Modern* to restore Wesley's original opening couplet.[53]

In the contemporary Episcopal *Hymnal 1982* there are seventeen hymns by Charles Wesley. They are listed below in a chronological sequence according to the sources in which they first appeared:

Hymns and Sacred Poems (London: Strahan, 1739).

> "Hail the day that sees him rise"
> "Hark! the herald angels sing"
> "Love's redeeming work is done"
> (second stanza of "Christ the Lord is risen today")

Hymns and Sacred Poems (London: Strahan, 1740).

> "Christ, whose glory fills the skies"
> "Jesus, lover of my soul"
> "O for a thousand tongues to sing"

Hymns and Sacred Poems (Bristol: Farley, 1742).

> "Come, O thou Traveller unknown"

Hymns for the Nativity of Our Lord (London: [Strahan, 1744]).

"Come, thou long-expected Jesus"

Hymns for Times of Trouble and Persecution (London: [Strahan], 1744).

"Ye servants of God"

Hymns for Our Lord's Resurrection (London: Strahan, 1746).

"Rejoice, the Lord is King!"

Graces Before Meat ([London, 1746]).

"Glory, love, and praise, and honor"

Hymns for those who Seek, and those that have, Redemption in the blood of Jesus Christ (London: Strahan, 1747).

"Love divine, all loves excelling"

Hymns and Sacred Poems (Bristol: Farley, 1749).

"Soldiers of Christ, arise"

Hymns of Intercession for all Mankind (Bristol: Farley, 1758).

"Lo! He comes with clouds descending"

Funeral Hymns [Second Series] (London: [Strahan], 1759).

"Let saints on earth in concert sing"[54]

Short Hymns on Select Passages of the Holy Scriptures (Bristol: Farley, 1762).

"O thou who camest from above"

Hymns for Children (Bristol: Farley, 1763).

"Come, let us with our Lord arise"

It is interesting to note that of the first thirteen in the above list, that is, those published by 1753, five are also found in Whitefield's collection, first published that year.

After two hundred years or more, therefore, the Episcopal Church regards the production of a hymnal without including the hymns of Charles Wesley as unthinkable. The Anglican Church which once questioned Charles Wesley's Methodism now enthusiastically sings his hymns, and the man who regarded himself unquestionably a loyal son of the Church of England is perhaps beginning to be understood on his own terms.

Chapter 10

CHARLES WESLEY AND THE METHODIST TRADITION

Richard P. Heitzenrater

This title seems to imply an answer to the question, In what way was the Methodist tradition shaped by Charles Wesley? Such an endeavor immediately confronts certain ambiguities, however, as seen in the desire of some of John Wesley's friends in the 1750s to "thrust [Charles] out from the Methodists" while Charles himself felt that his heart was "more closely united to the true Methodists than ever."[1]

Any attempt to analyze Charles Wesley's relationship to the Methodist tradition, then, almost necessarily requires some definition of "Methodist" and some comparison with John Wesley. The story of Methodism is usually told as the story of John Wesley, with Charles at his side (if not in his shadow). In assessing the younger brother's role in the movement, Charles Wesley specialists frequently become very defensive; they point out Charles's special niche in Methodist history, emphasize his significance in the Wesleyan movement, and show that he has been mistreated if not forgotten by historians. Many would-be friends of Charles's approach their task with the intention of correcting what they see as unfair treatment of the man.

Such "corrective" approaches to history often strain the canons of objectivity in order to make a point. One recent example of such an approach is Frederick Gill's book, which exhausts the English vocabulary of its superlatives. Charles Wesley is viewed (as the title exclaims) as "the first Methodist." But Gill goes beyond a claim for Charles's chronological priority in the Methodist movement. He claims that "Charles no less than John established Methodism"; their work was "indivisible," that Charles's contribution was "immeasurable," especially his hymns, "without which it is doubtful whether Methodism could have survived." In summary Gill asserts, "He was a Methodist in the truest sense, not only the First Methodist, but the complete Methodist."[2] In a saner moment, the author comments that "the work of the brothers was complementary,"[3] but is careful to point out that their correlative position has not been properly recognized or commemorated by successive generations.

Other Methodist historians offer a careful corrective to such exaggerated views of Charles's significance. Such is Frank Baker's appreciative but careful observation that "Charles Wesley's preaching and poetry were important factors in the spread of Methodism, but without John's administrative genius and calm statesmanship, the fire might easily have burned itself out in a generation with little to show where it had been."[4]

The usual treatment of Charles Wesley (somewhere between the poles of neglect and exaggeration) is typified by the index subheadings under Charles Wesley in a recent survey of *Religion in England, 1688–1791*: "Founder of the 'Holy Club' at Oxford; mission to Georgia; first hymnbook; return to England; conversion; under harassment; marriage; children; hymns."[5] The entry for "first hymnbook" is actually a reference to John, with only an oblique comment about Charles—John's translations from the German creating "hymns as fine as anything his brother would ever write."[6] Some Charles Wesley enthusiasts may challenge such relative evaluations, just as other historians may challenge many of the typical encomia heaped upon Charles.[7]

The truth of the matter is that most surveys of Methodist history simply mention Charles as the hymnwriter of Methodism and leave it at that. Some of the more detailed studies occasionally portray Charles also as a thorn in his brother's side on issues relating to the question of separation from the Church of England: lay preachers, ordinations, perfectionism, etc. Very few actually ask about the particulars of Charles's constructive role in the development of the Methodist tradition.

Such a task would entail a preliminary evaluation of what is meant by "the Methodist tradition," especially in its eighteenth-century context. No matter how difficult, this question is perhaps the right place to start our analysis. Let us assume from the outset that the term "Methodist" is to be understood in an eighteenth-century sense, in order to shortcut any possible discussion of prior uses of the nomenclature. The use of the term "Methodist tradition" assumes the existence of such a definable phenomenon—a recognizable exhibit of a particular "method" of theology, organization, and/or mission (I would say, all three).

One common approach is to define the "Methodist" tradition as the "Wesleyan" tradition and to equate Wesleyan with John Wesley. Typically, when someone comments that "Wesley" said something or other, the assumption is that John Wesley is the one being referenced. There is some traditional rationale for this: John Wesley was the founder and leader of the movement called Methodism; he had an actual priority in the movement, both chronologically and hierarchically; he became the focal point of printed and personal attacks against Methodism; he inspired a long succession of studies of his life, his theology, his organization, his mission.

What are the crucial elements of this traditional view of Methodism in the eighteenth century?

(1) Its *theology* had a characteristic shape, formed by a central concern with soteriology. It exhibited a typically Protestant view of salvation, basically Arminian, with certain distinctive emphases: the presence of prevenient grace, the expectation of assurance, the possibility of perfection. It also manifested certain paradoxical tensions: faith/works, evangelism/sacramentalism, knowledge/vital piety, and the like. It was based on certain doctrinal standards: Wesley's *Sermons on Several Occasions*, his *Explanatory Notes upon the New Testament*, and his explanations of key doctrines in the *Minutes* of his conferences with the preachers. The Methodist theology also had a characteristic methodology, based upon the fourfold authority of scripture, early church tradition, reason, and the experience of the Holy Spirit.

(2) Its *organization* consisted of a connexional structure within the Church of England. The characteristic features were lay preaching, itinerant leadership, regular conferences, annual minutes, far-flung circuits of societies, and a plethora of small groups for Christian nurture (eventually also some ordinations). All of these elements were basically to implement the theology, through edification, conversion, nurture, ministry, and mission.

(3) Its *mission* was to reform the nation (especially the Church) and to spread scriptural holiness (love of God and love of neighbor) across the land. This goal resulted in specific patterns of concern and outreach for the poor, the sick, the imprisoned, the ignorant, the spiritually starved, through institutions like schools, clinics, orphan houses; through programs of visitation and economic assistance; through opportunities for worship, spiritual formation, and nurture (love feasts, watch nights, field preaching, Bible study, class and band meetings).

An important and complicating consideration that must not be forgotten is that this tradition (with its distinctive theology, organization, and mission) did not arise full-blown overnight. As John Wesley said, the rise of Methodism was not the result of a previous design but was a sign of unfolding providential activity in response to needs that developed. The Methodists' theology was different in 1733 from what it was in 1740, or 1765, or 1771. Their organization was different in 1732 from what it was in 1738, or 1744, or 1763, or 1784. The same is true for their mission.

In a sense, the Methodist tradition also then includes a view of history that tries to understand human developments in the light of the unfolding of God's providence. As John Wesley said to Charles, when writing his four-volume *History of England*, "My view in writing history (as in writing philosophy) is to bring God into it."[8]

Given this view of the Methodist tradition (a certain constellation of concerns, approaches, views, and structures), we can then ask: In what areas did Charles add his own unique contribution? In what areas did Charles help shape John's contribution? In what areas was Charles unable to make any impact?

The answers to these questions cannot be easily given here. The queries do, however, present a framework within which I would hope that Charles Wesley studies could provide responses, especially in some specific major areas. The assigned topic (as well as the prevalent approach, as we have said) is to look at Charles Wesley in relation to John Wesley, in relation to Methodism, in relation to issues, ideas, and events largely initiated by others. But at the same time, it would be useful to try to look for Charles Wesley, the individual, as he was himself, with his feet firmly planted in his own shadow, for a change. This may be hard to do at the present time, given the present state of Charles Wesley studies. The best we may hope to do at this point is to stimulate serious thinking in that direction on some particular issues.

However, some specific observations are in order before starting an examination of the three areas outlined above.

(1) We need not establish a false significance for Charles. We should set aside the idea of Charles Wesley as the "first Methodist." The term is inappropriate by almost any definition, either in terms of *chronology* of naming or in *priority* of leadership. The evidence usually cited to support Charles as being "first" in time (as "founder of the Holy Club") is wholly inadequate—a letter[9] written late in life at a time when he was challenging his brother's leadership on several important issues. There is no contemporary evidence for the terms "Holy Club" or "Methodist" being applied in the first instance to Charles—the terms were not used earlier than 1730 and 1732 respectively (the former being directed at Bob Kirkham and the latter seeming to be associated with John Wesley).[10] Charles did, in fact, seem to be satisfied (perhaps a somewhat natural tendency) to defer to his older brother in most things, though he was not always or necessarily submissive. He never exhibited any desire for the limelight and increasingly seemed somewhat eager to stay in the shadows, relishing a degree of quiet retirement.[11] None of these reflections, however, should detract from his individual significance. He does not have to be

made a founder of the movement in order to be worth looking at for his own sake.

(2) Having placed him in a secondary role, we must hasten to add that Charles (the younger brother) anticipated some of the important developments in John Wesley's own biography, though typically some ambiguity concerning the significance of those instances remains. Charles does, in fact, seem to have been the first to implement the Wesleyan vision of holy living in a corporate context—Charles did convince someone else to join with him in studying and going to the sacrament at Oxford, just about a month before John arrived for the summer of 1729 (though the pattern of thought and action they followed were consciously derived from John). Charles was the first to experience assurance in May 1738, three days before John at Aldersgate. Charles also was the first to marry—in 1749, just weeks before John was engaged to Grace Murray (his "first wife" and "last love").

But in each of these instances, John turns out to have a certain priority. John was the first to have a serious bent of mind and spirit at Oxford and helped shape Charles's approach to religious bibliography, spiritual habits, and pietist disciplines. John had the experience of assurance that became paradigmatic in the tradition—Methodists remember John's "strangely warmed" heart rather than Charles's "strange palpitation of heart." John's thoughts on marriage (in spite of his stormy experiences) get much more play within the Methodist Connexion than Charles's quiet and happy marriage.

All of this is to say that we should deal straightforwardly with the sibling relationship, recognizing that Charles was the younger brother, but remembering that such a position holds some advantages as well as disadvantages. We need not only recognize that Charles deferred to and learned from John in many ways, but also that he did not shrink from challenging John on several important issues that were crucial to the ultimate shape of Methodism, especially the overarching question of separation from the church. And although they probably were not close friends during their adolescent years, they grew close to each other at the University and continued for many years to work together to hammer out answers to tough theological and organizational questions.

Having sorted through these observations, now let us look at the three areas of theology, organization, and mission, and see Charles Wesley's role in the development of the Methodist tradition.

Theology

Any discussion of Charles Wesley's role in the development of Methodist theology immediately raises the question of how well hymns serve as a vehicle for expressing and transmitting theological ideas. There is no doubt that poetry is Charles's primary means of expressing his theology. And hymns, as poetry put to music, are often seen as "the ordinary man's theology."[12] But such truisms should not deter us from asking the question of whether such materials give an adequate or clear theology, and whether this form is a successful means of communicating theological ideas, then and/or today.

One practical problem in dealing with Charles Wesley's theology as seen in the hymns is that many of them were produced in pamphlets co-published with John and were thus filtered through his ear. It is therefore difficult at best to distinguish a distinctive Charles Wesley theological perspective from these sources alone. And generally there has not been much other material available until recently.[13]

What can we derive from Charles's other writings in order to correlate broader expressions of theology with that of the poetry and hymns? A very few authors have tried to use a collection of sermons published in 1816 by Charles's widow as a source of his thought and found it somewhat difficult to distinguish a perspective distinctive from John's. The reason has more recently become obvious. It turns out that most of those sermons were actually written by John, then copied and used by Charles. One at least seems to have been written by John especially for Charles's use.[14] Charles apparently had no problem preaching John's sermons (even in his presence on October 3, 1736), continuing to do so after his return to England, even after Aldersgate.[15] It should also be remembered that John had no problem using (at least publishing in his own works) Charles's sermon on "Awake, Thou that Sleepest."[16] It is unfortunate that there are apparently no extant sermons of Charles beyond the six early shorthand ones and this latter sermon of 1742; these sources correlate very closely with John's views and it is difficult to discern Charles's mature theology from anything other than the poetry and hymns.

As for Charles Wesley's theology as seen in those sources, there are several themes and emphases that can be delineated as characteristic. First and foremost among these is Charles's insistence that the Methodists hold to the doctrines and discipline of the Church of England. In this regard, he was even more stringent than John, who at times seemed to be implementing practices and structures that moved toward, or implied separation from, the Church. For instance, it was Charles's task

181

during the early years of the revival to help maintain the standards of preaching in the movement through examination of the preachers. One would assume that Charles would be especially concerned that the preachers stay within the parameters of doctrine outlined by the Thirty-Nine Articles, exposited in the Book of Homilies. It is interesting to note that, when Charles effectively gave up the task of examining preachers, John in 1763 shifted the responsibility to the trustees of the United Societies, requiring (in the Model Deed) that they make sure the preaching houses were used only for the propagation of "good Methodist doctrine" as delimited by John's four volumes of *Sermons on Several Occasions* and his *Explanatory Notes Upon the New Testament*. It would be interesting to know more about Charles's attitude toward this apparent development of distinctive doctrinal standards for the Methodists. How did Charles view John's imposing these writings upon Methodists as the definitive measures and boundaries of preaching, requiring that no doctrine be preached other than those in the *Sermons* and *Notes*? John protested to all alike that the Methodists taught nothing other than what was in the Thirty-Nine Articles, the Homilies, and the Book of Common Prayer. This claim was aimed perhaps as much at Charles as at the outside critics. In any case, Charles was not willing to abdicate totally the definition of "Methodist" to John's standards of concern or performance. To the end of his life, Charles seems to have been constantly on guard lest any doctrinal development in Methodism result in even implicit separation.

As for some of the particular doctrines that were emphasized within Methodism, there have long been acknowledged some identifiable differences between the two Wesley brothers. Their basic view of the nature of salvation was similar, but the understanding of the nature of faith may have had some important differences.[17] The eucharistic views of the two brothers were occasionally expressed in different terms.[18] Charles and John also developed different relationships with the Moravians and therefore seem to have adapted or modified their own views in slightly different ways vis-à-vis some of the doctrines (such as assurance) emphasized by the Moravians. Charles's views of the nature and effects of sanctification can be distinguished at some length from those of John.[19]

Many of these and other areas of Charles's theology could bear further investigation. Almost no work has been done in any area that stresses the developmental approach: what are the sources of his ideas, how did his theology grow, change, respond to challenges? Typically, Charles is portrayed as holding a particular idea (as if he always had), and a verse of poetry is quoted as an exemplary prooftext—no date, no context, no internal comparison or contrast. This inadequate method of study differs from the usual approach to John only in the type of sources quoted. We have a long way to go in our understanding of Wesleyan theology in order to know just what Charles's distinctive contribution to the shaping of the Methodist tradition might have been.

Organization

One of the ironies of this story is that, although Methodism was intended to provide, not a challenge, but a means of revitalizing the Church of England, almost every distinctive feature of the developing Methodist organization that was designed to promote and protect that vitality *could* be seen as contributing to the impression that they were separating from the church. They were developing separate meeting places, local society structures, membership tickets, small group forms, leaders, rules; they were becoming a distinctive connexional organization with conference and circuit structures, general rules, doctrinal standards, worship forms, hymns, a type of ministry, and eventually ordination. John Wesley, while accepting and implementing these innovations, constantly reiterated that Methodists were not separating (i.e., they were neither leaving the Church through conscious dissent nor being kicked out of the Church by those in power). Charles was much more sensitive to the separatist implications of many of these developments; he frequently pointed out to John that he was in danger of crossing the line of separation *de facto* in spite of his expressed intentions.

The Methodist organization was basically typified as a connexion of itinerant lay preachers among a union of societies within the Church. In spite of Charles's recognition that the use of lay preaching posed the possibility of "partial separation," he seems to have supported it as a necessity to be kept within limits. He and John differed on the level of qualifications and expectations for the preachers. Worried about supplying the societies with enough preachers, John was clear about one thing: "I prefer grace before gifts." Charles, however, worried more about preachers' qualifications and felt that both gifts and grace were "indispensably necessary."[20] Charles wanted to prepare as many of their preachers as possible for ordination within the Church, afraid that otherwise Methodism would become a "seminary for dissenters." He was not hesitant to send an inept preacher back to his trade. It was, as we have seen, Charles's task to examine the preachers in the 1750s, a chore that he seems to have taken up with some zeal. It was during this period and in the midst of such ventures that Charles felt his heart was with "the true Methodists," but that some of John's advisers ("bad men") desired "to thrust me out from the Methodists," which in Charles's way of thinking was the plainest argument for his continuing within the movement.[21]

Charles participated in the itinerancy more in his earlier years than after his fiftieth birthday, when he desired a more settled life. As early as 1753, John recognized the growing distance from his brother, wishing that he "would really act in connexion . . . or leave off professing."[22] After marrying and settling in Bristol (and later in London), Charles travelled much less frequently[23] and after 1765 virtually stopped going to the annual conferences called by John.[24] The older brother was the visible "centre of union," in spite of the rhetoric about preachers in connexion with "the Rev. Messrs. John and Charles Wesley."[25] Although many expected that Charles would succeed his brother as leader of the movement, Charles declined any such responsibility, claiming that he was not fit for such a position.[26] Charles's reticence to participate in the leadership of the movement irritated John, who felt that his own efforts to stem the tide of criticism could be transformed into an effective turning of the tide with his brother's active assistance. Any possibility of sharing responsibility for leadership was lost after John's decision to ordain preachers for America in 1784. Charles's persistent but generally loyal criticism became an incessant cry that *de facto* separation had now taken place. John of course disagreed and tried to manipulate his brother: "If you will go hand in hand with me, do. But do not hinder me if you will not help."[27]

Charles represented the loyal opposition on many organizational issues. He was not just a footdragger, but rather conscientiously tried to promote what he thought was right, as well as oppose what he thought was wrong. His willingness to challenge authority on the basis of firmly held principles is basically similar to John's outlook, although their differing opinions on what represented separation from the Church occasionally brought them into direct opposition with each other, John being the authority that Charles was challenging. Charles's influence may have been the crucial factor in delaying until after both of their deaths (1795) what seemed to some as the inevitable reality of organizational separation from the Church.

Mission

In the development of the Methodist tradition, Charles seems to have had the least impact in the shaping of the specific methods and patterns whereby the Methodist mission reached out to society. He did, as we have seen, participate in some of the forms, itinerating for a while, and was occasionally persecuted by mobs of angry critics.[28] But in many of the common forms of the mission to spread scriptural holiness he did not participate. He was reticent to print any of his prose writings—no collections of his sermons, journals, or letters were published during his lifetime. He is not remembered as one who visited the poor, the sick, the imprisoned;[29] instead, he seems to have been the connection with the small group of "churchly" Methodists of the middle and upper class. His brother's involvement in promoting education and health is not matched in Charles's activities.

In all of these concerns, Charles seems to have focused his energies in expressing the vision of their mission through poetry. Why he was not more actively involved in the developing social program of the movement is something of a mystery. But some of his hymns, carried on the wings of singable tunes developed by others, may have had an impact on the development and spread of the Methodist mission, in spite of Charles's own personal distance from the missional activities characteristic of the movement.

Conclusion

What role did Charles Wesley play in the formation of the Methodist tradition? Many are willing to grant that Charles had an important role in the early development of Methodism (the first two or three decades, the 1730s–1750s). But the Methodist tradition was not fully shaped by 1760—the two brothers had about thirty years each yet to live. If John's mature expressions of theology during those later years tend to be overlooked (as is generally the case), Charles's have been almost totally ignored. Any serious evaluation of Charles's role in this story awaits further study of both brothers' work, especially in their later years.

A key to the future of Wesley studies (of Charles in particular) is the careful preparation and editing of their works. For Charles, that task would include especially those works that have not been generally available, such as his letters. Several important contributions to this ongoing process have already been made. I would hope that in the next decade, we would see even greater strides in the preparation and production of this material, in part to make possible a better understanding of Charles Wesley's role in the development of the Methodist tradition.

Chapter 11

CHARLES WESLEY
AND THE CALVINIST TRADITION

Horton Davies

At the outset, the topic, "Charles Wesley and the Calvinist Tradition" would seem to be a particularly unpromising one, since the relationship seems so antagonistic. This seems inevitable in view of the great hymn-writer's bitterly sarcastic verses against predestination, his quarrel with Calvinist George Whitefield, which was all the more acute because of their original comradeship, and the repeated reminders in his hymns of the boundless universality of divine love revealed in the incarnation of Christ,

> Our God contracted to a span,
> Incomprehensibly made man.[1]

In fact, Charles Wesley's attitude to Calvinism seems to be a record of calculated insults, sheer metrical kicks in the face. That is, indeed, a considerable part of the story, but far from being the whole, and I shall begin with the negative aspects of the relationship.

A Critique of Calvinism

It was common for the brothers Wesley to agree doctrinally, and for John to prepare a forceful sermon and for Charles to provide a hymn to express the conviction in verse and thus to bring it home to the minds and hearts of the Methodist societies. In the beginning of the relationship between George Whitefield and the Wesleys from the time that Whitefield joined the Holy Club when Charles describes him as "a second Timothy,"[2] and Whitefield pioneered both open-air preaching and using lay preachers, all was cordial amity, but when Whitefield preached *predestination* and *the perseverance of the saints*, despite their continuance in sin, and did so in the preaching places of the Wesleys even in their presence, explosions were to be expected, and the fireworks came.

The most impressive and explosive of these fireblasts was John Wesley's *Free Grace. A Sermon preach'd at Bristol* on April 29, 1793.[3] Its text is Romans 8:32: "He that spared not his own Son, but delivered him up for us all, how shall He not with him also freely give us all things?" Its opening words challenge: "The Grace or Love of God, whence cometh our Salvation, is free in all, and free for all." This is contradicted by *predestination* which is defined thus:

> By virtue of an Eternal, Unchangeable, Irresistible Decree of God, One part of Mankind [*sic*] are infallibly saved, and the rest infallibly damn'd: It being impossible that any of the former should be damn'd, or that any of the latter should be saved.[4]

Then John Wesley draws out the consequences as he sees them. First, all preaching is vain. Second, it destroys all holiness in taking away the motives: the hope of future reward and the fear of Hell. Third, it tends to inspire or increase a sharpness of temper contrary to the meekness of Christ and issues in treating these thought to be outcasts from God with contempt or coldness. Fourth, it destroys all zeal for good works because the majority of mankind is evil and ungrateful, and also "what avails it to relieve their temporal wants who are just dropping into Eternal Fire?"[5] Fifth, it tends to overthrow the whole Christian revelation as seeming unnecessary, and "In making the Gospel thus unnecessary to all sorts of men, you give up the whole Christian cause."[6] The sixth argument against *predestination* is that it makes Scripture contradict itself and leads to the misinterpretation of some promises in Scripture which are without qualifications, so that they are supposed to apply only to the elect, and this contradicts "the whole Scope and Tenor of Scripture."[7] The seventh and climactic final argument accuses *predestination* of blasphemy, in representing Jesus Christ "full of grace and truth, as an Hypocrite, a Deceiver of the People, a Man void of common Sincerity. For it cannot be denied that he everywhere speaks *as if he was willing* that all Men should be saved. Therefore to say that *He was not* willing that all Men should be saved is to represent him as a mere Hypocrite and Dissembler."[8] *Predestination* also dishonours God the Father and destroys his attributes of justice, mercy, and truth, and to create humanity only to destroy them makes him more cruel than the devil. The "*Horrible Decree* of predestination,"[9] Wesley calls it, modifying slightly Calvin's sense of it as a dreadful or terrifying decree (*decretum horribile*).[10] This God, says Wesley, is worse than Moloch, for "God . . . by His Eternal Decree, fixed before they had done Good or Evil, Causes not only *Children of a Span long*, but the Parents also to pass thro' the Fire of Hell: That *Fire which never shall be quenched.*"[11]

Attached to this devastating critique was a hymn of Charles Wesley's entitled, "Universal Redemption." It included the following verses:

> Thy darling Attribute I praise
>   Which all alike may prove,
> The Glory of thy boundless Grace,
>   Thy universal Love.
>
> Mercy for All thy Hands have made
>   Immense, and Unconfin'd,
> Throughout thy every Work display'd,
>   Embracing all Mankind.
>
> And shall I, Lord, confine thy Love,
>   As not to others free?
> And may not every Sinner prove,
>   The Grace that found out me?
>
> Lord, if indeed, without a Bound,
>   Infinite Love Thou art,
> The HORRIBLE DECREE confound,
>   Enlarge thy People's Heart![12]

Now "the HORRIBLE DECREE"—those words are printed in capitals in the hymn—was the text of some of Charles Wesley's most ironical, abusive, and at this distance of time and ecumenical cooling of tempers, amusing verse. Under that very title Charles produced a poem of fifteen verses and a hundred and twenty lines, included in the *Hymns on God's Everlasting Love* published in 1741 as a theological military offensive charge against Calvinism.

Charles Wesley begs his hearers not to hear this other gospel of Calvinism:

> Sinners, abhor the fiend:
>   His *other* gospel hear—
> *The GOD of truth did not intend,*
>   *The Thing His Words declare,*
> *He offers Grace to All,*
>   *Which most cannot embrace,*
> *Mock'd with an ineffectual Call*
>   *And insufficient Grace.*

He continues:

> *The righteous GOD consign'd*
> *Them over to their Doom,*
> *And sent the Saviour of mankind*
> *To damn them from the Womb;*
> *To damn for falling short*
> *Of what they could not do*
> *For not believing the Report*
> *Of that which was not true.*

. . . .

> They think with Shrieks and Cries
> To please the Lord of Hosts,
> And offer Thee in Sacrifice
> Millions of slaughter'd Ghosts:
> With New-born Babes they fill
> The dire infernal Shade,
> *For such* they say, *was thy Great Will,*
> *Before the World was made.*

The climax is reached in the petition:

> Arise, O God, arise,
> Thy glorious Truth maintain,
> Hold forth the Bloody Sacrifice
> For every Sinner slain!
> Defend thy Mercy's Cause,
> Thy Grace divinely free,
> Lift up the Standard of thy Cross,
> Draw all men unto Thee.

And in the closing verse which typically, moodily, and morbidly expects martyrdom:[13]

> O take me at my Word,
> But arm me with thy Power,
> Then call me forth to suffer, LORD,
> To meet the fiery Hour:
> In death will I proclaim
> That all may hear thy Call,
> And clap my Hands amidst the Flame,
> And shout—HE DIED FOR ALL.[14]

Another poem which adapts Psalm 80 to the condition of the Church of England appeared in a *Collection of Psalms and Hymns* (1743) displaying how enemies of the Church of England had wrecked its vineyard and beguiled its members, including the Moravians, with their quietism, as well as the motley collection of Deists, Sectarians, Calvinists, and Unitarians, in the following verse:

> The Boar out of the German Wood
> Tears up her Roots with baleful Power;
> The Lion roaring for his Food,
> And all the Forest Beasts devour.
> Deists and Sectaries agree,
> And *Calvin* and *Socinus* join
> To spoil the Apostolic Tree
> And Root and Branch destroy the Vine.[15]

Professor Frank Baker has also reprinted from "manuscript Thirty" a fascinating poem, "Universal Redemption," with some very controversial lines. As we might expect, Calvinism and Calvin are blasted, demanding of God,

> "Silence his reprobating Roar,
> Cancel his Horrible Decree."

What is intriguing, however, is the following verse, which traces the spread and sources of determinism in religion to the Church of Scotland (the Kirk), the Eleatic School of Zeno, Mohammedanism, Dominic the Friar and founder of the Order of Preachers in his Cell, and Calvin on Geneva's lake Leman. Oddly enough he does not trace *predestination* back to St. Augustine. Here is his Litany of Hate:

> Drive the Old *Fatalist* to Hell
> Nor longer let him Refuge take
> In Kirk, or School, or Mosque, or Cell,
> Not ev'n in his own Leman-Lake.[16]

Charles Wesley has two other criticisms of Calvinism, and in each case it was the consequences of *antinomianism* that fed his ire. His pastoral soul had seen the terrible effects of claiming to be elect, without any spiritual or ethical transformation, and he had seen that the doctrine of the perseverance of the saints could lead not merely to the loss of any dynamic in religion, but even to persistence in evil and cruelty. This is, of course, a misrepresentation of Calvinism, which was as concerned for sanctification as Methodism was for Christian perfection. At the moment I wish us to see Calvinism through Charles Wesley's theological spectacles. In *An Epistle to a Friend Written in the Year 1743* he castigated the doctrine of the perseverance of the saints thus:

> No longer now their watch the Watchmen keep,
> But love to slumber, and lie down to sleep,
> Their eye-lids in *Poor Sinnership* they close,
> Or, rock'd in Calvin's Arms, supinely doze.
> *"Always in grace, if once!"* their foot stands sure,
> Their Lives unholy, and their Hearts impure. . . . [17]

He had seen a disgusting example of this attitude, for his *Journal* reports on June 8, 1741 how a man who was a Predestinarian, who accepted "the *other Gospel*" and—I quote: "Came home *elect* and in proof of it *beat his wife.*" Wesley says of this former Methodist: "His seriousness was at an end. His work was done. God doth not behold iniquity in Jacob; therefore his iniquity and cruelty towards her abound."[18]

The hymnwriter had already heard George Whitefield preach rudely against *Christian perfection* as held by the Wesleys in asserting the necessity of sin and the perseverance of the saints nonetheless, as his letter of March 16, 1741 attests:

> G.W. came into the desk while I was showing the believer's privilege. After speaking something, I desired him to preach. He did—predestination, perseverance, and the necessity of sinning. Afterwards mildly expostulated with him, asking if he would commend me for preaching the opposite doctrines in his Orphan-house . . . and labouring for peace to the utmost of my power.[19]

One is bound to share his abomination of the hypocrisy of the defaulter and of Whitefield's discourtesy, and to admire the spirit of reconciliation he so often exhibited.

In the same year, 1741, on May 19, Charles reports at length (too long for citation) the desperate confusion of a man who believed in reprobation yet who was unwilling to say that God made even Judas to be damned, and would not say that God made him to be saved. Charles Wesley finally asked him: "Why does God command all men everywhere to repent? Why does He call, and offer his grace to, reprobates?" and, getting no answer, "and so read him one of his friend Calvin's: 'God speaketh to them, that they may be the deafer; He gives light to them, that they may be the blinder; He offers instruction to them, that they may be the more ignorant; and uses the remedy that they may *not* be healed' " (*Institutes* I.iii.24). Charles adds: "Never did I meet with a more pitiful advocate of a more pitiful cause . . . I told him *his* predestination had got a millstone about its neck, and would infallibly be drowned, if

191

he did not part it from reprobation."[20] There Charles Wesley had divined the Achilles heel of Calvinism—the injustice of reprobation, predetermined in eternity independently of the consideration of an individual's future conduct.

Far more important than the negative and critical poems were the numerous hymns of Charles Wesley which lyrically lauded God for limitless and universal grace, and love to all humanity. It is remarkable how he rings the changes on universal redemption and perfect love which should be its consequence eventually. He recognizes it in its origin as divine law, as the single basic need of humanity supplied by God, as the responsive rendering of that which is due God, as effecting humility leading to the adoration of God, as the cause of which human love is the effect—indeed, the love of God is of human love "its pattern, principle, and end."[21] From a treasure of choices I will elect three verses which seem excellent of their kind. There is the Athanasian theology of the hymn that begins "Let earth and heaven combine" to be sung on the Sunday after Christmas, where Wesley celebrates that God became flesh that we might become Godlike:

> He deigns in Flesh t'appear,
>   Widest Extremes to join,
> To bring our Vileness near,
>   And make us All divine;
> And we the Life of GOD shall know,
> For GOD is manifest below.[22]

The long historical record of divine Love and its reach to all kinds and conditions is emphasized in the next citation:

> Thy sovereign grace to all extends
>   Immense and unconfined;
> From age to age it never ends;
>   It reaches all mankind.
>
> Throughout the world its breadth is known,
>   Wide as infinity!
> So wide, it never passed by one,
>   Or had it passed by me.[23]

The universality of Christ's redemption is vividly recalled in Holy Communion together with the costliness of the gift:

> Who would not with thy Burden stoop,
> And bow the Head when Jesus dies!

Yet in this Ordinance Divine
We still the sacred Load may bear;
And now we in Thy Offering join,
Thy Sacramental passion share.

Thou art with *all* thy members here,
In this tremendous Mystery
We jointly before God appear,
To offer up ourselves with Thee.[24]

This is Arminianism soaring to the blue empyrean with matchless out-spread wings!

Charles Wesley, like John, took seriously the divine command "to love the Lord thy God with all thy heart, and all thy soul, and all thy mind, and thy neighbor as thyself." This was the doctrine of *Christian perfection* which Calvin had maintained was only possible to experience at death at the immediate entry into God's presence. Both the Wesley brothers believed that the experience of perfect love could be known, instantly said John, rarely and gradually said Charles. It was a doctrine derided by Calvinists.

The experience, however, was not absolute, nor did it remain permanently, except in eternity. Frank Whaling interprets *Christian perfection* as implying "that all one's thoughts, words, and deeds were governed by pure love, but did not imply perfection in knowledge or freedom from infirmities or freedom from temptation. Nor did it imply an inability to grow further in grace, nor an inability to fall from grace."[25]

If anything, Charles's requirements for *Christian perfection* were higher than John's, but he was careful to examine any who claimed to have reached *Christian perfection*. On Monday, June 22, 1741 the *Journal* of Charles Wesley records that he visited a woman on her death-bed who claimed that Christ would fill up what was lacking in her faith. Two days later she told him she would receive it with the sacrament, which he administered to her. When she assured him that God had then taken away the evil heart, and said that she had no sin in her, he reported, "I told her that time and temptation would show."[26] Yet on May 6th of the same year, he had been profoundly impressed by the death-bed behavior of Sister Hooper whose joy was much greater than her acute sufferings. His journal entry reads:

I asked her whether she was not in great pain. "Yes," she answered, "but in greater joy. I would not be without either." "But do you not prefer life or death?" She replied: "All is alike to me; let Christ choose; I have no will of my own."

Charles concludes: "This is that holiness, or absolute resignation, or Christian perfection!"[27] In this respect he was readier to believe that perfect holiness might be achieved at death rather than before it, and he changed his earlier view of 1739, and utterly denied any instantaneous achievement of Christian perfection. A later hymn, based in part on Romans 13:10 insists upon the gradualness of holiness:

> Thou dost not say, the seed springs up
> Into an instantaneous crop;
> But waiting long for its return,
> We see the blade; the ear; the corn;
> The weak; and *then* the stronger grace,
> And *after that* full holiness.[28]

In *A Plain Account of Christian Perfection*, which went through six editions during his life, John Wesley claimed that it was a doctrine the brothers had always taught and that this was the whole point and purpose of his life. Its continuity in their teachings he illustrates by citations from *Hymns and Sacred Poems* published in 1740. One of these hymns goes:

> Lord, I believe a rest remains
> To all thy people known,
> A rest where *pure enjoyment* reigns,
> And Thou art *lov'd alone*.
>
> A rest where *all* our soul's *desire*
> Is fixed on things above:
> Where doubt, and pain, and fear expire,
> Cast out by *perfect love*.

And the hymn ends:

> Come, Father, Son, and Holy ghost
> And seal me thine abode!
> Let all I am in thee be lost:
> Let all be lost in God.[29]

The very purpose of all Christ's work on earth was perfect love and this is consummately expressed in one verse:

> Heavenly Father, Life divine,
> Change my nature into thine!
> Move and spread throughout my soul,
> Actuate and fill the whole!
> Be it I no longer now
> Living in the flesh, but Thou.[30]

Its most sublime expression is contained in the following verse:

> Finish, then, thy new creation,
>   Pure and sinless let us be;
> Let us see thy great salvation
>   Perfectly restored in thee;
> Changed from glory into glory,
>   Till in heaven we take our place,
> Till we cast our crowns before thee,
>   Lost in wonder, love and praise.[31]

Having examined where Charles Wesley says a resounding "No" to the Calvinist tradition, we shall now consider where he says a genuine "Yes" to that tradition. We cannot claim that it was from the Reformed tradition that the Wesleys came to accept justification by faith, since it was by the help of the Moravian Peter Böhler, and after reading Luther's Commentaries, that both brothers accepted justification by faith, a doctrine also central to Calvinism. Nor can we claim that the conviction of original sin and the need to be delivered from it was a borrowing from the Calvinist tradition: this is as Lutheran and Anglican as it is Calvinist. The same is also true of the primacy of Scripture over tradition, and the secondary but important guidance offered by the primitive church.

Interestingly enough, both the Wesleys accepted the doctrine of *election*, without its negative aspect: *reprobation*. How could they not with John's dramatic experience of being plucked from the burning Epworth Rectory, which his mother Susanna, the daughter of a distinguished English Presbyterian minister, encouraged him to believe was a sign that he had a singular religious destiny ahead of him? It is important to recognize that Charles believed that the seal of *election* is being called to suffer with Christ. This becomes clear in a hymn written for St. Stephen's Day:

> Saved is the Life for JESUS lost,
>   Hidden from Earth, but found in GOD,
> To suffer is to triumph most,
>   The highest Gift on Man bestow'd,
> Seal of my sure Election This,
> Seal of mine everlasting Bliss.

195

The Touchstone, and the Proof of Grace,
The Standard of Perfection here,
The Measure of my Heavenly Place,
When CHRIST and all his Saints appear,
The Mark Divine, by JESU'S art
Imprinted on my faithful Heart.[32]

Parallels with Calvinism

There are two areas of Calvinism in which I believe we can find parallels with the thought and lyricism of Charles Wesley, and in one case a borrowing from Calvinism: these I now propose to explore. The first is in the exposition of the mystery of the Eucharist. The second is in the concept of the covenant which was taken from a Puritan source for the renowned Methodist service for renewing one's covenant with God now used on the first Sunday of the new year.

It is clear that Charles Wesley cannot accept the Roman Catholic explanation of the mystery of Christ's presence as due to a change in the substance of the elements of bread and wine, at the consecration, which converts them into the body and blood of Christ, while the accidents remain bread and wine. Nor could he accept the Lutheran theory of consubstantiation, which maintains that after the consecration the substances of both the body and blood of Christ and the bread and wine coexist in union with each other (and requires a curious belief in the ubiquity of Christ's human body), since this is hardly an explanation. He was even less likely to accept the bare memorialism associated with Ulrich Zwingli, who claimed that the Lord's Supper had two values: one was that of the reminiscence of Christ's passion and death, and the other was that it functioned as a badge of membership in the body of Christ, the church, although Wesley incorporated both aspects in his eucharistic hymnody. The only other acceptable theory of the mystery—and it remained a wondering mystery to Charles Wesley like the incarnation itself—was that of John Calvin, who repudiated the idea that the Holy Communion was a *nudum signum*, but gratefully acknowledged that it was a seal of the promises of salvation in Christ. This has been termed "instrumental symbolism" because the bread and wine are symbols that the Holy Spirit uses to bring to believers the benefits of Christ's atoning death and resurrection, which are forgiveness and eternal life. Another term for this theory is "virtualism" because it asserts the strength (or *virtus*) as being the spiritual, dynamic, and real presence of Christ at the Sacrament. It should also be noted that the presence of Christ in the preaching of the Word of God is corroborated for the believer by the *testimonium internum Spiritus sancti* (the interior witness of the Holy Spirit) and the same is true for the sacrament of the Eucharist for both Calvin and the Wesleys, who stressed the importance of confirmatory experience in sermon and sacrament.

Calvin's own exposition of his interpretation of the Lord's Supper can be found at length in the *Institutes* and also in his Strasbourg and Genevan Liturgy. In the former it is expressed in concise form:

> To summarize: our souls are fed by the flesh and blood of Christ in the same way that bread and wine keep and sustain physical life. For the analogy of the sign applies only if the souls find their nourishment in Christ—which cannot happen unless Christ truly grows into one with us, and refreshes us by the eating of his flesh and the drinking of his blood. Even though it seems unbelievable that Christ's flesh, separated from us by such great distance, penetrates to us, so that it becomes our food, let us remember how the secret power of the Holy Spirit towers above all our senses, and how foolish it is to wish to measure his immeasurableness by our measure. What, then, our mind does not conceive, let faith conceive: that the Spirit truly unites things separated in space.[33]

We should note that Calvin insists upon the mysterious power (*virtus*) operating in the sacrament of the Lord's Supper, which, as Ford Battles points out, is why his theory is called "virtualism."[34] Calvin also insists that the sign or symbol is not empty or nude:

> Now, that sacred partaking of his flesh and blood by which Christ pours his life into us, as if it penetrated our bones and marrow, he also testifies and seals in the Supper—not by presenting a vain and empty sign, but by manifesting there the effectiveness of his Spirit to fulfil what he promises. And truly he offers and shows the reality there signified to all who sit at that spiritual banquet, although it is received with benefit by believers alone, who accept such great generosity with true faith and gratefulness of heart.[35]

Charles Wesley also insisted on the need for faith, and both Wesleys believed that the Lord's Supper was a confirming ordinance.

In his *The Form of Church Prayers* prepared for the Reformed French Church in Geneva in 1542 and in Strasbourg in 1545, Calvin includes the following explanatory words in the exhortation:

> Above all, therefore let us believe those promises of which Jesus Christ, who is the unfailing truth, has spoken with his own lips: He is truly willing to make us partakers of His body and blood, in order that we may possess Him wholly, and in such wise that He may live in us and we in Him. And though we see but bread and wine, we must not doubt that He accomplishes spiritually in our souls, all that He shows us outwardly by these visible signs,

namely, that he is the bread of heaven to feed and nourish us into eternal life.[36]

In his book, *The Eucharistic Hymns of John and Charles Wesley*, J. Ernest Rattenbury indicates that John Wesley repudiated both *transubstantiation* and *consubstantiation*, while accepting the doctrine of the *real presence* as both brothers did in their Oxford days, and his conclusion is: "It is possible that Charles may have held a doctrine more akin to Luther's; but John's doctrine of the presence, and I think that of Charles's too, seems rather to have approximated to Calvin's."[37]

The *Hymns on the Lord's Supper* appeared in 1745.[38] Hymn CXVI makes it very clear that Christ's is not a "Hidden Presence" (*Latens deitas* as the Catholic Mass on Corpus Christi Day has it, which Gerard Manley Hopkins translated as "Godhead here in hiding, Whom I do adore, Masked by these bare shadows, Shape and nothing more.")[39] The words of Charles are:

> We need not now go up to Heaven
>   To bring the long-sought Saviour down,
> Thou art to All already given:
>   Thou dost ev'n Now thy Banquet crown,
> To every faithful Soul appear,
> And shew thy Real Presence here.[40]

As Rattenbury insists, Charles Wesley believed that Christ's was a "special" Presence as when he maintains "*If chiefly here* Thou mayst be found" and in another hymn: "His Presence makes the Feast."[41]

Charles Wesley, presumably aided by John, divided the *Hymns on the Lord's Supper* into five categories, following the Preface by Dean Brevint. These were: "As it is a Memorial of the Sufferings and Death of Christ" (Hymns I to XXVII); "As it is a Sign and a Means of Grace" (Hymns XXVIII to XCII) (by far the largest category); "The Sacrament a Pledge of Heaven" (Hymns XCIII to CXV); "The Holy Eucharist as it implies a Sacrifice" (Hymns CXVI to CXXVII); "Concerning the Sacrifice of our Persons" (Hymns CXXVIII to CLVII), with nine additional Hymns "After the Sacrament" (CLVIII to CLXVI). Each one of these categories would be approved by Calvin, but he might have thought strange the emphasis on the oblation Christ offers permanently to God, together with the smaller oblation offered by the members of the Body of Christ.

It even seemed strange to Charles Wesley, since one hymn queried: "How can the two Oblations join?" to which the answer is offered:

> Thy Offering doth to Ours impart
> Its Righteousness and Saving Grace,
> While charg'd with all our Sins Thou art,
> To Death devoted in our Place.[42]

Yet the problem is not wholly solved, since two themes which do not agree are stressed in these hymns: one is the once-for-all historic atonement made on the cross; while the other is the notion that this sacrifice is eternally presented by the Son to the Father in heaven:

> The Sacrifice is all-compleat,
> The Death Thou never canst repeat,
>   Once offer'd up to die no more.
>
> Yet may we celebrate below,
> And daily thus thine Offering shew
>   Expos'd before thy Father's Eyes;
> In this tremendous Mystery
> Present Thee bleeding on the Tree
>   Our everlasting Sacrifice;
>
> Father, behold thy dying Son!
> Ev'n now He lays our Ransom down,
>   Ev'n now declares our Sins forgiven:
> His Flesh is rent, the Living Way
> Is open'd to Eternal Day,
>   And lo, thro' Him we pass to Heaven![43]

One cannot know whether it was John or Charles who was responsible, but it was probably Charles, and it is fascinating to discover that one hymn indicates that the author believed that consecration was effected, as in the Eastern Orthodox Church, by the invocation of the Holy Spirit (the *epiklesis*):

> Come, Holy Ghost, thine Influence shed,
>   And realize the Sign,
> Thy Life infuse into the Bread,
>   Thy Power into the Wine.[44]

Furthermore, this sacrament is clearly recognized as the supreme means of grace:

> The Prayer, the Fast, the Word conveys,
>   When mixt with Faith, thy Life to me,
> In all the Channels of thy Grace,
>   I still have Fellowship with Thee,
> But chiefly here my Soul is fed
> With Fulness of Immortal Bread.
>
> Communion closer far I feel,
>   And deeper drink th'Atoning Blood.
> The Joy is more unspeakable,
>   And yields me larger Draughts of God,
> 'Till Nature faints beneath the Power,
> And Faith fill'd up can hold no more.[45]

Here Charles is the God-intoxicated hymnologist!

With Calvin, Charles Wesley reverently acknowledges the mystery:

> O The Depth of Love Divine
>   Th' Unfathomable Grace!
> Who shall say how Bread and Wine
>   God into Man conveys?
> *How* the Bread his Flesh imparts,
>   *How* the Wine transmits his Blood,
> Fills his Faithful People's Hearts
>   With all the Life of God.
>
> . . . .
>
> Sure and real is the Grace,
>   The Manner be unknown;
> Only meet us in thy Ways
>   And perfect us in One,
> Let us taste the heavenly Powers,
>   Lord, we ask for Nothing more;
> Thine to bless, 'Tis only Ours
>   To wonder, and adore.[46]

The sacrament is also both a means of unity and a pledge of heaven:

> So dear the Tie where Souls agree
>   In JESU's Dying Love;
> Then only can it closer be,
>   When all are join'd above.[47]

Let me conclude this part by endorsing the judgment of a modern moderate Calvinist and ecumenist, Bernard L. Manning. In praising the *1780 Collection*, which is comprised almost exclusively of Charles Wesley's hymns, Manning evaluated it as ranking "in Christian literature with the Psalms, the *Book of Common Prayer*, the Canon of the Mass. In its own way, it is perfect, unapproachable, elemental in its perfection. . . . It is a work of supreme devotional art by a religious genius." The same historian justified his judgment by analyzing the three basic elements in the hymnody: "There is the solid structure of historic dogma; there is the passionate thrill of passionate experience; but there is, too, the glory of a mystic sunlight coming directly from another world."[48]

The clearest debt to the Calvinist tradition is the borrowing not only of the idea of the renewing of the covenant, but the original wording and even a summary of the directions for it from either Richard or Joseph Alleine, two Puritan divines of the seventeenth century, who both include exactly the same covenant in their published writings. It appears in Richard Alleine's *Heaven Opened, Or, A Brief and Plain Discovery of the Riches of Gods Covenant of Grace* in 1666, and is the third part of the author's renowned *Vindiciae Pietatis*, and it also appears in Joseph Alleine's *An Alarme to Unconverted Sinners* in 1672, when it sold 20,000 copies and on its reissue with a different title, *A Sure Guide to Heaven*, in 1675, it sold 50,000 copies.[49] It would be difficult to decide which book had influenced John Wesley more, but since he was a man who admired concision, he might well have preferred the abbreviated "Directions" in Richard Alleine over the almost interminable directions offered by Joseph Alleine.

As planned by John Wesley, the Covenant Service had two parts. The first was devoted to directions by which the members of his societies were to make this covenant: (1) Set aside time for secret prayer to seek God's help, to consider the terms of the covenant, and to search the heart. (2) To see that one's spirit is composed "into the most serious frame possible, suitable to a transaction of so high importance." (3) The believer is adjured to "lay hold on the Covenant of God and rely on His promise of giving grace and strength, whereby you may be enabled to fulfil your promise." (4) Make a resolution to be faithful. Finally, the believer must "set upon the work."[50]

Part II of the Service was the solemn taking of the covenant itself. In its original form it began: "O most dreadful God, for the Passion of Thy Son, I beseech Thee to accept of Thy poor prodigal . . ." and it ended, "And the Covenant which I have made upon earth, let it be ratified in Heaven."[51] These were the very words of the covenants of both Alleines.

201

The first Covenant Service was held in the autumn of 1755, but John Wesley later felt it more appropriate to hold it on the first Sunday of the New Year. It was so used in 1766 and at the start of every year from 1770 to 1778, with the exception of 1774. The first printed edition of the Service appeared in 1779. Wesley had always required his congregation to assent to the covenant by standing, but in the first printed order of the service he followed Joseph Alleine's advice that the covenant should be signed. In later years, the service was always followed by the Lord's Supper.[52] This practice has continued to the present.

The ecclesiology of Puritanism was built firmly upon the taking of covenants. Indeed, you could not become a member of an Independent or Particular Baptist Church (both Calvinistic) without signing or reciting its covenant of membership. While a creed may be accepted with the top of the mind, a covenant involved a solemn commitment from the bottom of the heart and a firm resolution of the will. Joseph Alleine advised that it should be in writing "and that you would with all possible Reverence spread the Writing before the Lord, as if you would present it to him as your Act and Deed."[53] Indeed, the very words in the covenant described it as a "Marriage Covenant" with Christ.[54]

It seems appropriate to conclude by citing a hymn by Charles Wesley which first appeared in *Short Hymns* and became attached to the service of covenant renewal:

> Come, let us use the grace divine,
>   And all, with one accord,
> In a perpetual covenant join
>   Ourselves to Christ the Lord.
>
> Give up ourselves, through Jesu's power,
>   His name to glorify;
> And promise in this sacred hour
>   For God to live and die.
>
> The covenant we this moment make
>   Be ever kept in mind;
> We will no more our God forsake,
>   Or cast his words behind.
>
> We never will throw off his fear
>   Who hears our solemn vow;
> And if thou art well-pleased to hear,
>   Come down, and meet us now!

Thee, Father, Son, and Holy Ghost,
   Let all our hearts receive!
Present with the celestial host,
   The peaceful answer give!

To each the covenant-blood apply
   Which takes our sins away;
And register our names on high,
   And keep us to that day![55]

APPENDIX

Loyal Anglican as Charles Wesley always remained, he might have been delighted that John proposed for the use of the American Methodists an abridgment of the *Book of Common Prayer*, when British and American Methodists were separated by the American War of Independence. Yet, in fact he took John to task for making the abridgement.

> Your Liturgy so well-prepared
> To E[ngland]'s Church proves your regard,
> Of churches national the best,
> By you, and all the world confest:
> (Why shou'd we then bad counsel take
> And for a worse the best forsake?)
> You tell us, with her Book of prayer
> No book is worthy to compare;
> Why change it then for your Edition,
> Deprav'd by many a bold omission?
> We never will renounce our creed,
> Because of Three but One you need,
> No longer the Nicene approve,
> The Athanasian Mound remove,
> And out of your New book have thrown
> God One in Three, & Three in One.[56]

A highly probable source for this abridgment was the summary of suggestions for revision put forward by the Presbyterians at the Savoy Conference with the Anglicans in 1661 as recorded in Edmund Calamy's *Abridgment of Mr. Baxter's History of His Life and Times.* Of this proposal put forward by Frederick Hunter,[57] Robert C. Monk judiciously observes "that other Wesley scholars, such as Wesley Swift and J. E. Rattenbury, question the emphasis Hunter gives to Calamy's influence on Wesley, but there is little question that the revisions *are* those suggested by the Presbyterians whether or not Wesley was dependent upon Calamy for these suggestions."[58] In any case, while the Communion Order of the abridged Book of Common Prayer had a long influence on American Methodist worship, the other services were quickly dropped.

Chapter 12

CHARLES WESLEY
AND ROMAN CATHOLICISM

Teresa Berger

The subject matter described by the simple title "Charles Wesley and Roman Catholicism" is a complex, multilayered issue which has to be addressed on a number of very different levels. For the purposes of the present chapter, I have chosen the following: First, Charles Wesley's actual contacts with Roman Catholicism will be identified in order to ascertain the depth (or non-depth) of his confrontation with this particular ecclesial tradition. Wesley's knowledge of Roman Catholic devotional literature, his position vis-à-vis the "young Pretender," his stay in Ireland, his attitude during the Gordon Riots, and his reaction to the reception of his son Samuel into the Roman Catholic Church will be analyzed. Second, Charles Wesley's views of the Roman Catholic tradition—sketchy and unsystematized as they are—will be characterized. Third, what has been called a "Catholic spirit" will be examined as a source in the hymns of Charles Wesley. In the last part of this chapter, the focus will shift beyond Charles Wesley's lifetime to the question of whether and where Wesley can be identified as a source of dialogue between the Methodist and the Roman Catholic traditions. Remaining true to the subject matter of this chapter, I will close with a hymn of Charles Wesley which can be considered an ecumenical hymn *par excellence*. It is worth noting at the outset that although a number of studies have been done on John Wesley and the Roman Catholic tradition,[1] none, to my knowledge, has been done on Charles Wesley so far.[2] Before looking in detail at Charles Wesley's position vis-à-vis Roman Catholicism, however, it is important first to outline briefly the place of the Roman Catholic Church in the society in which Charles Wesley lived.

The Roman Catholic Church in Eighteenth-Century England

Without Charles Wesley's stay in Ireland and the reception of his son Samuel into the Roman Catholic Church, the "Singer of the Evangelical Revival" would not necessarily have had any sustained contact with Roman Catholics at any given point in his life. The English Catholic Community[3] of Charles Wesley's time was a minority in English society. One estimates its numbers at roughly 80,000 in the year 1767, with somewhat less than 400 priests in ministry. Administratively, the Roman Catholic community was organized along the lines of a mission, not along traditional diocesan lines.

The legal position of Roman Catholics in England in the eighteenth century was still one of discrimination—a position Roman Catholics shared with Dissenters—although the relevant laws often were not enforced. A "pattern of harassment"[4] nevertheless seems to have been the order of the day. Probably as important, if not more important to the life of the English Catholic community than its actual legal standing, were popular (mis)conceptions of Roman Catholicism in the minds of many non-Roman Catholics. The Church was seen as superstitious, cruel, tyrannical and bloody. These views were fed not only by religious convictions, but also by political presuppositions (Roman Catholics were usually identified as Jacobites supporting the "Young Pretender"), and by ideological motivations (the Enlightenment, on the whole, did not look favorably on the Roman Catholic Church). The outcry against Roman Catholicism, "No Popery," became—neither for the first nor for the last time—a battle cry during the so-called Gordon Riots in 1780. Protesters violently opposed to the Catholic Relief Act of 1778, which had granted Roman Catholics the right to own property and repealed life imprisonment for Roman Catholic priests and for those keeping Roman Catholic schools, marched to Parliament. The demonstration turned violent with houses and chapels being destroyed and set on fire. About 300 people were killed. Nevertheless, further Catholic Relief Acts followed in the next years, which amongst other things allowed Roman Catholic worship and schools, and—at least in theory—opened up most professions and public office to Roman Catholics. But these Catholic Relief Acts were introduced after Charles Wesley's death in 1788 and therefore do not directly concern the subject of this article.

It is worth noting that, particularly in the early days of the Methodist revival, Methodists were not infrequently charged with being "Papists," "Jacobites," and "Jesuits in disguise"[5]—and suffered for the equation. The charges were not confined only to mob slogans, they also made it into print. To name but one example: in the years 1749–1754, George

Lavington (1684-1762), the Bishop of Exeter, published a treatise in three parts under the title "Enthusiasm of Methodists and Papists compar'd" in which he paralleled aspects of Roman Catholic and Methodist spirituality—with a view towards discrediting the latter by association with the former (these comparisons between "Papism" and "Methodism" were by no means confined to the eighteenth century. The nineteenth century still saw publications with titles like "The Popery of Methodism; or The Enthusiasm of Papists and Wesleyans Compared," "John Wesley, the Papa of British Rome" or "John Wesley an Unconscious Romanist"). The suspicion of ties between Methodism and Roman Catholicism was denied vigorously not only from the Methodist side. In 1760, the Roman Catholic Bishop Richard Challoner (1691-1781) published his "Caveat Against the Methodists," the purpose of which is stated in the subtitle as "Shewing how Unsafe it is for any Christian to Join Himself to their Society, or to Adhere to their teachers"—a caveat which provoked a long reply from John Wesley.

When looking at Charles Wesley's contacts with and views of the Roman Catholic tradition, both the not infrequent denunciations of Methodism as "Papist" and the anti-Roman Catholic sentiments at the time of the Methodist revival will have to be borne in mind.

Charles Wesley's Contacts with the Roman Catholic Tradition

As is to be expected of a minister of the Church of England in the eighteenth century, Charles Wesley's contacts with members of the Roman Catholic Church were neither regular nor sustained—but there are a few instances in his life where these contacts went beyond a superficial encounter.

Devotional Literature

Wesley's first contact with Roman Catholicism, as far as we can tell, came not through personal acquaintance with members of the Roman Catholic Church, but through Roman Catholic devotional material from the European Continent—which had a wide impact in England in the eighteenth century. Charles Wesley was familiar with Blaise Pascal (1623-1662) and with the medieval ascetic writer Thomas à Kempis (1380-1471) who were both read in his parental home. In all likelihood, he also read Lorenzo Scupoli's *Spiritual Combat* at an early age, since this work was one of the spiritual classics his mother studied.[6]

In addition, Charles Wesley will also have known at least some of the Roman Catholic spiritual writers which were included in the readings of his brother John and of the Methodist cell groups in Oxford (e.g. Antoinette Bourignon, Jeanne Marie Guyon, François Fénélon, Nicholas Malebranche, Miguel de Molinos, Pasquier Quesnel, Alonso Rodriguez, Francis de Sales, Johannes Tauler, Gaston Jean Baptiste de Renty). Since, however, we do not have much detailed information about Charles's time in Oxford (his diary begins only in 1736, and his letters from Oxford are not informative on the point in question), one cannot claim with any degree of certainty which of these Roman Catholic writers he knew and which not.[7] The same applies to the works of Roman Catholic mystics which John Wesley included in his "Christian Library" between 1750 and 1756. It seems wise not to presume Charles's familiarity with these authors simply on the basis of John's knowledge of them.

There was, of course, an implicit ecumenical impetus in the reception of Roman Catholic classics of spirituality in other ecclesial traditions, but as far as Charles Wesley is concerned we have no record of this ever becoming an explicit ecumenical sharing in another tradition's spiritual riches. Charles Wesley was, however, not insensitive to the Roman Catholic roots of some of his spiritual reading. In Ireland, we will find him consciously drawing on Thomas à Kempis for his Roman Catholic audience.

The "Young Pretender"

In 1745, the grandson of King James II, Charles—commonly known as the "Young Pretender"—landed in Scotland with the intention of claiming the English crown. He was supported by France and by "Jacobites" within England. As a Roman Catholic, he also had the blessing of the Roman Catholic Church. The young Pretender's "invasion" naturally did nothing to quench anti-Roman Catholic sentiments in England, even if it was only a brief episode (after an initial victory, Charles's forces were defeated). The whole incident spelled trouble for the emerging Methodist societies because they were identified as "Papists" and as "Jacobites" in disguise. Consequently the year of 1745 finds Charles Wesley vigorously proclaiming his allegiance to the present King, and his opposition not only to the Young Pretender but also his religious affiliation. On September 26, 1745, for example, Wesley describes in his *Journal* his message to a group of Methodists:

> I warned them, with all authority, to flee to the mountains, escape to the strong tower, even the name of Jesus. We seemed to have strong faith, that the Romish Antichrist shall never finally prevail in these kingdoms.[8]

Charles Wesley also wrote a number of hymns "for times of trouble" during this year. On the whole, these hymns see the invasion of the

Young Pretender as a chastisement of God for the sins of the nation which is thereby called to repentance, but one also finds the occasional reference to "bloodthirsty *Rome*" and the "*Romish* wolf."[9] After the Young Pretender was defeated in April of 1746, Charles Wesley wrote a number of hymns for the scheduled public Thanksgiving Day. One of them, which opens with the line "THANKS be to God, the God of power," describes "danger's hour" in the following way:

> His [God's] eye observed the dark design,
> To blast our rightful monarch's line,
> The scheme in Satan's *conclave* laid,
> Improved by *Rome's* unerring head,
>
> To gall us with their yoke abhorr'd,
> And plant *their* faith with fire and sword.[10]

Altogether, it is obvious that the whole episode of the invasion of the Young Pretender would find Charles Wesley—not only by conviction but also by necessity—articulating a strongly anti-Roman Catholic position. When in 1758–1759 similar alarms of a French (and thereby Roman Catholic) invasion were prevalent, Wesley published some further hymns which echo the tenor of the hymns from the previous decade.[11]

Ireland, 1747–1748

Charles Wesley had encountered members of the Roman Catholic Church before going to Ireland in 1747, as we know from his *Journal*. He tells us, for example, that on April 5, 1736 while in Georgia, his congregation for the evening service "consisted of two Presbyterians and a Papist" (adding that he went home that evening with his "distemper being much increased with the little duty I could discharge"[12]). In 1739, while ministering in the prison at Newgate, he "talked in the cells to two papists, who renounced all merit but that of Jesus Christ." Two days later, Wesley finds "one of the Papists full of peace and joy in believing."[13]

The only sustained contact with Roman Catholics in Charles Wesley's ministry, however, came with his two stays in Ireland, the first for six months from September 1747 to March 1748, the second for two months from August to October 1748. There are numerous references to the "poor Papists" or "poor Romans" in his journal, but one does not get a sense of Wesley having confronted the Roman Catholic tradition itself in any depth. The content of his preaching continues to be the challenge to a living faith through justification by grace, although for the sake of his audience Wesley now explicitly includes references to Roman Catholic devotional material. His quotations from Thomas à Kempis, he notes, made some of his hearers "confident I am a good Catholic."[14] But not everybody was convinced, as is clear from Wesley's repeated references to "Popish mobs," and to Roman Catholic priests (as well as Protestant ministers) trying to prevent people from coming to hear him.

Out of the many relevant *Journal* entries from Wesley's time in Ireland, one shall here be quoted at greater length. Charles Wesley wrote under the date of September 20, 1747:

> I spoke with great freedom to the poor Papists, urging them to repentance and the love of Christ, from the authority of their own Kempis, and their own liturgy. None lifted up his voice or hand. All listened with strange attention. Many were in tears. I advised them to go to their respective places of worship. They expressed general satisfaction, especially the Papists.[15]

These sentences give an indication of Charles Wesley being familiar with not only à Kempis but also some part of the Roman Catholic liturgical tradition. They also suggest that the heart of his preaching ministry in a predominantly Roman Catholic context was not primarily the undoing of affiliation with the Roman Catholic Church, but rather the challenge to the acceptance of a living inward faith instead of a "formal religion." This is supported by another *Journal* entry from Wesley's second stay in Ireland in August 1748:

> I exhorted all alike to repentance toward God, and faith in Jesus Christ; and staked my own salvation upon it, that he who believes, whether Papist or Protestant, shall be saved.[16]

As is to be expected, Charles Wesley also conscientiously records whenever someone left the Roman Catholic Church after hearing a Methodist preacher—and he records this with satisfaction. But there is little trace of blind triumphalism, with Wesley usually insisting that "coming over to the power of godliness" was much more important than "coming over to the Church of England."[17] Occasional "Papists" joining the Methodist societies also seem to have provided Charles Wesley with some further contacts with members of the Roman Catholic Church beyond his two stays in Ireland.[18]

The Gordon Riots (1780)

Having moved to London in 1771, Charles Wesley experienced the Gordon Riots rather closely. He describes them vividly in letters to both his brother and his daughter Sally. One of his letters to Sally contains the draft of a poem later published as one of the *Hymns written in the Time of the Tumults*.[19] Although some people seem to have expected

Charles Wesley to be a part of the initial crowd asking for a repeal of the Catholic Relief Act, Wesley indeed had never signed the petition[20] and took quite the opposite position from the crowd once the riots broke out. In a letter to his brother John (who had earlier vigorously supported the Protestant Association which had called for the repeal) he writes:

> Imagine the terror of the poor papists. I prayed with the preachers at the Chapel, and charged them to keep the peace. I preached peace and charity, the one true religion, and prayed earnestly for the trembling, persecuted Catholics. Never have I found such love for them as on this occasion.[21]

The truth of the last statement is borne out by a hymn written during this time in which Charles Wesley pleads with God:

> With pity's softest eye behold
> The sheep which are not of this fold,
> The church in *Babylon*.[22]

Wesley also lashed out against the riots in a bitter satire called *the Protestant Association, written in the Midst of Tumults.*[23]

The Reception of Samuel Wesley into the Roman Catholic Church[24]

Charles Wesley's most immediate personal confrontation with Roman Catholicism was in all likelihood the reception of his youngest son into the Roman Catholic Church. Samuel (1766-1837), a talented composer and organist, was received into the Roman Catholic Church in his late teens, only to drift out again soon—a story that was repeated in a few other notable temporary receptions into the Roman Catholic Church[25] during the second half of the eighteenth century (for example those of the historian Edward Gibbon [1737-1794], James Boswell [1740-1795], the biographer of Samuel Johnson, and the poet Christopher Smart [1722-1771]). Samuel Wesley's reception into the Roman Catholic Church has been called "surely one of the oddest conversions to that church of which record has been preserved."[26] It was apparently more a question of musical attraction than of spiritual or doctrinal convictions. Be that as it may, the incident was kept from Charles Wesley for a time, but the news later evoked a number of poems[27] from Charles Wesley which show the bitter shock his son's decision spelled for him.

It is to these and other poems, as well as to Charles Wesley's *Journal* entries, letters, and sermons that one must turn in order to identify more clearly Wesley's views of the Roman Catholic tradition.

Charles Wesley's Views of the Roman Catholic Tradition

"Papists"

In Charles Wesley's writings one not infrequently encounters Roman Catholics, or "Papists" as he would call them, named alongside other non-Anglican Christians in lists of people Wesley guards against. In a *Journal* entry for October 1756, for example, one finds the following sentences:

> I showed [the Methodist society in Manchester] the melancholy state of the members of the Established Church, who are the most unprincipled and ignorant of all that are called Protestants; and therefore exposed to every seducer who thinks it worth his while to turn them Dissenters, Moravians, or Papists.[28]

Although these sentences are hardly complimentary for Charles Wesley's own Church, they indicate that Roman Catholicism together with a number of other non-Anglican ecclesial traditions was seen as an aberration—at least if a member of the Church of England was "seduced" by them. In fact, in the same *Journal* entry, Charles also notes having written a letter to his brother John, insisting that Methodist preachers be properly tested as to their love and affection to "our desolate mother," the Church of England. As one test, Charles suggests: "to try what he can answer a Baptist, a Quaker, a Papist, as well as a Predestinarian or Moravian."[29] Further quotes along the same lines could be added, but the general picture is already clear: Charles Wesley's scattered references to members of the Roman Catholic Church do not usually appear in favorable contexts.

"Babylon" and the "true invisible church"

In a hymn written after his son Samuel was received into the Roman Catholic Church, Charles Wesley pleads with God:

> Surely Thou hast in Babylon,
> Where Satan fills his favourite throne,
> Thy worshippers sincere
>
> Who pure as Lot in Sodom live,
> Glory to their Redeemer give
> And love the God they fear.
>
> To These my murder'd (?) son unite,
> Give him with these to walk in light,
> Where hellish darkness reigns.[30]

212

It would be easy to charge Wesley with a pervasive anti-Roman Catholicism here and see him as only one more spokesperson of a vehement polemic which equated the Roman Catholic Church with the whore of Babylon of the Book of Revelation (Rev. 17 and 18). Certainly this theme is present in the poem—as in some others which further characterize the Roman Catholic Church as a "lion's den" and its members as "Sodom's hellish sons."[31] These characterizations, moreover, cannot simply be interpreted as the result of Wesley's grief over his son's reception into the Roman Catholic Church. The identification of Rome with the "Babylonish Beast" already appears in Charles Wesley's hymn for Roman Catholics in Ireland, written in 1748.[32] But it should not be overlooked that Wesley does acknowledge that there are "sincere worshipers"—"walking in the light"—in the Roman Catholic Church which his son joined. The conviction of the presence of "real Christians" in other communities of faith making up an invisible community of true believers across denominational lines was (and is) particularly strong in pietist and evangelical circles with their emphasis on a shared experience of conversion and "inward religion," rather than on shared dogmatic, liturgical and ecclesial elements. In Charles Wesley's poems about his son, it is striking how intensely he pleads with God to grant to Samuel "the power of godliness" and thereby unite him to the "universal Church" and "true religion"—even as a member of the Roman Catholic Church.[33] Looking to the future, Wesley can say about himself and his son:

> Redeem'd from earth, renew'd in love,
> To the Jerusalem above
> By different paths we came.[34]

This insistence on the importance of "true [inward] religion" over affiliation with a particular ecclesial tradition may have been caused or heightened by the fact that Charles Wesley was not convinced of his son Samuel having "experienced the new birth." Certainly John Wesley's letter to his nephew Samuel on the occasion of him having become a Roman Catholic is motivated by this. But one finds a similar insistence already in Charles Wesley's ministry in Ireland nearly forty years earlier. He writes about two Roman Catholics with whom he had come into contact:

> Two others, in whom I found a real work of grace begun, were Papists till they heard the gospel; but are now reconciled to the church, even the true, invisible church, or communion of saints, with whom is forgiveness of sins.[35]

213

That the "different path" of Roman Catholicism nevertheless has its particular problems for Charles Wesley becomes evident when one looks for more specific objections beyond the charges of the Roman Catholic Church being like "Babylon."

"A papistic jumble of faith and works"

From the previous observations one may get the impression of a rather unspecific opposition to the Roman Catholic Church in Charles Wesley—and this is not an entirely false impression. In the ecclesial atmosphere of Charles Wesley's days an often unreflective anti-reaction to most things Roman Catholic was certainly prevalent. Some of Wesley's statements simply mirror this general attitude. There are a number of other statements, however, in which Charles Wesley addressed individual negative points more specifically.

One of them clearly relates to his understanding of faith and justification. In a sermon on Romans 3:23–25, preached before the University of Oxford on July 1, 1739, Charles Wesley outlined his understanding of justification by faith alone. He charges that even within the Church of England, this doctrine is no longer understood and accepted, rather "a papistic jumble of faith and works" has taken its place. Wesley challenges:

> Let not those therefore who deny this doctrine any longer call themselves of the Church of England. They may be of the Church of Rome, but cannot be of ours, who allow works any share in our justification with God. Papists indeed they are, though they may not know it, for they lay the wood, hay, stubble of their own works, not as the superstructure, but as the very foundation, of their acceptance with God. . . . This is our Church's censure of all that bring any other doctrine than justification by faith only; she calls them antichrists who presume to say they can by their own works justify themselves.[36]

The charge leveled against the Roman Catholic position is clear: it makes human works a part of justification, rather than an outcome of it. Obviously, sentences like these will have to be seen in their proper context: Charles Wesley was not preaching to Roman Catholics and addressing them as antichrists. His audience was his own ecclesial communion which he tried to challenge out of its rampant Pharisaism, as he saw it. One of his charges to his own community was the (then offensive) suggestion of a crypto-Papist attitude. However, the suspicion that the Roman Catholic tradition relies on works where only faith will do was ingrained in Charles Wesley. In a journal-letter to his brother John three years after his Oxford sermon, he identifies the "worst error of Popery" as "Justification by Works,"[37] and in one of the hymns written after his son was received into the Roman Catholic Church, Wesley pleads for Samuel to be "Free from the partial, blind respect, The *shibboleth* that marks his Sect":

> Not like the simple croud misled,
> Who leaning on a broken reed,
>   Refuse a pardon *given*,
> But hope the grace by works to *buy*;
> Or on a friar's Cowl rely
>   To carry them to heaven.[38]

It is ironic in this context that the Wesleys were charged with being Papists by other Protestant groups because they did allow for a positive place for "works" in the overall *ordo salutis*. The Wesleys' charge against Roman Catholicism was that it allowed a place for works where there simply can be none: in the act of a sinner being justified.

"Doctrines of the hellish foe"

The poem quoted above gives a glimpse of another issue which Charles Wesley obviously identified as particularly problematic in the Roman Catholic tradition:

> Thy power be in his weakness seen,
> Nor let him the commands of men
>   Rashly mistake for thine,
> Nor heed to lying wonders give,
> Or legendary tales receive
>   As oracles divine.
>
> Preserve, that he may never know
> Those doctrines of the hellish foe
>   Which contradict thy word.[39]

Underlying this plea for his son is clearly Wesley's suspicion that the Roman Catholic Church has added "legendary tales" and doctrines—and ones which *contradict* the Scriptures—to God's all-sufficient word.

There are some other hints in Charles Wesley's writings of popular charges against the Roman Catholic tradition: that priests attempt to forgive sins, that the Papacy has been set up over and against Christ's lordship in the Church, that the Dominicans propagated predestinarian views long before Calvin, and that Jesuits invariably are villains. But all these charges are never spelled out at length and might best be read as supporting an *argumentum ex silentio*: There are no long and sustained attacks on the Roman Catholic Church in Charles Wesley's writings as a whole because tensions with the Roman Catholic tradition were not in the forefront of theological struggles within the Methodist revival, and were not a primary concern of Charles Wesley. This observation in turn encourages a look beyond the occasional charges against Roman Catholicism in Charles Wesley's writings to more positive points of contact with the Roman Catholic tradition.

The Catholic Tradition as a Source in Charles Wesley's Hymns

There is another possible approach to the general topic "Charles Wesley and Roman Catholicism" than simply looking at Wesley's explicit statements on the matter. The claim could be made that one finds a quite positive *implicit* relationship to the Roman Catholic tradition particularly in the Wesleyan hymns, which somewhat counterbalances the *explicit—* not infrequently negative—statements about Roman Catholicism in the Wesleyan corpus as a whole.

It is not the place here to analyze in detail the theological tenets of the Wesleyan hymns and the degree of their affinity with the Roman Catholic tradition. It would not be difficult to show—especially in an age of heightened ecumenical sensibilities—that on the fundamentals of the faith there is indeed an obvious convergence between the two traditions.

Granted that this is the case, it is worth noting that there are also some more direct positive links with the Roman Catholic tradition in the hymns of Charles Wesley. Henry Bett has noted a number of instances where Charles Wesley seems to be directly dependent on medieval authors, particularly Thomas Aquinas and Adam of St. Victor.[40] Whether Charles Wesley really knew the Roman Breviary, as Bett claims, should, however, not be deduced from Wesley's acknowledgment that he quoted to Roman Catholics "their own Liturgy." By this, Wesley may just as well have been referring to the Missal or another Roman Catholic liturgical book. After all, the Breviary at that time was the prayer book for priests; lay people would mostly not have been familiar with any more than its name. For Wesley to quote from it certainly would not have provided his hearers with familiar material.

Maybe more important than prooftexting direct Roman Catholic sources in the hymns is the fact of a "Catholic spirit"[41] (note that I am not speaking of a *Roman* Catholic spirit) pervading many of the hymns. Rather than analyzing this "Catholic spirit" in detail here, let me suggest two factors which I consider to be at the roots of it. There are, first of all, remnants of what can be called a traditional Catholic spirituality evident in Charles Wesley's hymns. To name but four of its characteristics: a high regard for the sacramental life of the Church, a deep appreciation for the liturgical year, a continuous commitment to "Mother Church," and a reverence for the Tradition of the Church, particularly that of the early church. These characteristics obviously are not the exclusive property of the Roman Catholic tradition, but are a heritage shared with, amongst others, the Eastern Churches (both "Chalcedonian" and "non-Chalcedonian") and the high church tradition within Anglicanism. Charles Wesley's "Catholic spirit"—as is to be expected—does not contain much that can be characterized as distinctly Roman,[42] but does breathe a deep catholicity as defined along the lines suggested above.

Another root of this "Catholic spirit" is provided by the category of doxological language operative in most Wesleyan hymns—at least those which have developed any kind of sustained reception history. Doxological language—the language of adoration, praise, and thanksgiving—usually does not lend itself to confessional polemics. Rather, it provides a doxological "bond" even where theologically traditions may still differ substantially (it has been noted before how hymns transcended confessional boundaries long before Christians of different ecclesial communities were able to engage in meaningful theological dialogue[43]). The category of doxological language may also provide a clue to Bernard Manning's comparison of the hymnbook of 1780 with the Canon of the Mass(!), the *Book of Common Prayer*, and the Psalms. Not only are all four works of "supreme devotional art,"[44] all four are also doxological material, used in the community of faith to praise the triune God. In this praise of God, "Real Christians of all Denominations"[45] find a degree of communion usually not found around dogmatic compendia.

Conclusion

"Charles Wesley and Roman Catholicism" is not a subject Wesley ever chose to say anything about in an ordered fashion or a lengthy treatise. We only have some brief remarks, and a few rather emotional reactions to particular situations in his life as the basis from which to gather information on "Charles Wesley and Roman Catholicism." If the nature of the material allows for any conclusion at all, it would, I suggest, have to be the following:[46]

Charles Wesley, never having personally confronted the Roman Catholic tradition in any real depth, in many respects simply mirrors the attitude of his age, his society, and his ecclesial communion. There is a largely unreflective unease with the Roman Catholic Church in most of

217

his writings. Where Charles Wesley names specifics, he repeats the typical charges against Roman Catholicism: of having added Tradition to Scripture, and works to faith. On the other hand, however, Wesley also reflects the implicitly ecumenical impetus of the pietist and evangelical revival movements of his age. There is the overall importance of "strangely warmed hearts"—whether they beat in Roman Catholics or not, and there is a deep concern with holy living—whether practiced by Roman Catholics or others. The two positions—one of general bias against Roman Catholicism, and one of pietist indifferences towards ecclesiastical divisions—are not always consistent with each other, but when both are held they would seem to lead to what we find in Charles Wesley: sometimes general unease, sometimes specific criticisms, sometimes acceptance and positive drawing on the Roman Catholic tradition, but—due to the lack of in-depth confrontation with the Roman Catholic tradition—no sustained effort at dialogue.

A sustained effort at dialogue between the two traditions had to await the coming of the Ecumenical Movement in the twentieth century. It is to this "century of ecumenism" that we now turn with the question of whether and where Charles Wesley can be seen as a source of dialogue between the Methodist and the Roman Catholic traditions. To do justice to the subject in all its depth, one would of course also need to explore more thoroughly Charles Wesley's lifelong affiliation with the Church of England on the one hand, and acknowledge more systematically the rediscovery of the Anglican Wesley among some Anglicans and Episcopalians in our time. The broadening of horizons beyond the "Methodist captivity" of the Anglican/Methodist Charles Wesley, however, exceeds the confines of this paper.

Charles Wesley as a Source of Dialogue
Between the Methodist and the Roman Catholic Traditions

Even if Charles Wesley himself should not be interpreted as a radical ecumenist bridging the waters between Anglicanism/Methodism and Roman Catholicism long before the Ecumenical Movement, there are nevertheless aspects to the reception history of this one Anglican/Methodist which can properly be highlighted as a welcome signpost on the ecumenical journey. Three areas are worth mentioning here:

Roman Catholic Scholarship and the "Singer of the Evangelical Revival"

The interest of Roman Catholic scholarship in Charles Wesley in a way parallels Wesley's reflections on Roman Catholicism; there is not a lot of material to draw on. A number of works on *John* Wesley's position vis-à-vis Roman Catholicism have already been mentioned.[47] There are a couple of other scholarly works by Roman Catholic authors worth pointing out here, such as the book by the Belgian Franciscan Maximin Piette *La Réaction de John Wesley dans l'Evolution du Protestantisme*. It is a sympathetic treatment of the Methodist Revival, born out of an ecumenical impetus truly unusual for its time.[48] Charles Wesley, however, only is mentioned in passing in Piette's book. More sustained attention is paid to him in an article by the Roman Catholic priest Francis Frost, "Biblical Imagery and Religious Experience in the Hymns of the Wesleys,"[49] and in the recent dissertation by a German Roman Catholic on the *1780 Collection*.[50] But these works by Roman Catholic scholars are rather isolated instances of interest in Charles Wesley. This lack of interest should not be astonishing when compared to the relative lack of interest in Charles Wesley, say in comparison with John Wesley, even in Methodist scholarship. Lastly, the lack of scholarly attention given to the particular subject of "Charles Wesley and Roman Catholicism" could also be read as a tribute to Charles Wesley's relative moderation and reservation on the issue.

Roman Catholic Hymnals

Charles Wesley's presence in Roman Catholic hymnbooks is more noticeable than in Roman Catholic scholarship (a quite appropriate imbalance one might add). The presence of Wesleyan hymns in Roman Catholic hymnbooks seems to be dependent directly on the presence of the Methodist tradition in the culture in which the Roman Catholic Church finds itself. In other words: in North America, for example, where the Methodist influence is quite noticeable and where the Wesley hymns are accessible in their original language, one finds a sizeable number of them being incorporated into Roman Catholic hymnals. In Great Britain Wesley hymns have appeared in Roman Catholic hymnbooks only very recently. In Germany or Peru on the other hand, where Methodists are a minority and utterly marginal in the life of the local culture, and where Methodists themselves only have access to Charles Wesley through translations, none of his hymns has made its way into Roman Catholic hymnbooks.

The presence of Charles Wesley's hymns in Roman Catholic hymnals, then, has relatively little to do with questions of doctrinal compatibility between the two traditions—at least in this day and age. The real motivating factor seems to be the strength of a community faithfully living with the hymns of one of its founding fathers and thereby offering these hymns as vessels of worship to other communities. In North America, this offering has been accepted by a number of Roman Catholic worship books and hymnals. To name just three examples: the standard resource in the United States, *Worship II*, contains amongst its over 300 hymns nine by Charles Wesley, one given twice with two different melodies.[51] The *St. John the Baptist Book of Catholic Worship* contains eight Wesleyan hymns, with three of them appearing with different melodies.[52] The Canadian *Catholic Book of Worship* lists five Wesley hymns, two of them again appearing twice, with differing melodies.[53] Wesleyan hymns centering on the liturgical year, such as Christmas or Easter hymns, quite naturally are particular favorites in Roman Catholic hymnals, while hymns celebrating an evangelical conversion experience do not enjoy the same popularity. "O for a thousand tongues to sing," for example, is conspicuously absent from the Roman Catholic hymnals named above. Absent also are Wesley's eucharistic hymns, but this certainly has more to do with their overall non-reception history in Methodist hymnals than with a particular Roman Catholic bias. In fact, the "Roman Catholic bias" would work in favor of most of them.

The Ecumenical Dialogue

There is a third area where Charles Wesley is finding a positive reception history in the ongoing journey of Methodism and Roman Catholicism, namely in the ecumenical dialogue between the two ecclesial communions. Particularly the Methodist—Roman Catholic Conversations on a world level have repeatedly drawn attention to the hymns of Charles Wesley. In the so-called Denver Report of 1971, the dialogue partners state:

> If a Methodist ideal was expressed in the phrase "a theology that can be sung," it was appreciated on the Roman Catholic side that the hymns of Charles Wesley, a rich source of Methodist spirituality, find echoes and recognition in the Catholic soul.[54]

Especially the eucharistic hymns of Charles Wesley are repeatedly alluded to in the dialogue,[55] and under the suggestions for further ecumenical projects one finds a plea for "sympathetic commented editions of the works of one side by members of the other," with the hymns of Charles Wesley mentioned as the first example.[56] Altogether, there is no single point in the dialogue where Charles Wesley and his hymns are seen as a point of division between the two ecclesial traditions. On the contrary, Charles Wesley is more often than not interpreted as a point of bridging the distance between the two.

The positive reception of the hymns of Charles Wesley in both Roman Catholic hymnals and the ecumenical dialogue between the Roman Catholic Church and the World Methodist Council seems to support the contention of a "Catholic spirit" pervading the Wesleyan hymns. In order not to read this "Catholicity" in too one-sided a direction (namely the direction of Roman Catholicity—which would be misinterpreting Wesley), I want to close with a hymn by Charles Wesley which not only expresses a truly "Catholic" but a profoundly ecumenical spirit. It may not be amongst the best poetic texts of Charles Wesley, but it evidences an ecumenical motivation long before the Ecumenical Movement as we know it began:

No, they cry, it cannot be!
Christians never will agree!
All the world Thy word deny,
Yet we on the truth rely,
Sure, in that appointed day,
Thou wilt give us all one way,
Show us each to other join'd,
One in heart, and one in mind.

Hasten then the general peace,
Bid Thy people's discord cease,
All united in thy name,
Let us think, and speak the same:
Then the world shall know and own
God Himself hath made us one,
Thee their Lord with us embrace,
Sing Thine everlasting praise.[57]

221

Contributors

Thomas R. Albin is Assistant Professor of Christian Formation and Faith Education, Dubuque Theological Seminary, University of Dubuque, Dubuque, IA.

Frank Baker is Professor Emeritus of English Church History, The Divinity School, Duke University, Durham, NC.

Oliver A. Beckerlegge is a supernumerary British Methodist Minister, author, and Wesley scholar, York, England.

Teresa Berger is Associate Professor of Ecumenical Theology, The Divinity School, Duke University, Durham, NC.

Horton Davies is Henry W. Putnam Professor Emeritus of the History of Christianity, Princeton University, Princeton, NJ.

Richard P. Heitzenrater is Albert Outler Professor of Wesley Studies, Perkins School of Theology, Southern Methodist University, Dallas, TX.

S T Kimbrough, Jr. is Founder and President of The Charles Wesley Society, Madison, NJ.

Thomas A. Langford is William K. Quick Professor of Theology and Methodist Studies, The Divinity School, Duke University, Durham, NC.

Robin A. Leaver is Associate Professor of Church Music, Westminster Choir College, Princeton, NJ.

Kenneth D. Shields is Associate Professor of English, Southern Methodist University, Dallas, TX.

Laurence Hull Stookey is H. L. Elderdice Professor of Preaching and Worship, Wesley Theological Seminary, Washington, DC.

Abbreviations

Poet. Works = *The Poetical Works of John and Charles Wesley*, 13 vols., ed. George Osborn (London: 1868–72). Citations from these volumes will be made by the volume and page number, e.g. *Poet. Works* 10:198–9.

Rep. Verse = *Representative Verse of Charles Wesley*, ed. Frank Baker (Nashville: Abingdon, 1962). Poems from this volume will be cited by their number followed by the page number, e.g. *Rep. Verse*, no. 245, pp. 272–4.

Short Hymns = Charles Wesley, *Short Hymns on Select Passages of the Holy Scriptures*, 2 vols. (Bristol: Farley, 1762). Citations from these volumes will be made by the volume and page number, e.g. *Short Hymns* 1:64.

Journal = *The Journal of The Rev. Charles Wesley, M.A.*, 2 vols., ed. Thomas Jackson (London: Mason, 1849). Citations from these volumes will be made by volume and page number, e.g. *Journal* 2:22.

Unpub. Poetry = *The Unpublished Poetry of Charles Wesley*, 3 vols., ed. S T Kimbrough, Jr. and Oliver A. Beckerlegge (Nashville: Abingdon Press/Kingswood Books, 1988–1991). Citations from these volumes will be made by the volume and page number, e.g. *Unpub. Poetry* 1:155.

Shorthand Sermons = *Charles Wesley's Earliest Evangelical Sermons*, transcribed from the original shorthand by Thomas R. Albin and Oliver A. Beckerlegge (Ilford: Wesley Historical Society, 1987). Citations from this volume will be made by page number, e.g. *Shorthand Sermons*, 42.

1780 Collection = *A Collection of Hymns for the Use of the People Called Methodists*, ed. Franz Hildebrandt and Oliver A. Beckerlegge with the assistance of James Dale, in the series *The Works of John Wesley*, vol. 7 (Oxford: Clarendon Press, 1983). Citations from this work will be made by page number, e.g. *1780 Collection*, 475.

Proceedings = *Proceedings of the Wesley Historical Society* published currently by Robert Odcombe Associates of Ilford (Essex), England. Citations from this periodical will be made by volume, year, and page number, e.g. *Proceedings* 37 (1970):110.

Works = *The Works of John Wesley*, begun as "The Oxford Edition of the Works of John Wesley" (Oxford: Clarendon Press, 1975–1983), continued as "The Bicentennial Edition of the Works of John Wesley" (Nashville: Abingdon Press, 1984–). Citations from this series will be made by volume and page number, e.g. *Works* 11:123, except for volume 7 which is abbreviated as above: *1780 Collection*.

Notes*

Preface

1. Frank Baker, *Charles Wesley as Revealed by His Letters* (London: Epworth Press, 1948).
2. See p. 108 below.
3. See p. 111 below.
4. See p. 159 below.
5. For the influence of the Moravian and Lutheran traditions see Franz Hildebrandt, *From Luther to Wesley* (London: Lutterworth Press, 1951); John L. Nuelsen, *John Wesley und das deutsche Kirchenlied*, English translation, *John Wesley and the German Hymn*, by Theo Parry, Sydney H. Moore, and Arthur Holbrook (Calverley, Yorkshire: A. Holbrook, 1972); J. Ernest Rattenbury, *The Conversion of the Wesleys: A Critical Study* (London: Epworth Press, 1938), 25, 72, 89, 164, 171, 183, 231. For the importance of the doctrine of justification by faith see the chapter by Robin A. Leaver, "Charles Wesley and Anglicanism."

Chapter 1
Berger, *Charles Wesley: A Literary Overview*

1. This is an English translation of Teresa Berger's article "Charles Wesley und sein Liedgut: eine Literaturübersicht," which originally appeared in *Theologische Revue* 6 (1988):442–50. Some minor revisions and editorial changes have been made for publication of the article in this form.
2. Cf. Richard P. Heitzenrater, "The Quest of the First Methodist: Oxford Methodism Reconsidered," *Mirror and Memory: Reflections on Early Methodism* (Nashville: Abingdon Press/Kingswood Books, 1989), 63–77.
3. One seldom finds works which attempt to deal with both brothers simultaneously. The following should be cited as exceptions: Mabel Richmond Brailsford, *A Tale of Two Brothers: John and Charles Wesley* (New York: Oxford University Press, 1954), where the author operates primarily from an historical perspective; Samuel J. Rogal, *John and Charles Wesley* (Boston: Twayne Publishers, 1983), which is dedicated to the literary production of the brothers; and theologically most important, Frank Whaling, ed., *John and Charles Wesley: Selected Prayers, Hymns, Journal, Notes, Sermons, Letters and Treatises* (New York: Paulist Press, 1981). One bibliography is available: Betty M. Jarboe, *John and Charles Wesley: A Bibliography* (Metuchen: Scarecrow Press, 1987).

* Only the first citation of a work is given with full bibliographical information. Throughout the volume subsequent references to a work are generally cited only by author and title.

227

4. A good overview of the current state of Wesley research (with, as one might expect, an emphasis on John Wesley) is offered by Richard P. Heitzenrater, "The Present state of Wesley Studies," *Methodist History* 22 (1984):221–33.

5. See the *1780 Collection*.

6. The mammoth project with its thirty-five planned volumes was begun in 1975 by Oxford University Press under the title "The Oxford Edition of the Works of John Wesley." Frank Baker functioned as editor-in-chief. Since 1984 the project has been entrusted to Abingdon Press (Nashville, TN) as "The Bicentennial Edition of the Works of John Wesley." Richard P. Heitzenrater is currently editor-in-chief. A two-volume interpretive bibliography of the complete works of John Wesley is planned as a part of this series.

7. See *Unpub. Poetry*.

8. Cf. the research overview on John Wesley in Vilem Schneeberger, *Theologische Wurzeln des sozialen Akzents bei John Wesley* (Zürich: Gotthelf-Verlag, 1974), 18.

9. Cf. for example, John Whitehead, *The Life of the Reverend Charles Wesley, M.A., late Student of Christ Church, Oxford, Collected From His Private Journal* (Dublin: J. Jones, 1793 [1st edition], 1805 [2nd edition]); John Telford, *The Life of Rev. Charles Wesley, M.A.* (London: Religious Tract Society, 1886 [1st edition], 1900 [2nd edition]).

10. Charles Adams, *The Poet Preacher: A Brief Memorial of Charles Wesley, the Eminent Preacher and Poet* (New York: Carlton & Porter, 1859).

11. John Kirk, *Charles Wesley, the Poet of Methodism: A Lecture* (London: John Mason, 1860).

12. Frank Colquhoun, *Charles Wesley, 1707–1788: The Poet of the Evangelical Revival* (London: Church Book Room Press, n.d.). This pamphlet is only 40 pages in length but presents a precise and balanced introduction to Charles Wesley.

13. F. Luke Wiseman, *Charles Wesley, Evangelist and Poet* (New York: Abingdon Press, 1932); similarly, F. Luke Wiseman, *Charles Wesley and his Hymns* (London: Epworth Press, n.d. [1938?]).

14. Elmer T. Clark, *Charles Wesley: The Singer of the Evangelical Revival* (Nashville: The Upper Room, 1957).

15. Elizabeth P. Myers, *Singer of Six Thousand Songs: A Life of Charles Wesley* (London/New York: Thomas Nelson, 1965).

16. Frederick C. Gill, *Charles Wesley, the First Methodist* (New York: Abingdon Press, 1964).

17. See *Poet. Works*. The volumes included 4,600 published individual pieces of both Wesleys and approximately 3,000 of the, until then, unpublished texts of Charles Wesley which, however, did not represent his entire legacy. Also, certain of the texts published by Osborn were abridged without being identified as having been shortened.

18. See *Journal*. This edition of the journal was not complete. Some sixty years later appeared *The Journal of the Reverend Charles Wesley: The Early Journal, 1736–1739*, ed. John Telford (London: Culley, 1910). Actually, a three-volume edition of the journal was planned of which only the first volume ever appeared. In 1977 this volume was reprinted under the same title by The Methodist Reprint

Society in Taylors, SC. The Jackson edition of 1849 has in the meantime been newly reissued (Kansas City: Beacon Hill Press, and Grand Rapids: Baker Book House, 1980).

19. Thomas Jackson, *The Life of the Rev. Charles Wesley, M.A., Sometime Student of Christ-Church, Oxford: Comprising a Review of his Poetry; Sketches of the Rise and Progress of Methodism; with Notices of Contemporary Events and Characters*, 2 vols. (London: John Mason, 1841 [1st edition]). An American edition appeared three years later in New York published by G. Lane and P. P. Sanford.

20. *Sermons By the Late Reverend Charles Wesley, M.A.* (London: Baldwin, Cradock, and Joy, 1816).

21. See *Shorthand Sermons.*

22. Thus, for example Franklin Wilder, *The Methodist Riots: The Testing of Charles Wesley* (Great Neck: Todd & Honeywell, 1981). The author concentrates on the struggles of the nascent Methodist movement between the years 1739 and 1756.

23. Arnold A. Dallimore, *A Heart Set Free: The Life of Charles Wesley* (Westchester: Crossway, 1988).

24. Ibid., 73.

25. Wesley's hymns had certainly received considerable attention in work done on Methodist hymnbooks. Cf. for example, David Creamer, *Methodist Hymnology; Comprehending Notices of the Poetical Works of John and Charles Wesley* (New York: Joseph Longking, 1848).

26. Henry Bett, *The Hymns of Methodism in Their Literary Relations* (London: Epworth Press, 1913 [1st edition], 1920 [2nd edition], revised 1945 [3rd edition]).

27. Ibid., 2.

28. Ibid., 129–35.

29. Robert Newton Flew, *The Hymns of Charles Wesley: A Study of Their Structure* (London: Epworth Press, 1953).

30. See *Rep. Verse.*

31. Frank Baker, *Charles Wesley's Verse: An Introduction* (London: Epworth Press, 1964 [1st edition], 1988 [2nd edition]). Baker's preliminary work for an edition of the letters of Charles Wesley is also important; see *Charles Wesley as Revealed by His Letters* (London: Epworth Press, 1948), and "The Prose Writings of Charles Wesley" in *London Quarterly and Holborn Review* 182 (1957):268–74.

32. Donald Davie, *Purity of Diction in English Verse* (New York: Chatto and Windus, 1953), 70–81.

33. Among others, see especially Davie (ibid.) and Dale (see note 38 below). Frederick C. Gill, *The Romantic Movement and Methodism: A Study of English Romanticism and the Evangelical Revival* (London: Epworth Press, 1937 [1st edition], 1957 [2nd edition]) makes the case for the connection with Romanticism, still more for the influence of Methodism on emerging Romanticism. Cf. also Mark A. Noll, "Romanticism and the Hymns of Charles Wesley," in *Evangelical Quarterly* 46 (1974):195–223.

34. J. Ernest Rattenbury, *The Evangelical Doctrines of Charles Wesley's Hymns* (London: Epworth Press, 1941 [1st edition], 1942 [2nd edition]).

35. J. Ernest Rattenbury, *The Eucharistic Hymns of John and Charles Wesley* (London: Epworth Press, 1948). A reprint has recently been published by the Order of Saint Luke Publications in Cleveland, Ohio.

36. Bernard L. Manning, *The Hymns of Wesley and Watts* (London: Epworth Press, 1942 [1st edition], 1948 [2nd edition]).

37. George H. Findlay, *Christ's Standard Bearer: A Study in the Hymns of Charles Wesley as They are Contained in the Last Edition (1876) of A Collection of Hymns For the Use of the People Called Methodists by the Reverend John Wesley, M.A.* (London: Epworth Press, 1956).

38. James Dale, *The Theological and Literary Qualities of the Poetry of Charles Wesley in Relation to the Standards of his Age* (Dissertation, Cambridge, 1960). Cf. also James Dale, "Some Echoes of Charles Wesley's Hymns in His Journal," in *London Quarterly and Holborn Review* 184 (1959):336–44.

39. Gilbert L. Morris, *Imagery in the Hymns of Charles Wesley* (Dissertation, University of Arkansas, 1969; Ann Arbor, MI: University Microfilms, 1981).

40. Barbara Ann Welch, *Charles Wesley and the Celebrations of Evangelical Experience* (Dissertation, University of Michigan [1971], Ann Arbor, MI: University Microfilms, 1973).

41. James C. Ekrut, *Universal Redemption, Assurance of Salvation, and Christian Perfection in the Hymns of Charles Wesley, With Poetic Analyses and Tune Examples* (M.Mus. thesis, Southwestern Baptist Theological Seminary, Fort Worth, TX, 1978).

42. James A. Townsend, *Feelings Related to Assurance in Charles Wesley's Hymns* (Dissertation, Fuller Theological Seminary, Pasadena, CA, 1979).

43. John R. Tyson, *Charles Wesley's Theology of the Cross: An Examination of the Theology and Method of Charles Wesley as Seen in His Doctrine of the Atonement* (Dissertation, Drew University, Madison, NJ, 1983; Ann Arbor, MI: University Microfilms, 1986). A summary is offered by John R. Tyson, "Charles Wesley's Theology of Redemption: A Study in Structure and Method" in *Wesleyan Theological Journal* 20 (1985):7–28.

44. John R. Tyson, *Charles Wesley on Sanctification: A Biographical and Theological Study* (Grand Rapids: Francis Asbury Press, 1986). Along the same lines cf. also A. Harold Wood, "Charles Wesley's Hymns on Holiness" in *Dig or Die: Papers Given at the World Methodist Historical Society Wesley Heritage Conference, 1980*, ed. James S. Udy and Eric G. Clancy (Sidney: World Methodist Historical Society, 1981), 67–76.

45. *Charles Wesley: A Reader*, ed. John R. Tyson (New York: Oxford University Press, 1989).

46. Teresa Berger, *Theologie in Hymnen? Zum Verhältnis von Theologie und Doxologie am Beispiel der "Collection of Hymns For the Use of the People Called Methodists" (1780)* (Altenberge: Telos-Verlag, 1989).

47. Craig Gallaway, *The Presence of Christ With the Worshipping Community: A Study in the Hymns of John and Charles Wesley* (Dissertation, Emory University, Atlanta, GA, 1988; Ann Arbor, MI: University Microfilms, 1989). Also see his article on the influence of Charles Wesley's hymns on *The United Methodist Hymnal*: Craig Gallaway, "Tradition Meets Revision: The Impact of the Wesley

Hymn Corpus on the New United Methodist Hymnal" in *Quarterly Review* 9 (1989):64-79.

48. Wilma Jean Quantrille, *The Triune God in the Hymns of Charles Wesley* (Dissertation, Drew University, Madison, NJ, 1989; Ann Arbor, MI: University Microfilms, 1989).

49. See especially the publications in the series "Beiträge zur Geschichte des Methodismus" and "Beiträge zur Geschichte der evangelisch-methodistischen Kirche."

50. The only biography known to me comes from Karl G. Eissele, *Karl Wesley, Sänger des Methodismus* (Bremen: Anker Verlag, 1932). To Eissele's credit, he includes in this biography translations of a few chosen Charles Wesley hymns. See also Henry Bett, "German Books on Wesley's Hymns," *Proceedings* 21 (1938):180-181, which contains a discussion of the books of Eissele and Nuelsen.

51. Cf. Karl Dahn, "Die Hymnologie im deutschsprachigen Methodismus" in *Der Methodismus*, ed. Carl Ernst Sommer (Stuttgart: Evangelisches Verlagswerk, 1968), 166-84.

52. Nuelsen, *John Wesley und das deutsche Kirchenlied* (English translation: *John Wesley and the German Hymn*). On this theme see also Oliver A. Beckerlegge, "John Wesley and the German Hymns," *London Quarterly and Holborn Review* 165 (1940):430-439; and Henry Bett, "John Wesley's Translations of German Hymns," *London Quarterly and Holborn Review* 165 (1940):288-94. For Charles Wesley, see John R. Tyson, "Charles Wesley and the German Hymns" in *The Hymn* 35 (1984):153-57, where additional literature is listed.

53. Erika Mayer, *Charles Wesleys Hymnen. Eine Untersuchung und literarische Würdigung* (Dissertation, Tübingen, 1957).

54. Franz Hildebrandt, *From Luther to Wesley* (London: Lutterworth Press, 1951); also his *Christianity According to the Wesleys* (London: Epworth Press, 1956); *Wesley Hymn Book*, ed. Franz Hildebrandt (London: A. Weekes and Co., 1958 [1st edition], 1960 [2nd edition]). See also note 5 above.

55. Cf. Martin Schmidt, *John Wesley*, 2 vols. (Zürich: Gotthelf-Verlag, 1953–1966); English translation: *John Wesley: A Theological Biography* (London: Epworth Press, 1962-1973); Martin Schmidt, "Methodismus" in *Religion in Geschichte und Gegenwart* (1960), 4:913-19; Martin Schmidt, "Methodismus" in *Konfessionskunde*, ed. Friedrich Heyer (Berlin: de Gruyter, 1977), 595-605.

56. At least one article from the abundance of literature in 1988 is referred to here: Frank Baker, "Charles Wesley's Productivity as a Religious Poet" in *Proceedings* 47 (1989):1-12.

57. See, for example, S T Kimbrough, Jr., *Lost in Wonder. Charles Wesley: The Meaning of His Hymns Today* (Nashville: Upper Room Books, 1987); and Timothy Dudley-Smith, ed., *A Flame of Love: A Personal Choice of Charles Wesley's Verse* (London: Triangle, 1987). J. Alan Kay, ed., *Wesley's Prayers and Praises* (London: Epworth Press, 1958), is representative of earlier anthologies in this style.

58. However, cf. Richard L. Fleming, *The Concept of Sacrifice in the Eucharistic Hymns of John and Charles Wesley* (Dissertation, Southern Methodist University, Dallas, TX, 1980). As to the latter theme, see Kathryn Nichols, "Charles Wesley's

Eucharistic Hymns: Their Relationship to the Book of Common Prayer" in *The Hymn* 39 (1988):13–21.

59. Also important here are the non-Wesleyan sources from the early stages of the Methodist Renewal movement, e.g. journal entries about Charles Wesley. Cf. Geoffrey F. Nuttall, "Charles Wesley in 1739. By Joseph William of Kidderminster" in *Proceedings* 42 (1980):181–85.

60. See S T Kimbrough, Jr. "Charles Wesley as a Biblical Interpreter," *Methodist History* 26 (1988):139–53. The brief book published by John W. Waterhouse, *The Bible in Charles Wesley's Hymns* (London: Epworth Press, 1954), is not an adequate appraisal of the subject.

61. See Elizabeth [Hannon] Hart, *The Influence of Paradise Lost on the Hymns of Charles Wesley* (M. A. Thesis, University of British Columbia, 1985).

62. H. A. Hodges and A. M. Allchin, eds., *A Rapture of Praise: Hymns of John and Charles Wesley*, (London: Hodder and Stoughton, 1966).

63. Francis Frost, "Biblical Imagery and Religious Experience in the Hymns of the Wesleys" in *Proceedings* 42 (1980):158–66.

Chapter 2
Beckerlegge, *Charles Wesley's Poetical Corpus*

1. T. W. Herbert, *John Wesley as Editor and Author* (Princeton: Princeton University Press, 1940), 37.

2. Baker, *Charles Wesley's Verse*, 6.

3. Ibid., 14.

4. Alan Dunstan, "The Use of Wesley's Hymns in Contemporary Worship," *The Epworth Review* (May 1988), 56.

5. *The Methodist Hymn Book* (1933), Preface.

6. *Unpub. Poetry* 1:108.

7. Rattenbury, *Evangelical Doctrines*, 60.

8. *Rep. Verse*, 167–68.

9. *Poet. Works* 8:xv-xvi.

10. Bett, *The Hymns of Methodism*, 21–33.

11. *Rep. Verse*, 93–97.

12. Herbert, *John Wesley as Editor and Author*, 58.

13. Ibid., 128.

Chapter 3
Shields, *Charles Wesley as Poet*

1. *1780 Collection*, 44.

2. *Unpub. Poetry* 1:11.

3. *1780 Collection*, 74–75.

4. J.E. Rattenbury, *The Evangelical Doctrines of Charles Wesley's Hymns* (London: Epworth Press, 1941), 48.

5. MS Psalms; *Poet. Works* 8:46.

6. Richard Crashaw, "On our crucified Lord Naked and bloody," *The*

Complete Poetry of Richard Crashaw, ed. George Walton Williams (New York: New York University Press, 1972), 24.

7. *Hymns for the Use of Families, on various occasions* (Bristol, 1767), no. 161; *Poet. Works* 7:194-95.

8. *Hymns and Sacred Poems* (London, 1740), 120-123; *Poet. Works* 1:299-300.

9. *Unpub. Poetry* 1:172.

10. Ibid., 173.

11. Ibid., 176.

12. Ibid., 177.

13. Ibid., 252.

14. Ibid., 254.

15. Ibid., 304.

16. *Hymns and Sacred Poems* (Bristol, 1742), 115-18; *Poet. Works* 2:173-76.

17. Isaac Watts, *Hymns and Spiritual Songs* (London, 1709), 2nd edition, no. 74, pp. 57-58.

Chapter 4

Baker, *Charles Wesley's Letters*

1. *Proceedings* 25 (1945-1946):17-23.

2. Ibid., 97-104.

3. Another reader of my article was not so generous, but in two newspaper columns claimed that I had falsified the evidence because of my willingness to sacrifice Charles rather than John; see *Irish Christian Advocate,* September 26 & October 10, 1947.

4. Frank Baker, *John Wesley and the Church of England* (London: Epworth Press, 1970), 109.

5. *Proceedings* 47 (1989):8-9.

6. Baker, *Charles Wesley as Revealed by His Letters,* 56-57.

7. Ibid., 63-67.

8. *Rep. Verse,* 201-3.

9. Ibid., 200-1; *cf.* 198-99.

10. The Methodist Archives (Manchester), CW Letters I, 106, containing an endorsement by Sally which it might be possible to decipher.

11. We give the dating clues for these letters, together with the tentative numbers assigned to them, followed by some brief elucidatory notes: "December 23. London" [112], "Friday Night. Ln."[113], "Tues. Morn."[114], "December 27. Tues. Even."[114/3], "Fri. Dec 30."[115], one completely undated [116], "London, January 3."[117], "Shoreham Thur. Night"[118], "Shoreham. Sat. Morn"[119], "Sun. Morn."[120], "Tues. Nit." [121], "To S.G."[122].

The notes: 116 contains some potential internal clues. 118 offers some internal clues indicating January 5, 1749, as the most likely date; 119 seems to be January 14: Wesley's *Journal* for Friday January 13 notes the receipt of Mrs. Gwynne's rejection of John Wesley's offer of annual assistance, and the following day Charles visited Shoreham to seek Perronet's support. 120, four closely written pages, probably a draft of a letter written January 15, with a reference to

"Mrs. D[ewal]," probably visited at Lewisham the previous day. This may well lead to the short letter beginning "Tues. Nit." [121], i.e. January 17, announcing, "On Sat. & Mon. you shall hear from me again." 122, an octavo scrap, perhaps written Saturday, January 21, "to S.G. I have nothing to add, only pray for our happy meeting here. . . ."

12. See Baker, *Charles Wesley as Revealed by His Letters*, 82–87.

13. *Works* 26:479. The surviving copy of Charles's letter was endorsed by him "August 4, 1752," but John's reply shows that this was an error for "August 4, 1751."

14. Baker, *John Wesley and the Church of England*, 161–63.

15. Ibid., 164–67, 326–40.

16. *Works* 26:582–86; *cf.* Baker, *John Wesley and the Church of England*, 169–71.

17. Baker, *Charles Wesley as Revealed by His Letters*, 96–97 (October 23, 1756).

18. Ibid., 97–103; *cf.* Baker, *John Wesley and the Church of England*, 174–79.

19. Ibid., 272–82.

20. The Methodist Archives (Manchester), Wesley Family Letters, IV, 15.

21. The Methodist Archives (Manchester), CW Letters II, 39.

22. The Methodist Archives (Manchester), Wesley Family Letters, IV, 59.

23. Copy in hand of Dr. Adam Clarke in album of James Kirkby, Leeds, at Duke University, Durham, NC.

24. Wesley's Chapel, London, Dodsworth Legacy.

25. The Methodist Archives (Manchester), Wesley Family Letters, IV, 62.

26. Moravian Archives (London). First and second sentences adapted for the Adams-Acton monument to the Wesleys in Westminster Abbey.

27. *Methodist Magazine*, 3rd Series, 5 (1826):33.

28. Emory University, Atlanta, GA.

29. The Methodist Archives (Manchester), Charles Wesley's Letter-book, 30–31.

30. Jackson, *Life of Charles Wesley*, 2:430. For Vincent Perronet see *Proceedings* 16 (1927):40–47, and *Wesley's Chapel Magazine* (Summer 1985), 9–14.

Chapter 5

Albin, *Charles Wesley's Other Prose Writings*

1. Letter to John Wesley (January 22, 1729), *Works* 25:236.

2. "Letters" and "letter days" were part of the early Methodist experience. The terms are a short form of jargon referring to letters of spiritual autobiography and significant religious experience. The Wesley brothers continued this tradition found among Puritans, Pietists and Moravians before them. It came into the eighteenth century through organizations like the corresponding membership of the SPCK. On April 9, 1739, John Wesley wrote to ask members of the London society for letters about their spiritual experience; and a second letter of the same date requested that the four spiritual letters already in existence be forwarded immediately; *Works* 25:628ff. Charles had a similar practice of collecting accounts of personal religious experience; see the two manuscript volumes of Early Methodist Letters now housed in the Methodist

Archives, University of Manchester, England. John Bennet's "Minutes" show that the very first Methodist Conference established a monthly "letter day" for the public reading of these documents; *Wesley Historical Society Occasional Publication* no. 1, p. 17; also p. 27, for the 1745 "letter days" and p. 51 for 1747. Evidence from the journals of John and Charles Wesley makes it clear that this Methodist practice began no later than December of 1738 and continued throughout their lives; see *Journal*, 1:285, 401; 2:73, 182; and *The Journal of the Rev. John Wesley*, ed. Nehemiah Curnock, 8 vols. (London: Epworth Press, 1909-1916), 3:219-24, 485; 4:259; 5:398 n.; 6:373; hereafter *Journal JW*.

3. *Journal*, 1:143f. (February 21, 1739); 192f. (October 30, 1739).

4. I am indebted to Frank Baker's article on "The Prose Writings of Charles Wesley," *London Quarterly Holborn Review* 182 (1957):268-74.

5. See Richard P. Heitzenrater, "John Wesley's Early Sermons," *Proceedings* 37 (1970):110-128.

6. I have listed this sermon here because it was omitted from the new edition of John Wesley's *Sermons*, edited by Albert Outler (*Works*, vols. 1-4). The evidence to suggest that it is actually John's sermon is presented below.

7. See my article in *Methodist History* 21 (1982):60-62, for a more complete discussion of the documents.

8. *Shorthand Sermons*, 73.

9. Ibid., 66-68.

10. John Wesley to Charles Wesley (June 27, 1766), *The Letters of John Wesley*, ed. John Telford, 8 vols. (London: Epworth Press, 1931), 5:16; hereafter *Letters JW*.

11. This observation can be verified in the manuscript letters and journals of the early Methodists who recorded their reflections on the preaching of John and Charles Wesley.

12. Jackson, *Life of Charles Wesley*, 1:275.

13. Charles Wesley, *A Short Account of the Death of Mrs. Hannah Richardson* (London: Strahan, 1741), *passim*.

14. Haliburton was a Scottish puritan of the late seventeenth century; see no. 10 in Richard Green's *The Works of John and Charles Wesley, A Bibliography* (London: Methodist Publishing House, 1906), 13-14.

15. De Renty was a French Roman Catholic nobleman who was a Christian mystic, an active servant of the poor in Paris and a Christian witness at court. See Green's *Bibliography*, no. 21, pp. 17-18.

16. Sermon 46, "The Wilderness State" (1760), *Works* 2:202-21.

17. Tyson, *Charles Wesley on Sanctification*.

18. See 2:140-166.

19. MSS CW, Box III, Colman 5 and 170. All references to manuscript materials are located in the Methodist Archives of the John Rylands University Library at Deansgate, Manchester, England.

20. MS CW Box III, Colman 8.

21. MS CW Box III, Lamplough, 618.

22. MS CW Box III, Lamplough, 667, MSS page [8b].

23. *Rep. Verse*, 387-94.

24. MS CW Sermon.

25. MS Lamplough, 666, 673, 674, 675.

26. MS CW Box III, Colman 4.

27. MS CW Box III, Colman 13, 66, 201.

28. This is a ten page journal fragment for the period from August 14 to October 9, 1769.

29. I am grateful to Alan Rose for sharing this information.

30. Frank Baker has noted that "130 sermons and outlines are preserved in the Colman Collection," see *Charles Wesley as Revealed by His Letters*, 38. This material, of course, must be scrutinized.

Chapter 6

Langford, *Charles Wesley as Theologian*

1. Rattenbury, *Evangelical Doctrines*; Baker, *Charles Wesley as Revealed by His Letters*; and Berger, *Theologie in Hymnen?*

2. *Wesley's Sermons*, ii, 342, quoted in Rattenbury, *Evangelical Doctrines*, 61. In this article I have refrained from quoting Wesley's verses because of the danger of "prooftexting" and inappropriate simplifying of his complex message. Only unusual control of his corpus would justify selective use of his hymns.

3. Rattenbury, *Evangelical Doctrines*, 61.

4. One reason for the lack of systematic presentation is certainly due to Charles Wesley's practice, as Frank Baker describes it, "Throughout his life Charles Wesley kept up the practice of opening his Bible and reading the first sentence which presented itself as God's message. We remember, of course, that in his case this type of sermon preparation was not as dangerous as it would be for most people, for he knew the Scriptures as few have done, and at whatever page he opened he was almost certain to find himself on familiar ground. Even more than his brother John he was a man of one book." Baker also notes that "130 sermons and outlines are preserved in the Colman Collection" and these must be examined carefully in order to determine more clearly the nature of Charles Wesley's homiletical style, content, and practice. See Baker, *Charles Wesley as Revealed by His Letters*, 38.

5. It is clear that Charles provided a different interpretation of Christian perfection. This difference, although noted from the beginning, has been most extensively dealt with by Tyson in *Charles Wesley on Sanctification*; see especially 170–172. Mention must be made of Albin and Beckerlegge's edition of the *Shorthand Sermons*. This carefully done work adds to our knowledge of the thought of the early Charles, but I do not see it as adding any further evidence of a distinctive theological position. See also Richard P. Heitzenrater, "Early Sermons of John and Charles Wesley," *Mirror and Memory*, 150–161. See especially the closing paragraph of the article on 156.

6. Rattenbury (*Evangelical Doctrines*, 90) states roundly, "He showed no signs of originality or adventurousness of thought." See also 95. Thomas Jackson comments with some abrasiveness: "There was a peculiarity in his mental constitution which serves to explain many things in his conduct that would

otherwise appear inexplicable. Above almost every other man, he was the child of feeling; so that it was with the utmost difficulty he ever divested himself of a deep and solemn impression that had been made upon his mind. When once he had received any principles, and regarded them as true and important, he generally retained them to the end of his life. He indeed entertained counter principles, and cherished them with equal tenacity, but without abandoning the old ones. Through many years, therefore, he entertained on various subjects two sets of principles and alternately acted upon them, with equal sincerity: nor does it appear that he ever thought of reconciling them with each other, or even suspected their inconsistency." Thomas Jackson, *Memoir of The Reverend Charles Wesley, M.A.* (London: John Mason, 1862), 478.

7. *1780 Collection*, xi.

8. Ibid., 1. The best discernment of the relation of the work of John and Charles Wesley is found in Baker, *Charles Wesley's Verse* (2nd edition, 1988), 102–15.

9. *1780 Collection*, 5.

10. Ibid., 11.

11. Ibid., 234–36.

12. Ibid., 11–12.

13. Robert E. Cushman, *John Wesley's Experimental Divinity* (Nashville: Abingdon Press/Kingswood Books, 1989), 35f.

14. Arthur S. Gregory, *Praises with Understanding* (London: Epworth Press, 1936), and Berger, 147–55. In discussing his cultural-linguistic model of religious experience, George A. Lindbeck in *The Nature of Doctrine* (Philadelphia: Westminster Press, 1984), 35, describes entry into the religious experience of a particular tradition in ways which are congenial to the function of Charles Wesley's hymns. "To become religious—no less than to become culturally or linguistically competent—is to interiorize a set of skills by practice and training. One learns how to feel, act, and think in conformity with a religious tradition that is, in its inner structure, far richer and more subtle than can be explicitly articulated. The primary knowledge is not *about* the religion, nor *that* the religion teaches such and such, but rather *how* to be religious in such and such ways. Sometimes explicitly formulated statements of the beliefs or behavioral norms of a religion may be helpful in the learning process, but by no means always. Ritual, prayer, [we could add hymns] and example are normally much more important."

15. "The Paradoxes of Creativity," *The American Scholar* (Summer 1989), 342. In a recent article, "Grace, von Balthasar and the Wesleys," in *Freedom and Grace*, ed. Ivor H. Jones and Kenneth B. Wilson (London: Epworth Press, 1988), Ivor Jones makes some suggestive comments which have relevance at this point. Jones investigates von Balthasar's development of aesthetic judgment as integral to theological interpretation. On p. 101, von Balthasar's discussion of Bach's *Art of Fugue* is used as an illustration of the way the Wesley hymns could be approached. The article is suggestive but it does not develop its suggestions. I simply want to note this prospective possibility and hope that the author will extend his discussion.

16. Baker, *Charles Wesley as Revealed by His Letters,* 141. Any complete contextualization of Charles Wesley's hymns would have to include the hymn tunes used and what the combination of words and music might mean for a hermeneutic. I am incapable of doing this more inclusive work; although I have consulted with two persons who have expertise in music, this remains a task to be done by others.

Chapter 7

Kimbrough, *Charles Wesley and Biblical Interpretation*

1. G. H. Gilbert, *Interpretation of the Bible, A Short History* (New York: Macmillan, 1905), 259. See also the studies of Frederic W. Farrar, *History of Interpretation,* (published as the Bampton Lectures in 1885 and reprinted in Grand Rapids: Baker Book House, 1961), 357-96, 420-428; Gordon M. Hyde, editor, *A Symposium on Biblical Hermeneutics* (Washington, DC: Review and Herald Publishing Association, 1974), 61-65; 70-73; R. S. Cripps, "Two British Interpreters of the Old Testament: Robert Lowth (1710-1787) and Samuel Lee (1783-1852)," *Bulletin of the John Rylands Library* 35 (1953):385-404.

2. Ibid., 219.

3. *Short Hymns,* no. 973, 1:310.

4. Ibid., no. 1285, 2:56.

5. Ibid., no. 663, 2:337.

6. "Charles Wesley as a Biblical Interpreter," *Methodist History* 26 (1988):147. See here also the perceptive study of Francis Frost, "Biblical Imagery and Religious Experience in the Hymns of the Wesleys," *Proceedings* 42 (1980):158-66. On Charles Wesley's use of biblical metaphor see J. R. Watson, "Author, Faith, and Word: Biblical Text and Metaphor in Charles Wesley's Hymns," *Parole biblique et inspiration littéraire* (Paris: Groupe de recherche littéraire et religion dans les pays de langue anglaise, Université Paris-Nord, 1989).

7. Astruc's method of source criticism became the basis for Pentateuchal studies. See his *Conjectures sur les mémoires originaux dont il paraît que Moïse s'est servi pour composer le livre de la Genèse* (Bruxelles: Friex, 1753). The first edition was actually published in Paris.

8. Ernst Ludwig, *Schriftverständnis und Schriftauslegung bei Johann Albrecht Bengel* (Stuttgart: C. Schuefele, 1952).

9. See Johann Salomo Semler, *Abhandlung von freier Untersuchung des Canons,* ed. Heinz Scheible (Gütersloh: Mohn, 1967.) Semler gave new direction to exegesis by developing historical method.

10. Ernesti, whose approach to interpretation was primarily philological, maintained that the Bible may be interpreted only grammatically. See *Principles of Biblical Interpretation,* translated by Charles H. Terrot (Edinburgh: [s.n.], 1832-33), 2 vols.

11. See *Gotthold Ephraim Lessing Werke, Theologiekritische Schriften I und II,* vol. 7, ed. Helmut Göbel (Munich: Carl Hanser Verlag, 1976).

12. R. S. Cripps, see note 1 above. Lowth also provided the first developed view of parallelism as the primary characteristic of Hebrew poetry.

13. Gilbert, 259.

14. Amos N. Wilder, *Theopoetic, Theology and Religious Imagination* (Philadelphia: Fortress Press, 1976), 25. See also "Theology and the Symbolic Imagination: A tribute to Andrew Greeley," *The Incarnate Imagination: Essays in Theology, the Arts, and Social Sciences in Honor of Andrew Greeley*, ed. Ingrid H. Shafer (Bowling Green, OH, 1988), 235-47; John Bowker, *The Religious Imagination and the Sense of God* (Oxford: Clarendon Press, 1978), 308-18; Justus G. Lawler, *The Christian Imagination* (Westminster, MD: Newman Press, 1955); David Tracy, *The Analogical Imagination* (New York: Crossroad, 1981) especially the section "The Religious Classic: *Manifestation and Proclamation*," 193-202.

15. Keith Egan, "The Biblical Imagination of St. John of the Cross" (unpublished paper, dated July 21, 1989, presented at the Center of Theological Inquiry, Princeton, NJ), 27.

16. *Journal* 2:226.

17. Wilder, 41.

18. *Unpub. Poetry* 2:249.

19. Ibid., 120-121.

20. Ibid., 121.

21. Ibid.

22. Ibid., 122.

23. Ibid.

24. Ibid., 123.

25. Ibid., 91.

26. Ibid., 143.

27. Wilder, 87.

28. *Unpub. Poetry* 2:169.

29. Ibid., 169-70.

30. Egan, "The Biblical Imagination of St. John of the Cross," 15.

31. *Unpub. Poetry* 2:297-98.

32. Ibid., 276-77.

33. Ibid., 277.

34. Ibid., 88-89.

35. Samuel Wesley, *Poems on Several Occasions* (1736), 242.

36. William Romaine, *An Essay on Psalmody* (London, 1775), 105.

37. The original version has six verses; MS Select Psalms; published in the *Arminian Magazine* (1800); in *Poet. Works* 8:46.

38. *Unpub. Poetry* 2:441-42.

39. From *Hymns of Petition and Thanksgiving for the Promise of the Father* (1746) no. 28; *Poet. Works* 4:198-99; also in the *Pocket Hymn Book* (1785) no. 80. See *Rep. Verse*, no. 127, pp. 175-76.

40. See Psalm 104:2-4.

41. See Psalm 104:32.

42. See Psalm 104:29.

43. See the following poems of Charles Wesley in *Hymns and Sacred Poems*

(Bristol: Farley, 1742): "The Woman of Canaan," 96–98; "The Pool of Bethesda," 98–100; "The Good Samaritan," 101–3. While portions of each of these poems appear in the *1780 Collection*, none is published there in its entirety. They appear with significant omissions of verses.

44. At times his interpretations "beyond" the text have little or nothing to do with it. At others, however, he seems to be right on target.

45. See the poems listed in note 39 above and also in the same volume "David and Goliath," 173–75.

46. S. Laeuchli in *Parable, Myth and Language*, ed. Tony Stoneburner (Newton Centre, MA: National Institute for Campus Ministries, 1968), 13.

Chapter 8
Stookey, *Charles Wesley, Mentor and Contributor to Liturgical Renewal*

1. *1780 Collection*, no. 468, p. 651.
2. Ibid., no. 472, p. 656.
3. prove = experience
4. *1780 Collection*, no. 473, p. 657.
5. Ibid., no. 474, p. 658.
6. Ibid., no. 15, p. 98.
7. *Rep. Verse*, no. 146, p. 204.
8. *1780 Collection*, no. 471, p. 656.
9. Ibid., no. 86, p. 186.
10. Ibid., no. 85, p. 185.
11. *Rep. Verse*, no. 196, p. 231.
12. MS Scriptural Hymns (1783). See the *United Methodist Hymnal* (Nashville: United Methodist Publishing House, 1989), no. 595. Cf. *Poet. Works* 13:123–24.
13. *1780 Collection*, no. 240, pp. 381–82.
14. Ibid., no. 480, pp. 666–67.
15. Ibid., no. 371, pp. 541–42.
16. *A Collection of Hymns for the Use of the People Called Methodists* (London: Wesleyan Conference Office, 1877), no. 107, p. 52.
17. James Sanders (Philadelphia: Fortress Press, 1979).
18. *Rep. Verse*, no. 72, p. 99; and cf. *1780 Collection*, no. 2, p. 81.
19. *1780 Collection*, no. 131, pp. 242–43.
20. Charles Wesley, *Hymns on the Lord's Supper* (Bristol: Felix Farley, 1745), no. XCII, pp. 78–79.
21. *Journal* 1:140.
22. *Hymns on the Lord's Supper*, no. LXVI, p. 48.
23. Ibid., no. LVII, p. 41.
24. Ibid., no. V, p. 5.
25. Ibid., no. XLIV, pp. 32–33.
26. Ibid., no. CXVI, pp. 98–99.
27. Ibid., no. LIV, p. 39.
28. Ibid., no. CXXXV, p. 103.

29. Ibid., no. CXXXIX, pp. 105-6; *1780 Collection*, no. 415, p. 589. Charles Wesley has capitalized line three in verse four.

Chapter 9
Leaver, *Charles Wesley and Anglicanism*

1. Baker, *John Wesley and the Church of England*, 1.
2. *Journal* 1:129 (September 3, 1738).
3. It still has this double function. See Stanford E. Lehmberg, *The Reformation of Cathedrals: Cathedrals in English Society, 1485–1603* (Princeton: Princeton University Press, 1988), 87, 272.
4. *Journal* 1:84 (April 8, 1738).
5. Ibid., 320 (July 3, 1743).
6. Ibid., 88.
7. Ibid., 169.
8. For the period between August 1736 and September 1739, see *Journal* 1:126-28, 140, 144, 145, 156, 169, 178.
9. John Wesley, *A Sermon on Salvation by Faith* (London: James Hutton, 1738); see Sermon 1, *Works* 1:117-30.
10. See *Shorthand Sermons*.
11. Ibid., 71-86.
12. Ibid., 79-81, interpolating the earlier draft and ignoring editorial marks.
13. *Journal* 1:143.
14. *Shorthand Sermons*, 26-30, 36.
15. Ibid., 37-45.
16. See the discussion of Wesley's Trinitarian hymns in this chapter.
17. *Shorthand Sermons*, 51-70.
18. Ibid., 58.
19. Wesley again draws attention to those who subscribe to the Articles with mental reservation, as he had done in the previous sermon on justification; ibid., 66-67, see 46-47. For the background of the justification debate in the Church of England see Robin A. Leaver, *The Doctrine of Justification in the Church of England* (Oxford: Latimer House, 1979), and the annotation of Albin and Beckerlegge in *Shorthand Sermons*.
20. *Shorthand Sermons*, 66-67. The citation is from the homily on "Salvation" which Wesley had quoted earlier; see ibid., 61.
21. *Journal* 1:192 (October 27, 1739).
22. Letter, March 5, 1744; cited by Baker, *Charles Wesley as Revealed by His Letters*, 91.
23. Ibid., 96; cf. Charles Wesley's journal entry for October 27, 1756: "I went . . . to the old church, as usual. I preached at six; then met and lovingly reproved, the Society . . . and could find only two who would not take advice . . . the rest, a few Dissenters excepted, determined to live and die with us in the communion of the Church of England"; *Journal* 2:135.
24. *Journal* 2:135; also given in Tyson, *Charles Wesley: A Reader*, 420-421.
25. *Journal* 2:136.

26. Cited by Baker, *Charles Wesley as Revealed by His Letters*, 100.

27. Ibid., 135.

28. Loc. cit.

29. Letter, August 14, 1785; cited by Tyson, *Charles Wesley: A Reader*, 433.

30. *The Works of John Wesley*, ed. Thomas Jackson, 3rd ed, 14 vols. (London: Wesleyan Methodist Book Room, 1872; reprinted Grand Rapids: Baker Book House, 1979), 13:224-26.

31. Tyson, *Charles Wesley: A Reader*, 434.

32. Jackson, *Life of Charles Wesley*, 2:445.

33. In the week of Thursday, June 1 to Thursday, June 8, 1738, Wesley recorded in his journal that he attended the sacrament on all of these days except Sunday and the second Thursday. Nothing is recorded in the journal under June 4, but, since it was a Sunday, he probably communicated that day as well; see *Journal* 1:98-101.

34. For example: "At St. Paul's, the Psalms, Lessons, &c., for the day, put fresh life into me. So did the sacrament"; "I communicated at St. Paul's, as every Sunday"; *Journal* 1:155, 159 (Sun., June 24, and Sun., August 12, 1739, respectively).

35. *Journal* 2:15, 41, 53 (July 24, October 16, 1748, and March 26, 1749, respectively).

36. The Oxford "Holy Club" Methodists were accustomed to the strict observance of the Anglican "stationary fasts" on Wednesdays and Fridays (see Richard P. Heitzenrater, ed., *Diary of an Oxford Methodist: Benjamin Ingham, 1733-1734* (Durham: Duke University Press, 1985), and the second main section of John Wesley's Charlestown *Collection of Psalms and Hymns* of 1737 was comprised of twenty (out of a total of seventy) psalms and hymns for the two weekly fastdays: "Psalms and Hymns for Wednesday and Friday (see *Facsimile Copy of John Wesley's First Hymn Book: A Collection of Psalms and Hymns* [Nashville: United Methodist Publishing House, 1988], 40-58).

37. *Journal* 2:120, 123.

38. Ibid., 127 (Sun., October 17, 1756).

39. Ibid., 109.

40. This was a perspective Charles shared with his brother John; see Kenneth A. Wilson, *The Devotional Relationships and Interaction between the Spirituality of John Wesley, the Methodist Societies and the Book of Common Prayer* (Dissertation, Belfast: Queen's University, 1984) especially 291-313.

41. Reprinted by Rattenbury, *Eucharistic Hymns*, 176-249.

42. See Kathryn Nichols, "Charles Wesley's Eucharistic Hymns: Their Relationship to the Book of Common Prayer," *The Hymn*, 39, 2 (1988):17, 21, where the hymns are given in parallel with the respective texts of the Prayer Book.

43. *Rep. Verse*, 113-14; *cf.* the similar imagery, especially in stanzas 3 and 4, of the "upper" and "lower" choir, also found in the three Trinitarian hymns discussed later in the chapter.

44. See Nichols, 17 (see note 42 above).

45. Rattenbury, *Evangelical Doctrines*, 48.

46. J. R. Watson, "Author, Faith, and Word: Biblical Text and Metaphor in

Charles Wesley's Hymns," in *Parole biblique et inspiration littéraire* (Paris: Université Paris-Nord, 1989), 94.

47. On Charles Wesley's use of the *Book of Common Prayer*, see Bett, *The Hymns of Methodism* (3rd edition), 129-35; the critical annotation of the *1780 Collection*; and J. R. Watson, "Charles Wesley's Hymns and the Book of Common Prayer," in *Thomas Cranmer: Essays in Commemoration of the 500th Anniversary of his Birth*, ed. Margot Johnson (Durham: Turnstone Ventures, 1990), 205-8. S T Kimbrough, Jr., in his unpublished study of Wesley's *Short Hymns* has computed that in the section devoted to the Book of Psalms of the 104 psalm passages on which the 114 poems are based, 67 rely on the Prayer Book version of the Psalms, 20 on KJV, and 17 on passages that are identical in both versions. On John Wesley's debt to the Book of Common Prayer, see J. Brian Selleck, *The Book of Common Prayer in the Theology of John Wesley* (Dissertation, Madison: Drew University, 1983).

48. *Shorthand Sermons*, 49.

49. *Journal* 2:66 (December 18, 1749).

50. Ibid., 31 (September 8, 1748).

51. Toplady also included one of Charles Wesley's later hymns with the same opening first line (Fig. 1B) in his 1776 hymnal.

52. Misprint corrected to "King" in later editions.

53. For the details of the literary development of the text of "Hark! the herald angels sing," see *Rep. Verse*, 12-14; *Companion to Hymns and Psalms*, ed. Richard Watson and Kenneth Trickett (Peterborough, England: Methodist Publishing House, 1988), 94-95.

54. This is a rather jumbled version of the hymn which begins: "Come, let us join our friends above."

Chapter 10

Heitzenrater, *Charles Wesley and the Methodist Tradition*

1. Baker, *Charles Wesley as Revealed by His Letters*, 95; Gill, *Charles Wesley, the First Methodist*, 170.

2. Ibid., 231, 234. Another typical comment is that of F. L. Wiseman: "Methodism without Charles Wesley is just as unthinkable as Methodism without John Wesley." *Charles Wesley, Evangelist and Poet* (New York: Abingdon Press, 1932), 9.

3. Gill, *Charles Wesley, the First Methodist*, 234.

4. Baker, *Charles Wesley as Revealed by His Letters*, 117.

5. Gordon Rupp (Oxford: Clarendon, 1986), 583.

6. Ibid., 353.

7. For a rehearsal of some of these ringing words of praise, see *Rep. Verse*, ix-x.

8. *Letters JW* 6:67 (January 13, 1774).

9. Baker, *Charles Wesley as Revealed by His Letters*, 14.

10. Richard P. Heitzenrater "The Quest of the First Methodist," chapter 4 in *Mirror and Memory*, 63-77.

11. Charles seems to have enjoyed what John also desired: "How gladly could I spend the remainder of a busy life in solitude and retirement!" *Journal JW* 3:479.

12. George Sampson, "A Century of Divine Songs," the Warton Lecture on English Poetry, 1943, quoted in *Rep. Verse*, x.

13. Charles's unpublished poetry is now available in an edition by S T Kimbrough, Jr. and Oliver A. Beckerlegge; see *Unpub. Poetry*. Albin and Beckerlegge have published Charles's previously unpublished sermons, transcribed from shorthand, in *Shorthand Sermons*.

14. Heitzenrater, "Early Sermons of John and Charles Wesley," *Mirror and Memory*, 153, 154–55.

15. Ibid., 155–56.

16. Sermon 3 in almost every edition of John Wesley's collected sermons.

17. Bernard Holland has proposed that Charles's understanding of faith led to a two-step conversion and has become normative in the Methodist tradition, while John's implied three steps and has subsequently faded away. Holland's basic reading of the sources, however, is not beyond challenge. "The Conversions of John and Charles Wesley," *Proceedings* 38 (1971):46–53; cf. Heitzenrater, *Mirror and Memory*, 254, n. 196.

18. See John C. Bowmer, *The Sacrament of the Lord's Supper in Early Methodism* (London: Dacre Press, 1951), and Rattenbury, *Eucharistic Hymns*.

19. See Tyson, "A Brotherly Debate," in *Charles Wesley on Sanctification*, 227–301.

20. *Works* 26:472 (July 24, 1751).

21. See note 1 above.

22. *Works* 26:528 (October 31, 1753).

23. John's comment to Charles in 1785 reflects this trend: "I see fifty times more of England than you do." *Letters JW* 7:288.

24. In 1773, John complained to his brother: "You have *intended* again and again to stand by me at this and that Conference, and then left me to stand by myself. It is certain we two can turn the tide; I alone can only *stem* it." *Letters JW* 6:29. Except for four or five instances, the title of the annual ("penny") *Minutes* after 1765 generally do not refer to a conference with "the Rev. Messrs. Wesleys" but rather with "the Rev. Mr. [John] Wesley." Charles was at the conference in 1786 in Bristol, but took no part in the debate over separating from the Church "except to cry out a loud and angry 'No' to a suggestion that Methodist services should be held in church hours" (Gill, *Charles Wesley, the First Methodist*, 200).

25. During Charles's lifetime, this was the consistent entry in the title of the "Large" *Minutes*, containing the disciplinary standards of the connexion.

26. When the newspapers prematurely reported John Wesley's death, John Fletcher wrote to Charles that "The Methodists . . . have, I think, a right to expect that you will preside over them while God spares you in the land of the living" (Gill, *Charles Wesley, the First Methodist*, 182). Charles felt he had neither the strength nor the ability. Fletcher, of course, had been "designated" by John Wesley as his successor in January 1773, while Charles was still alive; both Charles's and Fletcher's reticence in this matter was made unnecessary by their predeceasing John Wesley.

27. *Letters JW* 7:285.

28. Baker, *Charles Wesley as Revealed by His Letters*, 34–35.

29. Charles's "Hymns for Malefactors" and his *Journal* 1:402, however, challenge this stereotype. See also Telford, *Life of Charles Wesley*, 78–79 and 276–77.

Chapter 11
Davies, *Charles Wesley and the Calvinist Tradition*

1. Charles Wesley, *Hymns for the Nativity of our Lord* (London: Strahan, 1745), 7.

2. Letter of 26 November 1737 to Count Zinzendorf translated from the Latin, in Baker, *Charles Wesley as Revealed by His Letters*, 29.

3. Published by S. and F. Farley, Bristol, 1739.

4. *Free Grace*, 10.

5. Ibid., 16.

6. Ibid., 8.

7. Ibid., 21.

8. Ibid., 22.

9. Ibid., 25.

10. John Calvin, *Institutes of the Christian Religion*, ed. John T. McNeill, tr. Ford Lewis Battles, 2 vols. (Philadelphia: Westminster Press, 1960), III.xxiii.7, p. 955: "The decree is dreadful indeed, I confess." In the Latin original: *Decretum quidem horribile, fateor*, and in the French: *Je confesse que ce decret nous doit épouvanter.*

11. *Free Grace*, 27.

12. The complete poem is found on pp. 31–35 of *Free Grace*. Verses 3, 4, 17, and 26 of the original are printed here. See also *Poet. Works* 1:310–315.

13. Charles is often an exaggerated romantic driven by his feelings, while John is rational. But the combined result of both approaches was effectual in the multitudes whom they attracted to and retained in Methodism.

14. *Rep. Verse*, 158–61.

15. Ibid., 161–65. It was excised from later editions of the *Collections of Psalms and Hymns*. By "The Boar out of the German Wood" in line one Wesley means the Moravians from Herrnhut.

16. Ibid., 167.

17. *Unpub. Poetry* 1:172; 3:160–161.

18. *Journal* 1:280.

19. Baker, *Charles Wesley as Revealed by His Letters*, 41.

20. *Journal* 1:276–77.

21. John Lawson, ed., *The Christian Year with Charles Wesley* (London: Epworth Press, 1966), 18.

22. *Hymns for the Nativity of our Lord*, 8.

23. Ibid., 76.

24. *Hymns on the Lord's Supper* by John and Charles Wesley (Bristol, 1745), no. 141. The same universal emphasis sounds also in the better known eucharis-

tic hymns, e.g. "Victim Divine, Thy grace we claim" in two separate lines: "Thou didst for *all* mankind atone" and "To *every* faithful soul appear."

25. Whaling, *John and Charles Wesley*, 54.

26. *Journal* 1:282.

27. Ibid., 272.

28. *Short Hymns*, 2:201.

29. See *Hymns and Sacred Poems* (London: Strahan, 1740), 204–7. I owe this reference to S T Kimbrough, Jr.

30. Whaling, *John and Charles Wesley*, 48.

31. Hymn IX of *Hymns for those that seek, and those that have Redemption in the Blood of Jesus Christ* (1747), 13–14.

32. Charles Wesley, *Hymns and Sacred Poems* (Bristol: Farley, 1749), 2:12.

33. Calvin, *Institutes*, IV.xvii.10, p. 1370.

34. Ibid., note 27.

35. Ibid.

36. Bard Thompson, ed., *Liturgies of the Western Church* (Cleveland: The World Publishing Co. 1961), 207.

37. Rattenbury, *Eucharistic Hymns*, 31.

38. *Hymns on the Lord's Supper*, see LXIII.

39. W. H. Gardner, ed., *Poems of Gerard Manley Hopkins* (London: Oxford University Press, 1948), 186. Wesley repudiates this view: see Hymn LXIII, "No Local Deity, We worship, Lord, in Thee."

40. *Hymns on the Lord's Supper*, CXVI.

41. Ibid. The first sentence comes from Hymn XCI, and the second from Hymn LXXXI.

42. Hymn CXLVII.

43. Hymn CXXIV.

44. Hymn LXXII.

45. Hymn LIV.

46. Hymn LVII.

47. Hymn CLXV.

48. *The Hymns of Wesley and Watts* (London: Epworth Press, 1942), 14, 29.

49. The covenant appears on pp. 293–97 of Richard Alleine's book (1666) and on pp. 164–70 of Joseph Alleine's book: *An Alarme to Unconverted Sinners, In a Serious Treatise* (London, 1672).

50. A Summary of *Directions for Renewing our Covenant with God*, by John Wesley (London: Paramore, 1794), 5th edition, 13–14.

51. Cited from John Bishop, *Methodist Worship in Relation to Free Church Worship* (London: Epworth Press, 1950), 108f.

52. Leslie F. Church, *More about the Early Methodist People* (London: Epworth Press, 1949), 240f.

53. Joseph Alleine, 170 (see note 49 above).

54. Ibid., 166–67.

55. *Short Hymns*, 2:36–37; Hymn no. 518 in the *1780 Collection*.

56. *Unpub. Poetry* 3:97.

57. Hunter's article is "Sources of Wesley's Revision of the Prayer Book in 1784-88," *Proceedings* 23 (1941-42):123-33.

58. Monk, *John Wesley: His Puritan Heritage* (Nashville and New York: Abingdon Press, 1966), 25.

Chapter 12
Berger, *Charles Wesley and Roman Catholicism*

1. See, for example, John M. Todd, *John Wesley and the Catholic Church* (London: Hodder and Stoughton, 1958); Robert G. Tuttle, *The Influence of the Roman Catholic Mystics on John Wesley* (Dissertation, University of Bristol, Bristol, 1969); Michael Hurley, S.J., "Salvation Today and Wesley Today," *The Place of Wesley in the Christian Tradition: Essays Delivered at Drew University in Celebration of the Commencement of the Publication of the Oxford Edition of "The Works of John Wesley,"* ed. Kenneth E. Rowe (Metuchen, NJ: Scarecrow Press, 1976), 94-116 (Michael Hurley, S.J. also edited John Wesley's *Letter to a Roman Catholic* in 1968); Mark S. Massa, "The Catholic Wesley: A Revisionist Prolegomenon," *Methodist History* 22 (1983):38-53. Aelred Burrows, O.S.B., "Wesley the Catholic," *John Wesley*, ed. John Stacey (London: Epworth Press, 1988), 54-66.

2. A look at Betty M. Jarboe, *John and Charles Wesley: A Bibliography* (Metuchen, NJ: Scarecrow Press, 1987) in the series "American Theological Library Association Bibliography," confirms this observation. The one exception she notes (A. S. Denyer, *The Catholic Element in the Hymns of Charles Wesley*, B.D. Thesis, University of Leeds, 1943) is unpublished, and was not available to me.

3. For the following, see John Bossy, *The English Catholic Community 1570-1850* (New York: Oxford University Press, 1976).

4. Ernest Gordon Rupp, *Religion in England 1688-1791* (New York: Oxford University Press, 1986), 184.

5. Donald Henry Kirkham, *Pamphlet opposition to the Rise of Methodism. The Eighteenth-Century English Revival under Attack* (Dissertation, Duke University, Durham, NC, 1973), 280-284. There is actually one reference to Charles Wesley being charged with being a "Jesuit" (as well as being "drunk, mad, an emissary, . . . a devil") already in 1736 (the *Journal* entry is September 4). See *Journal* 1:41.

6. See Charles Wallace, "'Some Stated Employment of Your Mind': Reading, Writing and Religion in the Life of Susanna Wesley," *Church History* 58 (1989):354-66, esp. 357.

7. From Benjamin Ingham's diary we know with certainty that Charles Wesley read Francis de Sales; see Heitzenrater, ed., *Diary of an Oxford Methodist*, p. 267. If the poem "On Reading M. de Renty's Life" (see *Poet. Works* 1:15f) is by Charles Wesley (though it may be by John), it is evidence that Charles had read the life of de Renty by Saint Jure, a fact which is borne out by John Wesley's Oxford diaries. The upcoming publication of these diaries will hopefully shed more light on the question of Charles's reading at Oxford.

8. *Journal* 1:405.

9. *Poet. Works* 4:88, 77.

10. Ibid., 95.

11. Ibid., 6:147–86.

12. *Journal* 1:16. Although terms like "Popish," "Popery," and "Papist" were certainly introduced as hostile designations, there is the possibility of them not always being used as that. In the register of the parish church where Bishop Richard Challoner was buried one reads: "Buried the Reverend Richard Challoner, a Popish Priest and Titular Bishop of London and Salisbury, a very pious and good man, of great learning and extensive abilities." Quoted in Eamon Duffy, "Richard Challoner 1691–1781: A Memoir," *Challoner and his Church: A Catholic Bishop in Georgian England,* ed. Eamon Duffy (London: Darton, Longman & Todd, 1981), 25.

13. *Journal* 1:145.

14. Ibid., 461; see also 2:31.

15. Ibid., 460.

16. Ibid., 2:22. Charles Wesley's hymn for the Roman Catholics in Ireland breathes a slightly different spirit until one gets to the last stanza; see ibid., 27–29.

17. Ibid., 36.

18. See, for example, the *Journal* entry of March 16, 1745: "I spake with one of the Society, lately a Papist, who is much haunted by her old friends, especially her confessor, who thunders out anathemas against her; and threatens to burn me—if he could catch me at Rome. I sent my respects to the gentleman, and offered to talk with him before her, . . . but received no answer." *Journal* 1:394; see also 354, 398.

19. *Poet. Works* 8:263–80.

20. In a letter to his daughter Sally, Charles Wesley writes on June 12, 1780: "No wonder y[ou]r Mother was terrified, when I was *proscribed* as a Popish Priest—for I never signed the Petition, or ranked among the Patriots." The letter is no. 504 in Frank Baker's collection of manuscript letters of Charles Wesley (see also *Journal* 2:281). I extend special thanks to Frank Baker for letting me consult this collection.

21. Jackson, *Life of Charles Wesley* (American edition), 677. For a different angle on the Gordon Riots see Ralph E. Reed, "From Riots to Revivalism: the Gordon Riots of 1780, Methodist Hymnody, and the Halevy Thesis Revisited," *Methodist History* 26 (1988):172–87.

22. *Poet. Works* 8:266.

23. Ibid., 449–78.

24. It seems theologically preferable to speak of a reception into a particular church rather than a conversion to it by baptized Christians. The term conversion/*metanoia* should be reserved for the initial radical turning of a human being to God.

25. For the beginning of the century see: Eamon Duffy, "'Poor Protestant Flies.' Conversions to Catholicism in early Eighteenth-Century England," *Studies in Church History,* Vol. 15: *Religious Motivation. Biographical and Social Problems for the Church Historian,* ed. Derek Baker (Oxford: Basil Blackwell, 1978), 289–304.

26. Erik Routley, *The Musical Wesleys* (New York: Oxford University Press, 1968) 65.

27. *Unpub. Poetry* 1:303-16. Unfortunately, there are no letters of Charles Wesley from that period making reference to this event. The only letter to Samuel (no. 564 in Frank Baker's collection) during that time is dated October 4, 1787, but is only a brief letter with general fatherly advice.

28. *Journal* 2:129.

29. Ibid., 131.

30. *Unpub. Poetry* 1:303.

31. Ibid., 306.

32. *Journal* 2:27; *Poet. Works* 8:398ff.

33. *Unpub. Poetry* 1:308.

34. Ibid., 313.

35. *Journal* 2:34.

36. *Shorthand Sermons*, 66f.; see also 46f. A similar attitude is taken in the "Hymns for a Protestant," *Poet. Works* 6:1-6.

37. In John R. Tyson, "Charles Wesley, Evangelist: The Unpublished New Castle Journal," *Methodist History* 25 (1986):49.

38. *Unpub. Poetry* 1:311.

39. Ibid., 310.

40. See Bett, *The Hymns of Methodism*, 39-70. I do not find the evidence Bett produces compelling. Analogies between certain Wesleyan formulations and some of the medieval writers can, to my mind, be satisfactorily explained by presuming that both draw on traditional images and terminology, rather than by Wesley directly borrowing from specific writers.

41. The expression, of course, is used by the Wesleys themselves (see, for example, its use in the preface to the *Hymns and Spiritual Songs, Intended for the Use of Real Christians of all Denominations*, [1753]).

42. To give just one example of the difficulties one labors under when talking about Charles Wesley's "Catholic spirit" and trying to define it more precisely in relation to the Roman Catholic tradition: Charles Wesley wrote a hymn based on the *Te Deum* (*Poet. Works* 4:224-27). One could easily claim that he is drawing on classic Roman Catholic liturgical material here. But the *Te Deum* is also prescribed in the *Book of Common Prayer* for use at Matins—so that Wesley is actually simply drawing on his Anglican liturgical heritage (which obviously in turn is derived from the Western liturgical tradition). Does Wesley's use of the *Te Deum* constitute a borrowing from the Roman Catholic tradition? I think not.

43. See Markus Jenny, "Vocibus unitis. Auch ein Weg zur Einheit," *Liturgie und Dichtung. Ein interdisziplinäres Kompendium*, vol. 2: *Interdisziplinäre Reflexion*, ed. Hansjakob Becker and Reiner Kaczynski (St. Ottilien: EOS-Verlag, 1983), 173-205.

44. Manning, *The Hymns of Wesley and Watts*, 14.

45. See the title of a hymnbook the Wesleys published in 1753: *Hymns and Spiritual Songs, Intended for the Use of Real Christians of all Denominations*.

46. I note that my brief assessment of Charles Wesley's position vis-à-vis Roman Catholicism parallels Richard Heitzenrater's brief assessment of John

Wesley's position. See Richard P. Heitzenrater, *John Wesley his own Biographer*, vol. I of *The Elusive Mr. Wesley* (Nashville: Abingdon Press, 1984), 201.

47. See note 1 above.

48. Maximin Piette, *La Réaction de John Wesley dans l'Evolution du Protestantisme*. Etude d'Histoire Religieuse (Bruxelles: La Lecture au Foyer, 1926 [1st edition], 1927 [2nd edition]). English translation: *John Wesley in the Evolution of Protestantism* (New York: Sheed and Ward, 1937).

49. Francis Frost, "Biblical Imagery and Religious Experience in the Hymns of the Wesleys," *Proceedings* 42 (1980):158-66; French trans., "Poésie biblique et expérience religieuse chez les frères Wesley," *Pluralisme religieux en Grande Bretagne*, ed. Christiane d'Haussy [Paris: Didier, n.d.], 95-109. Frost is also the author of an excellent dictionary article on Methodism, in *Catholicism, hier, aujourd'hui, demain*, vol. IX, 1, ed. G. Jacquemet (Paris: Letouzey et Ané, 1982), 48-71.

50. Berger, *Theologie in Hymnen?*

51. *Worship II. A Hymnal for Roman Catholic Parishes* (Chicago: G.I.A. Publications, 1975).

52. *The St. John the Baptist Book of Catholic Worship*, ed. by G. Paul Parr (Canton: St. John The Baptist Publishing Company, 1974).

53. *Catholic Book of Worship II*. The Officially Approved Hymnal for the English-speaking Catholics in Canada (Ottawa: Canadian Conference of Catholic Bishops/Toronto: Gordon V. Thompson, 1980).

54. *Growth in Agreement. Reports and Agreed Statements of Ecumenical Conversations on a World Level*, ed. Harding Meyer et al. (New York: Paulist Press/Geneva: WCC, 1984), 309. In this edition of the report, there is an unfortunate mistake which I corrected in the last sentence quoted: The very last word in "Growth in Agreement" reads "only" instead of the correct word "soul."

55. *Growth in Agreement*, 310, 321, 325, 352, 354. In the United Methodist-Roman Catholic Dialogue in the United States, the Wesleyan hymns as a whole are given no attention, but the eucharistic hymns are alluded to, see: *Building Unity. Ecumenical Dialogues with Roman Catholic Participation in the United States*, ed. Joseph A. Burgess and Jeffrey Gros (New York/Mahwah, NJ: Paulist Press, 1989), 314.

56. *Growth in Agreement*, 338.

57. *Poet. Works* 10:42f.